The AGE ꝏf DANTE

ILLUSTRATED BY FRED HAUCKE

ᕝ ᕝ ᕝ ᕝ

A CONCISE HISTORY OF ITALIAN CULTURE

The AGE

IN THE YEARS OF THE EARLY RENAISSANCE

# of DANTE

By DOMENICO VITTORINI ᐯ ᐯ ᐯ ᐯ

THE CITADEL PRESS • NEW YORK

To

MARY CURTIS ZIMBALIST

Founder of The Curtis Institute of Music

where I have happily taught since the

day of its opening in 1924

✿ ✿ ✿ ✿ ✿

Preface

The present work on the early centuries of Italian civilization has developed from a series of lectures given at the University of Pennsylvania over a period of many years. It aims at covering the culture and literature from the eleventh century to the death of Dante in 1321. We view these centuries as an age of radical change in every aspect of Italian life — political, social, religious, and cultural.

The term "Early Renaissance" applied to this epoch takes into consideration the new aspects that scholars, in increasing numbers, are recognizing in these centuries. The age of the Italian Communes bore the seed whence modern democracy developed. The merchants created a credit system that broke the hold exercised for centuries by the feudal lords over the lands that were gradually wrested from them. Modern historians, such as Giacchino Volpe and Luigi Salvatorelli, have realized how modern and dynamic the civilization of the Communes was. J. E. Staley's study on the guilds of Florence shows how far the social system prevailing in the republics of the time had advanced. Religiously, the faith in a humanized and vital Christianity was responsible for the rising of beautiful cathedrals and the fostering of sculpture and painting as well as the contribution to agriculture and culture in general by religious orders. Linguistically, the vernacular, in its local dialects, was extricating itself from the stately forms of Latin and becoming the everyday language. It became eventually the instrument of artistic expression employed by poets of the thirteenth century throughout Italy and finally attained its full beauty in the polished form that Dante Alighieri gave to it in the *Divine Comedy*. Taken as a whole, these political, social, religious, and cultural conditions form the basis for our belief that these early centuries were, in reality, the dawn of the Renaissance.

Contemporary scholars have gone beyond the conclusions that Jacob Burckhardt reached in his epoch-making work of 1860 on the Italian Renaissance. Yet there are many who, still caught in the web of those then admirable conclusions, continue to exclude the civilization of the early centuries of Italian history from the precincts of the Renaissance and look disdainfully upon the religious fervor of that time. Confusing culture and art, they reduce to classical culture the amazing activity of these centuries and fail to see the normal traits of Renaissance life viewed as human experience. In general, a broader view has been taken by today's historians and researchers in the field of culture, who have explored the eleventh, twelfth, and thirteenth centuries that were unknown quantities in the days of Burckhardt and of John Addington Symonds. Such American scholars as Charles Homer Haskins and George Sarton, in particular, have contributed greatly to a better understanding of the civilization of this time in its historical and cultural achievements.

The contributions of the Italian translators at Toledo in the twelfth century have been set forth here in detail, in accordance with the conclusions of Charles Homer Haskins and George Sarton. Although the contributions of Gerard of Cremona and of other translators at Toledo made a deep imprint on the history of European civilization, their humble yet glorious work has not been justly emphasized in Italian histories of culture and literature.

The presentation of the poetry of the thirteenth century represents our own analysis of the texts, begun in 1912 under the guidance of our beloved teacher Ernesto Monaci and pursued since in our work as a student of Italian literature. Whatever critical acumen we possess we owe to the training begun at the University of Rome under the guidance of Vittorio Rossi and Cesare de Lollis, and pursued at Princeton University under Christian Gaus, Frederick Vreeland, and Donald Stuart. We are happy to acknowledge here a great debt of gratitude to Edgar O. Singer, Jr., Hugo Rennert, James P. W. Crawford, and Felix Schelling of the University of Pennsylvania.

The present book is planned as the first of a series of ages which center around the dominant figures of particular epochs. With this in mind, we have called the study of the early centuries of Italian civilization *The Age of Dante*, for, as we see in retrospect, it is Dante Alighieri who stands out above all others of that time. We have attempted to present, in as great detail as the limited space permits, the literature of those years as well as a careful study of Dante as a man and as a poet, giving him a place of prominence without detracting, however, from the importance of others whose contributions to Italian civilization must not be disregarded. We trust that the reader will keep these aims in mind and will find within these pages a clear presentation of the literature of the dawn of the Renaissance.

We trust, too, that the reader will ponder over the words of Etienne

Gilson, one of the great scholars of our time, written on the period studied in these pages. They are found in his book *Les idées et les lettres*, published in Paris in 1932: *Pour savoir ce que furent le moyen âge et la Renaissance, il ne faut pas les définir a priori, puis en decrire l'histoire, mais en écrire l'histoire, puis les définir. C'est le contraire que l'on fait.* (In order to know what the Middle Ages and the Renaissance were, one must not define them *before-hand*, then write their history, but one must write their history, then define them. What is being done is the opposite.) Theories and definitions are not destined to replace historical facts. Each generation restudies and reappraises the past. This process constitutes the very essence of the history of culture.

Our basic goal is that of reaching the human pathos that glows in the depths of every existence, be it of today or of yesterday. Our book is addressed to the growing number of those who realize the necessity of culture as an integrating factor in our age of technology and gigantic industrialism. It is hoped that the present synthetic cultural interpretation will be of particular value to the increasing English-speaking public which in the last few years has discovered Dante and wishes to know more about the age that he illumines with his greatness.

We are very grateful to Antonio Pace, friend and scholar, of Syracuse University, for his interest in our manuscript and the suggestions he has offered us.

Domenico Vittorini

Preturo (L'Aquila), July 23, 1956

✿ ✿ ✿ ✿ ✿

Contents

XV

⟡ ⟡ ⟡ ⟡ ⟡

List of Illustrations

The AGE of DANTE

⟡ ⟡ ⟡ ⟡ ⟡

Introduction to the Literature
of the Renaissance

THE CHRISTIAN AGE AND THE RENAISSANCE

The history of Italian culture and literature would seem to have its beginning with the birth of national consciousness in the men and women of the Italian peninsula. This consciousness was revealed in the use of the new vernacular, first for practical purposes and then as a medium of artistic expression in poetry and prose. From a formal point of view, a new historical phase began with the fall of the Roman Empire in A.D. 476, but several centuries passed before national consciousness assumed a clear form and was expressed in literary works. The transition of Latin into the various Italian vernaculars[1] was very gradual and the new generations were slow in realizing that they were no longer Romans but part of a new element in European history. By the eleventh, twelfth, and thirteenth centuries, however, life was intimately Italian, even if in official circles there was an obstinate attempt to cover it with classical forms.

Persuaded that the light of Classicism glowed uninterruptedly throughout the whole "mediaeval" period and believing that each age should be evaluated through its own characteristics, we shall use the term "Christian Age" in referring to the ecclesiastical civilization that preceded that of the eleventh and later centuries. We notice its waning around the year 1000 because at that date civilization was gradually assuming the forms that are identified with the later Renaissance. We have discarded the term "mediaeval" in referring to the early centuries of the Christian Era since this nomenclature does not take into account the cultural impact of Christianity. The term "mediaeval," referring to the interlude between the Classical Age and the rebirth of Classicism, presupposes the belief that there is only one true civilization, the classical one, and ignores the indisputable fact that the history of man is not immutable, but is constantly new and diverse in its forms.

Historians are wont to extend the Christian Age in various ways: some to the appearance of the two great Humanists, Boccaccio and Petrarch in the fourteenth century; some to the discovery of America in 1492; some to the arrival in Italy of Francis I of France at the beginning of the sixteenth century. Modern scholars, however, have shown a distinctly different attitude toward the civilization of the eleventh and twelfth centuries. If one accepts the conclusions of Henri Pirenne[2] that civilization in Italy around the year 1000 had already assumed the forms in which we can recognize, be it in a rudimentary manner, the basic traits of our Western civilization, it is necessary to push back the limits of time which mark the end of the Christian epoch and the beginning of the Renaissance.

The Christian Age is customarily described as a barren and negative epoch, a long and dark night in which ascetic considerations obscured the joyous philosophy of living associated with Classicism. Modern scholarship is inclined to discount the darkness of the mediaeval night as well as the joyousness of Classicism and of the Renaissance. Civilization during the Christian Age was basically different from that of Greece and Rome. There was no reason why it should have continued toward the same goals and with the same forms. It was different from classical civilization just as the civilization of the Renaissance was different from it.

Culture was neither European nor national during the Christian Age. It was universal. In close contact through the Church with the basic ideas of Classicism, it relied on the Platonic principle of the oneness of truth. There was only one religion, Christianity; one language, Latin; one political head, the Emperor; one religious head, the Pope of Rome.

This condition changed markedly in the historical setting of the Renaissance. Its lay civilization was accompanied by an increasing interest in the sciences and in other cultures besides the classical one. By the twelfth century, new languages had appeared in Europe and the new peoples could boast of national lays and legends. The Empire had been replaced by many national states that were ruled by national kings.

The Christian Age saw the rise and expansion of Christianity in Europe as new peoples claimed a place in history. The Renaissance coincided with the historical moment when the Christian peoples took the place of the Arabs of Spain as the leading factors in the cultural as well as in the political history of the Mediterranean basin. The Crusades epitomized the challenge of Christian Europe to Islam and they testified to the renewed power of the Latins in defense of their civilization. The Normans wrested Sicily from the Saracens in 1072. Jerusalem fell to the Christians in 1099, Valencia in 1109.

Civilization during the Christian Age was largely agricultural; during the Renaissance, it was mostly industrial. The culture of the Christian Age, to a great extent monastic, was theological and mystic, reaching toward Heaven, while Renaissance culture was marked by scientific and practical interests, orienting itself toward the earth.

The principal interest during the civilization of the Christian Age lay in God the Creator and in the process of creation. Such a formula can be developed and clarified by the observation that men of culture, judging from the books of the time, were primarily interested in the consideration of the creation of the world as the book of *Genesis* presented it. Literary history is based on material documenting the emotions, sentiments, and ideas that the various epochs have left to us. The clerks wrote for the pious souls who sought in their books consolation from the distressing experiences of life. The emotions and reactions of the average man were not deemed worthy of becoming art material. The masses remained excluded from culture and from knowledge. Their books were the frescoes in the early cathedrals in which the artists told of the wonders of creation and the lives of the saints. God and the saints were the characters who acted and moved in that art. When man and his passions attracted the attention of men of culture, a new age had already dawned, the Renaissance. By the eleventh century civilization, although still very religious, was no longer monastic.

Records testify to a shift from the consideration of the creation of the world to the consideration of God's creations: the universe, the earth, man and his passions. During this period, one notices a constant intensification of literature in the vulgar tongue as well as the acceptance of the principle that the study of the human soul is the material for the art of the written word.

Literary production during the Christian Age was very limited. The most important original books were the *Exameron* by St. Ambrose, the *City of God* and the *Confessions* by St. Augustine, and the *Consolation of Philosophy* by Boethius. These works stand out among large collections of church hymns, didactic poems of very relative significance, sermons and theological treatises, lives of saints, legends, fables, and historical chronicles generally beginning with the creation of the world.

Quite different in extent and significance was the literature of the age that followed. It encompassed a vast body of fictional tales and lyric poems, that date back to the thirteenth century, and the works of Dante, Petrarch, Boccaccio, Ariosto, and Machiavelli.

After the fall of the Roman Empire, the Mediterranean basin lost every commercial importance. In the days of classical Rome, the Mediterranean had been the center of the economic activity of three continents: Europe, Asia, and Africa. When the German tribes, under pressure from the great migration from the East, spread themselves toward the north, west, and south, occupying modern England, France, Spain, and Italy, economic life was profoundly disturbed and trade suffered. A still greater disturbance was caused by the spread of Islam toward Europe from the northern coast of Africa. The Mediterranean had become a dead sea. It rose to a new life when there appeared a new social class, the merchants who, from the tenth century on, re-established trade between the Italian maritime cities and the French, English, and Flemish ones. The history of this reawakening is intensely dramatic.

Charlemagne, at the end of the eighth century, had given unity and security to the European continent, repulsing the Arabs of Spain south of the Pyrenees and imposing the feudal system on continental Europe. He had created an empire that was the shadow of imperial Rome — the Holy Roman Empire. European economy under the feudal system was an agricultural economy based on barter, since gold was not the medium of exchange under the Carolingians. The Italian maritime cities, on the fringe of the Carolingian Empire, had enjoyed a measure of independence. Only under pressure did they pay tribute to the Empire and receive its representatives. In the relative peace enjoyed around the year 1000, trading became more active, especially under the direction of the merchants. These far-seeing men produced merchandise destined to embellish life and make it more enjoyable. At first, they exchanged their goods for the agricultural products of the population of the fiefs, but very soon they learned how to attract the population of the countryside within the orbit of their economy and, with the weakening of the Empire, they absorbed the territory surrounding the cities, creating the *contado*.

Thus was born the "free city," or Commune, a child of the concept of the dignity of work and a forerunner of future democracy. Laws were proposed and discussed in the public squares and in the churches *a parlamento*, a phrase coined to refer to this democratic practice and which today finds its equivalent in the English word "parliament." A complex economic system displaced the barter system of the feudal days, and gold became again the medium of exchange. Merchants carried out their financial transactions behind *banchi* or counters, the forerunner of the modern bank. Of particular interest was the internal organization of the free cities into *arti* or guilds. The guilds included and regulated all the forces of production. There were the Major Guilds (*Arti Maggiori*) and the Minor Guilds (*Arti Minori*), a division that rested on the importance and activity of the members. The guilds greatly resembled our modern unions and developed especially in Florence, but were also organized in other Italian cities as well as in the rest of Europe.

The merchants were the first contributors to democratic civilization in the new phase of Western culture that we are about to study. They broke the chains of the feudal system, transporting their merchandise by sea in order to avoid payment of tolls to the feudal lords. In this way, they were able to undersell in the markets the merchandise produced in the fiefs, which was transported by land and was, therefore, more costly. The merchants laid the economic and political foundations of the civilization of the Renaissance. Far-seeing and silent, watchful and tenacious, they initiated a society in the midst of which there appeared a new culture and art which we identify with the Early Renaissance.

There is ample evidence to show that around the year 1000 life was very active, not only in Italy but also in the rest of Europe. In 989, the first Truce of God was proclaimed, whereby bishops forbade fighting on Sundays and church holidays. Land reclamation was carried out on a large scale in Central and Southern Europe. Even religious orders, such as the Benedictines and the Cistercians, turned to land reclamation. Such measures must have contributed to the great spurt in population at the end of the first millennium of our era.

It has been established that already in the year 900 Venice, Pisa, Genoa, Marseilles, and Bruges were important ports. In 1015, Genoa had a navy strong enough to conquer Sardinia and to challenge the Mohammedans in Bona, Africa. The economic growth of the free cities was accompanied by a strong desire for independence from both the bishops, who had replaced the Roman governors as political heads of the dioceses, and from the Empire that still had claims on these cities. Milan, the most powerful of the Communes, set the pattern for freedom and, in 1057, broke the rule of its bishop. In 1183, after a long war, the Empire was forced to recognize the juridical reality of the Communes.

Such, in brief, was the setting in which the Italian vernacular was first used.

HUMANISM AND RENAISSANCE

In using the term "Renaissance," we mean rebirth of civilization in new forms. We shall divide this epoch into various zones, determined by the cultural factors that influenced it, but keeping these factors separate from the creative activity that belonged to the field of the arts.

The distinction between the culture of an epoch and its literature is of fundamental importance in our study. The cultural background of an epoch is determined by the heritage of its past, by contacts with other cultures, and by the political and social changes that characterize a definite moment in history. Art, on the other hand, being primarily individual creation, is the projection of the poet's recollected experience or imaginative creations into the art-mold suited to him. In this sense, all the arts have a common origin. They are the sentiment arising from experience that flowers in forms of pure beauty. They differ only in the medium of expression that they use: words, sound, stone, color, and lines. The average man lives especially through practical activities in the daily experience that absorbs him. The artist lives more intensely than the average man in that he prolongs the duration of his experience by recreating in his fancy its data and fixing them in the mold of his art. In the cultural process, the artist absorbs what the environment offers to him, refining his taste, but without basically changing his genius and temperament. In the field of art, the artist reveals his inner self through forms that undergo the influence of the cultural environment, but the content of which stems from the creativeness of his temperament.

For this reason, the cultural zone of an epoch is more uniform and shows a greater unity than that of the literature and the arts of the same time. Culture is horizontal and cumulative. Art is vertical. Sophocles rises near Dante and Goethe, unmindful of the time that separates him from them. Great art lives outside the time in which it appears, though culturally it belongs to that time.

To understand the relation between culture and art during the centuries that we are about to study, it is necessary to distinguish very clearly between Humanism and Renaissance. Humanism constitutes the classical section of the cultural background of the Renaissance. Renaissance refers to and embraces the creative part of the artistic life of the time.

In studying the Renaissance, one readily becomes aware that Classicism was the main factor in the civilization of that epoch. There were, however, other cultural influences side by side with Classicism: Arabic, Jewish, Provençal, French, English. Lyric poetry from the Sicilian School to Romanticism took its forms, directly or indirectly, from the courtly love of Provence. The mock epic of the fifteenth and sixteenth centuries borrowed its material from France and England. In spite of this cultural parallelism, the richest cultural vein was the classical one. In all the theoretical treatises of the Renaissance on art and poetry, one finds a strong attachment to classical tradition. Only a few independent thinkers recognized the creative character of art. Most of the literati and the agencies of official culture clung, in general, to Classicism. Even a poet like Dante, although he borrowed greatly from

Provençal culture, followed the *Poetics* of Aristotle in theorizing about poetry. Aware that this was the general point of view during the Renaissance, we have used this attitude toward Classicism as the guiding light in our division of the cultural pattern of that age.

The crumbling of political Rome did not mean the end of classical culture. The new peoples that sprang up in Europe never lost their faith in and admiration for Classicism. Since their own culture was slowly and laboriously coming into being, the only culture that they recognized was that of the classical heritage transmitted by Greece and Rome. No one had yet formulated the problem of the creative character of art, and, hence, the independence of modern art from that of antiquity. It was not surprising, therefore, that artists produced their works keeping before their eyes the models of classical art. Dante looked upon Virgil as "my master and author, the only one from whom I took the beautiful style that has gained honor for me." In his *De Vulgari Eloquentia*, he referred to the epic style in the Aristotelian sense of the word.

Even in the eleventh and later centuries, when life changed substantially in language, feelings, society, and government, Classicism was the most revered culture in official and literary circles. The economic factor entered partly into that attitude, since, at a time when there was no copyright, men of letters were forced to seek the patronage of kings and noblemen. The literati functioned then much as the propaganda office of our day functions for governments. For this reason, thrones and Classicism were closely allied and remained so to the very end of the nineteenth century.

Classical culture survived without interruption all through the Christian Age and the Renaissance, and there were periodic returns to classical sources on the part of men of learning throughout those epochs. These returns determined various cultural zones of Humanism.

Humanism was synonymous with learning of a high and polished character, bearing close resemblance to the academic studies of our time. It had in no sense the connotation of humanity with which it is often associated today. In the sixteenth century, Ariosto, in one of his satires,[3] even referred to the Humanists in a most derogatory manner.

The first return to Classicism was made by the Schoolmen or Fathers of the Church who used the classics as sources. They read them with the purpose of extracting the theological elements that they passed on to the new religion. We call this return Religious Humanism.

In the Early Renaissance or Age of Dante (from the eleventh to the end of the fourteenth century), cultured men like Dante, Boccaccio, Petrarch, and

Salutati sought in the same books of the classics a moral lesson. This second return we call Moral Humanism.

In the fifteenth century, the books of the Ancients were read again, in greater number and in better editions, including those rediscovered at the end of the fourteenth century and after the fall of Constantinople in 1453. The goal of the new Humanists was neither religious nor moral, but aesthetic. This third return is herein called Aesthetic Humanism.

In the sixteenth century, the classics were reread by many of the serious-minded men of letters in order to find in them guidance both in the study of history and in the evaluation of human conduct. This constitutes Critical Humanism for us. These men were the real Humanists. They studied the past and felt reverence for it, but they looked at it from the historical perspective of their time, seeing in it the happy childhood of humanity. At the end of the sixteenth century they shouted with Bruno, "We are the Ancients, not they, the Greeks and the Romans. By climbing on their shoulders, we can see farther than they did."

However, there flourished at the same time, in the unhealthy political atmosphere determined by the invasion of Italy by the French, Spaniards, and Germans, a negative type of Humanism that we characterize as Rhetorical Humanism.[4] These false Humanists were rhetoricians who sought in the same books the rules of perfect poetry to justify their theory of imitation.

The division between true and false Humanism had also existed in previous centuries, but it became accentuated during the period of the political decadence of Italy in the sixteenth century. Pseudo-humanism assumed unhealthy and reactionary forms, which reached out toward the following century, when a new philosophical thought arose in open antagonism against the Aristotelian system.

These four zones that encompass the creative efforts of the generations that lived in and fashioned the civilization of the Renaissance are:

1. The Early Renaissance or Age of Dante, embracing the eleventh, twelfth, thirteenth, and fourteenth centuries.

2. The Aesthetic Renaissance, characterized especially by the achievements in painting, sculpture, and architecture during the fifteenth century.

3. The Critical Renaissance, that marked a great progress in philosophy and in theoretical concepts of art in the sixteenth century.

4. The Scientific Renaissance, that reached great heights in the field of physics and mathematics with Galileo, his pupil Torricelli, and those distinguished thinkers who, in the seventeenth century, rebelling against the principle of authority upheld by the Aristotelians, opened new paths, not only

in the scientific field, but also in the study of history, ethics, political economy, and aesthetics.

These divisions are included here because, from a cultural standpoint, European civilization remained largely influenced by Classicism until the Romantic Revolution in the eighteenth and nineteenth centuries changed the pattern of its culture.

CHAPTER ONE

Italian Culture in the Eleventh
and Twelfth Centuries

The civilization of the Renaissance was capitalistic in economics, Christian in religion, and predominatingly classical in the culture accepted by the Church and the official spheres of learning.

Cultural life in the Age of Dante, the first panel of the Renaissance, appears projected against a very stormy political background. The Wars of the Investitures, the rising of the national states where once the Empire ruled, the Communes and their clashes, both internal and external, contributed in creating a turmoil that exacted a large toll of blood and tears in Italy as well as in the rest of Europe.

The Church of Rome insisted that it was the sole dispenser of authority to the heads of the new states, and these, harassed by rival barons, welcomed its recognition and paid tithes to it in return for the stability that such recognition involved. The clashes between Pope Gregory VII and Henry IV of Germany in the eleventh century and between Henry II of England and the Church in the following one were typical in the struggle waged by the national states in achieving independence from the Church. The twelfth century closed with the restatement on the part of Innocent III (1198-1216) that the Church was above all European states.

The main factor in Italian life during this time was the Commune. Culture was deeply influenced by it. Communal life had its golden age in the eleventh and twelfth centuries and was characterized by simplicity and austerity, intense commercial activity, and patriotism. Unlike France, England, and Spain, Italy remained fractioned into these small and independent city-states.

In spite of inevitable imperfections, injustices, and even frauds, the Commune was a strikingly new form of political organization. The people were an integral and real part of the government. Through their activities, the gold of Europe was attracted to Italy, and that country became again the center of economic life in the Mediterranean. Although the Communes did not take a direct and vital part in the Crusades, they benefited greatly by the fact that troops going to fight in Palestine passed through Italy and were transported on ships belonging to the maritime cities of Venice, Genoa, Leghorn, and Amalfi. These republics traded vigorously with the Far East and the Middle East, thus restoring Italy to the vital function of serving as a link between the East and the West as in the days of the Roman Empire. In Constantinople and in other cities in the East they had established warehouses and autonomous quarters administered by Italian consuls. Venice was the mistress of the Mediterranean. In 1202, it occupied Zara and, two years later, obtained one fourth of the territory of the Byzantine Empire. Her supremacy lasted until the end of the thirteenth century when the republic of Genoa inflicted on her a deadly blow in the naval battle of the Curzola in 1298.

The Communes, during the twelfth century, fought against the claims of the German Empire on Italian territory. The victory of the Lombard Communes at Legnano in 1176 over the imperial forces of Frederick Barbarossa was an event of transcendent significance in European history. The Holy Roman Empire might have come to an end then, rather than lingering until 1806, had Italy continued to develop along the healthy ideals of communal civilization. However, during the age of the invasions of the fifteenth and sixteenth centuries by the French and the Spaniards, democratic institutions were so severely weakened under the despots that they were virtually destroyed.

In spite of the extremely active economic life in which the country was engaged and notwithstanding the turmoil of continuous wars, the interest in culture and in the arts was truly amazing in the eleventh and twelfth centuries.

In order to form an adequate idea of the conditions of learning of this time, it is well to realize that literature existed only in manuscript form and that to acquire even a limited culture required enormous effort. Since the means of communication were difficult, the number of schools restricted, and the cost of manuscripts very high, to join the not too large ranks of cultured persons constituted a truly heroic task.

The history of Italian culture offers a very clear documentation of the existence and growth of learning since the eleventh century. Latin was still the language of culture, but the vernacular was the language of everyday life.[1] The Capuan Charter of the year 960,[2] although it described court proceedings in Latin, registered in the crude vernacular the testimonies before the judges. Pious persons who went to confession used the vernacular, judging by the formula of confession at the end of the eleventh century.[3] The vernacular was also used in inscriptions on church walls.[4] It was a rudimentary language, primitive, strong, and not too clear, no longer pure Latin, but not yet the Italian vernacular which, at the beginning of the thirteenth century, had already become a powerful instrument of expression.

During the Age of Dante, there was not yet the clear distinction that the modern age has drawn between culture and poetry. The concept of poetry as an activity of the fancy had not yet been formulated. Poetry had not found a place in the curriculum of the schools. Men of letters aimed at being philosophers, theologians, and men of science, even when they wrote poetry. Science and knowledge stifled poetry, at least theoretically, in the official circles of culture. Whenever poetry blossomed forth in the writings of the time, it did so through poetic instinct, unaided by a clear consciousness of the nature and aim of this art.

Nor did cultured men distinguish between translation and personal creation. Our ancestors took from the Ancients and even from contemporary authors without scruples of any kind. Since there was no copyright, it was possible to do so with impunity and even with a certain degree of innocence.

The ideas of men of culture were largely patterned after those of Classicism. When they thought of the universe, they saw it as presented in the *Almagest* of Claudius Ptolemy (second century A.D.). Such a picture of the universe was accepted until Copernicus presented his heliocentric theory in 1543. Judging by the fact that in 1633 Galileo was made to recant his acceptance of the Copernican system before the tribunal of the Inquisition, it would not be unreasonable to conclude that the Ptolemaic system endured even later.

The prevailing moral code was also of classical derivation. The Church accepted from the classical tradition the four cardinal virtues although it added the three theological ones. Spurning the pleasures of life had been the basic tenet of stoicism, and Christian asceticism adopted it. The idea of the moral responsibility of the individual, that of reward and punishment, of the purification of the soul after death, were classical conclusions that the Church accepted and wove into the very fabric of the new faith.

UNIVERSITIES

During the Christian Era, teaching had been largely in the hands of the clergy. Schools were at first connected with monasteries and later with cathedrals, even up to the year 1000. Very scanty documentation remains of instruction imparted by and to laymen. Nevertheless, in the eleventh and twelfth centuries, there had already appeared universities independent of ecclesiastical institutions and different from the classical school oriented about great masters like Plato and Aristotle. The new schools were independent of the personality of the teacher. In the new age, it was the master who followed the school.

The university became a guild or society of teachers. Its full title was *universitas societas magistrorum discipulorumque* (General Association of Teachers and Pupils), from which our own universities have taken their name and form. It is interesting to note that the first time that the word *universitas* appeared was in a letter of Pope Innocent III written in 1209. Universities of that time were often called *studium*, a name kept by some Italian institutions of high learning. Pupils were trained according to the curriculum prescribed in the Trivium and the Quadrivium. In the Trivium, the subjects taught were: grammar, that offered Latin words; logic, that taught how to reason; and rhetoric, that embellished writing. In the Quadrivium the pupils studied arithmetic, music, geometry, and astronomy. Upon the completion of studies, the university conferred the degree of master (*magister*, master) and of doctor (*doctor*, he who teaches), terms that are still used in our universities.

The most famous and perhaps the oldest universities were those of Bologna and of Salerno. In the eleventh century, the University of Bologna was renowned for the study of law, the University of Salerno for the study of medicine. Elsewhere in Europe, the University of Paris was famous for the study of theology and that of Oxford for the study of rhetoric till the end of the thirteenth century.

THE STUDY OF LAW

Among the noteworthy contributions of the twelfth century was the study of law. Jurisprudence was not included in the Trivium or in the Quadrivium. The new interest in law began with the study of the *Digest*, a collection of Roman laws made by the Emperor Justinian and published at Constantinople in 529. It disappeared a few years later, but reappeared at the University of Bologna in the twelfth century, when illustrious teachers of that institution wrote marginal notes on it for the purpose of illustrating Roman laws. The work of these glossators has been viewed as a kind of appendix to rhetoric, originating in the desire to teach beautiful form to notaries and lawyers in the performance of their duties. We believe that the glossators did much more than this. In their theoretical study of the *Digest*, they initiated the historical presentation of law. They took part in the question of the Investitures, and they were able to conclude that inasmuch as the Empire, that is, the Roman

Empire, had existed long before the Christian Church and was a great historical reality, the Emperor had received his authority directly from God, without the intermediary action of the Pontiff. The *Digest* became the weapon that defended the rights of the Empire against the claims of the followers of the fiery Hildebrand, Gregory VII, during the eleventh century. The question of the sovereignty of the Empire and of the Papacy was a vital and live one. In this light, the early glossators were the first scholars who helped to extricate the modern concept of the state from the theocratic ideas entertained by the Church. Their interest in the *Digest* was more than strictly literary; it was also pragmatic.

Among these early glossators at Bologna there stands out Irnerius (*ca.* 1060-1140), who was the faithful counselor of the Countess Matilda, representative of the Empire in Tuscany, and, at her death in 1115, of Henry V of Germany. He argued the question of the sovereignty of the Empire and of the Papacy against Manegaldus of Lautenbach, an Augustinian monk of Alsace (d. *ca.* 1103) who had defended the rights of the Pope in the struggle of the Investitures. His work was carried on by his pupils, referred to as the "four doctors." They were Martino (d. *ca.* 1168), Bulgaro (d. *ca.* 1161), Ugo (d. *ca.* 1168) and Jacopo (d. 1178). These four jurists paved the way for the work of the famous Francesco di Accorso whose activity occupied the first half of the thirteenth century.

The study of Roman law was also accompanied by the organization of canon laws into a separate code. In 1139, Graziano issued the *Decretales,* a vast compilation of laws promulgated by the *Curia* of Rome. Both codes of Roman and canon laws circulated in abbreviated form in the *summae* which were condensed summaries.

THE STUDY OF MEDICINE

The Salernitan School of Medicine was made famous by such men as Constantine the African, Arcimatteo, Bartolomeo of Salerno, Matteo Plateario, Pietro of Musanda, and Trotula, a woman who wrote a treatise on obstetrics. Other teachers developed there the study of anatomy and *materia medica*. Still well-known today are the Latin distichs that enclosed principles of hygiene recommended by the school. To the University of Salerno we owe the anatomical charts of the pig. The pig was used for dissecting and its organs were studied because doctors were not permitted to use the human body for this purpose, lest they contaminate and offend the most perfect work of God's creation. The work accomplished in science at the Salernitan School was executed in a rudimentary manner; however, by their attempts in this field they succeeded in establishing experimental science as a subject for academic study.

THE STUDY OF HISTORY

One of the clearest manifestations of the new age was the appearance of historical works in which the study of the past, as well as of the present, was conceived as the making of man. The authors of such works were interested in events that pertained to their cities, the origin of these, their political struggles, and the factors that contributed to their growth or downfall. Modern history saw its dawn in these early centuries of our civilization. Historians wrote in Latin, but the content was new.

The immediate past had not contributed much, but, already in the tenth century, Liutprand (*ca.* 915-*ca.* 972) in his *Antapodosis* (Retributions to Friends or Enemies) and in his *Historia Othonis* (History of Otto) had written of contemporary political events in which he had taken part. He lived when political conditions, after the death of Charlemagne, were fluid in Italy as well as in Europe. Another chronicle of the tenth century was the *Gesta Berengarii Imperatoris* (The Exploits of the Emperor Berengarius), an anonymous work that shows concern over literary form together with a keen interest in the political events of the time.

Great progress is visible in the *Chronicon Venetum* (Venetian Chronicle), the first history of Venice, written by John the Deacon, that brings its account to the year 1009. In it, Venice is shown in all its glory as the queen of the seas. In the eleventh century, there appeared many works on contemporary history, such as the *Historia Mediolanensis* (History of Milan) by Landolfo the Elder and the *Panegiricus* (Panegyric) of Henry IV by Benzo, Bishop of Alba.

More important still and more numerous were the chronicles of the twelfth century, such as the *Historia Mediolanensis* (History of Milan) by Landolfo the Younger that dealt with events that took place in that city from 1005 to 1137. Sir Raul of Milan wrote a history of Frederick I (1100-1157). Caffaro related the important achievements of his Genoa, studying what happened between 1100 and 1163. Alessandro of Telese dealt with Sicily under Roger the Norman (1127-1137), while Ugo Falcando wrote about the court of Palermo in his *Liber de Regno Siciliano* (Book of the Sicilian Kingdom) that goes from 1154 to 1169.[5] The life of the Countess Matilda of Tuscany was sung in Latin hexameters by Donizzone, a Benedictine monk.

During the twelfth century, the famous *regesti*, chronicles written in monasteries, appeared in greater number than before. The most interesting of these was that of Farfa, a work by Gregory, a descendant of the counts of Catino. In these *regesti*, the interest of the compilers went beyond the walls of the monasteries and one finds in them the echo of the secular life of the time. Because of this, they are precious historical documents.

One of the most extraordinary books of that century is a work by Idrisi (or Edrisi), an Arab who lived in the court of the Norman kings at Palermo. He wrote in Arabic his *Sollazzo per chi si diletta di girare il mondo* (Pleasurable Entertainment for Those Who Find It Delectable to Roam the World). Written by order of Roger II who ruled from 1130 to 1154, it is a treatise on geography and contemporary history as well as on social conditions. It gives a living picture of such cities as Palermo, Genoa, Pisa, and Venice.

THE *PORTOLANI* AND THE STUDY OF GEOGRAPHY

The avowed and documented interest in this world and in this earth (it had always existed but had not been documented) was revealed by the new maps that appeared in the twelfth century. Guido the Geographer, who flourished

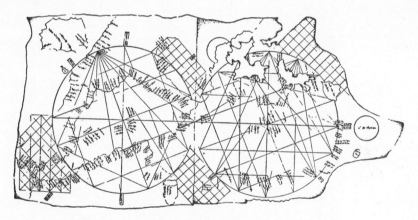

An Anonymous Portolano. First known of its kind,
it shows mariner's directions for the Mediterranean Sea
and part of Atlantic Ocean.

around 1119, wrote a book by the title of *Geographica* (Of Things Geographic) and drew two maps, one of Italy and one of the world.

Belardo of Ascoli, between 1112 and 1120, went to the Holy Land and wrote a Latin description of Palestine. Liutprand, in the tenth century, had also left a record of his trip to Constantinople.

The renewed interest in geography was due to two main causes. One was the transportation by sea, initiated by the merchants in the ninth century to avoid payment of tolls to the feudal lords who controlled land transportation. The other was the intensification of travel by sea due to the Crusades. The *portolani* indicated that traffic in the Mediterranean was very great. These guides for navigators contained descriptions of ports, outlined sea routes, gave sailing directions, and provided carefully marked charts.

THE FINE ARTS

Several styles are noticeable in the eleventh and twelfth centuries: Byzantine, Romanesque, and Gothic. We are particularly interested in the Romanesque and in the early and feeble attempts at Naturalism that appeared at that time and gradually replaced the Byzantine style. Byzantine art had penetrated into Italy at the beginning of the sixth century when the forces of the Eastern Empire dislodged the Lombards and conquered parts of Italy, placing the capital at Ravenna. As a result of this political event, Byzantine artists went to Italy and introduced into that country the ascetic and hieratic art that is characteristic of their style. The most beautiful Byzantine mosaics are found

Architectural Details. Capital, San Marco, Venice; Lion, doorway, Cathedral of Modena; Detail, Cathedral of Modena.

in the cathedral of Sant'Apollinare at Ravenna. They possess a beauty all their own, perfectly attuned to the religious atmosphere of a church. Byzantine artists were so much sought after that they eclipsed the local artists and the spontaneous naturalism that was so much a part of indigenous painting.

By the twelfth century, however, the local artists had clearly resumed their supremacy and they contributed greatly to both the architecture and to the frescoes that go by the name of Romanesque. The merchants turned to them, rather than to the Byzantines, whenever they wished to embellish the new cathedrals with mosaics and frescoes. The church of San Clemente in Rome, built between 1099 and 1118, shows clear signs of this new direction in art. In the frescoes that were executed in the last decades of the eleventh century, an unknown artist has depicted scenes of the life of the saint, replacing the static character of the Byzantine painting with action and motion. In the mosaic in the apse of Santa Maria in Trastevere, built in 1145, Christ and the Madonna are presented with a tenderness of feeling quite foreign to Byzantine art.

The twelfth century was especially noteworthy in architecture. The cathedral of Pisa was begun in 1063 and finished in 1118. The church steeple of San Marco in Venice was built between 1148 and 1154. Of Romanesque style, serene, simple, and eurhythmic, are the churches of San

The Betrayal, St. Apollinare Nuovo, Ravenna.
Mosaic, sixth century.

Miniato al Monte, San Zeno at Verona, Sant'Ambrogio at Milan, San Marco at Venice, and the baptistry of San Giovanni in Florence.

In Romanesque sculpture of the twelfth century, the use of animals, plants, and leaves as ornamental devices was an important contribution of that art. An excellent example of this is the pulpit of the basilica of Sant'Ambrogio in Milan, built in that century. The yielding of geometrical design to human figures full of movement is well exemplified in the façades of the cathedrals of Modena and Parma.

Of paramount importance in the history of art and civilization of this period is the presence of the Gothic style which flourished side by side with the Byzantine and the Romanesque. It came from northern Europe and was characterized by lines reaching upward, slender spires, and pointed arches, befitting architecture in countries where snow is abundant, in sharp contrast with the horizontal lines of the Romanesque style, the architecture of lands where roofs are not overtaxed by heavy snowfall. There are many beautiful examples of Gothic architecture in Italy, not the least of which are the Abbey of Fossanova and that of Casamari.

In these years of the Age of Dante the harmonious blending of intense religious fervor, flourishing economic conditions, and love for art contributed greatly to one of the most creative moments in Italian life.

CHAPTER TWO

The Transmission of Culture
in the Twelfth Century

The attitude of our ancestors toward learning was very different from our own. We take pride in extolling our modern culture while they took pride in obliterating themselves and their contributions to intellectual life. They looked at their civilization with a feeling of inferiority, as if persuaded that it would never attain the heights reached at the time of the Greeks and the Romans. For men of learning in high circles of the Age of Dante, the only culture recognized officially was the classical one. Their fervent desire was to master the works of antiquity. This attitude was accompanied by a sense of familiarity which allowed them to rehandle the texts without any thought of plagiarism. Many themes were taken from the history of Greece and Rome and recast in compilations in which fancy was given free rein.

The contacts which Italy enjoyed, for reasons of trade, religion, and politics, especially with Spain, France, and England, greatly enriched its culture. Spain facilitated Italy's contacts with Classicism through the great center of learning that existed at Toledo. This city was dominated by the Arabs who had gathered there many books of the classics. Arab scholars, whose idol was Aristotle, were particularly interested in science. Because of his famous commentary on Aristotle, Averroes, an Arab, was placed by Dante in the Christian Limbus with high praise for his great work. In the twelfth century, France had already wrested from the Arabs the intellectual leadership in the basin of the Mediterranean and had become a great cultural center. Two French schools, one at Cluny and the other at Chartres, were at the time focal points of a very intense cultural life.

In Italy the most important center of culture was Palermo where the Norman kings had a splendid court. Under Roger II, who reigned over Sicily from 1130 until his death in 1154, the culture of the island was distinctly Greek, and Greek was the official language of the court. Because of the close connections that Palermo had with both Toledo and Constantinople, work done in these cities by men of learning readily found its way into the Norman court. From Constantinople came many Greek and Arabic manuscripts as well as the translation of Aristotle's *Organon* (Logic) by Giacomo of Venice under the title of *Nova Logica* (New Logic), a book used as a school text as late as the days of Giambattista Vico at the beginning of the eighteenth century.[1] Other famous translations passed from Toledo to Palermo and from Palermo spread over Europe.

In the second half of the twelfth century, the nineteen translators known to be at Toledo were all Italian, with the exception of the French Guillaume Le Mire. The greatest of these translators was Gerard of Cremona who died in 1187. So great was his influence that George Sarton, the most renowned historian of science in our time, refers to the second half of the twelfth century by calling it the Age of Gerard of Cremona.[2]

CLASSICAL INFLUENCE

Gerard went to Toledo in quest of the *Almagest* for there was no copy to be had in continental Italy. A translation made of it in Sicily in 1160 was unknown to him. He found it at Toledo in an Arabic translation, learned Arabic, and translated the important work into Latin in 1175. He also translated many of Aristotle's works, as well as books on mathematics by Greeks, Arabs, works on astronomy and physics, and Galen's medical treatises. In the latter task he had as collaborator Burgundio of Pisa. Due, too, to Gerard was the translation of an Arabic commentary to the tenth book of Euclid, a treatise on salts and vitriol, and the *Spherics* of Theodosius of Bithynia. The translation of the pseudo-Aristotelian *De Causis et Proprietatibus* (Of Causes and Specific Properties of Bodies) that Vincent de Beauvais and Albert the Great used in the early thirteenth century was also the work of Gerard.

With Gerard there lived and worked at Toledo such men as Platone of Tivoli, Enrico Aristippo of Catania, Eugenio of Palermo, Burgundio of Pisa, Leone the Tuscan, and Pasquale of Rome. Among the translations into Latin that were made available to the West were the *Meteorologica* (Concerning Meteorology) by Aristotle, *Aphorism* (Aphorism) by Hippocrates, part of the *Digest*, and a treatise on agriculture, *Geoponica* (On Agriculture).

A very important page in the cultural life of the twelfth century was the interest in Plato's works. During the long and passionate disputes between the realists and the nominalists, a forerunner of the clashes between the idealists and the behaviorists of our time, Plato assumed a very important role in that he was adopted by the Church as the classical thinker who foreshadowed the Christian concept of God and His reality.

The two centers of these disputes were Chartres in France and Palermo in Sicily. In the famous school of Chartres, William of Conches wrote a new commentary on the *Timaeus* that replaced that of Chalcidius (fourth century), the Latin grammarian who kept alive in the West for centuries the only dialogue of Plato. Chartres remained throughout the twelfth century a center of Platonism.

The Norman court at Palermo added greatly to the study of Plato when Enrico Aristippo of Catania, archbishop of this city and prime minister of William I, translated directly from Greek into Latin two new dialogues of Plato, the *Meno* and the *Phaedo*. In the following century the writings of Plato attracted the attention of both Albert the Great and his pupil Thomas Aquinas. Very likely, the thought of Plato reached Dante through these translations as well as through the reading of the *Timaeus*.

The translation of Plato's three dialogues constituted an event of great significance because they were the only ones known in the West until Marsilio Ficino translated all of Plato's dialogues at the end of the fifteenth century.

Side by side with this great interest in the translation of scientific and philosophical books was the interest in classical lore. During the twelfth century, it is to France that we owe the greatest contribution to the transmission of this material. Classical subject matter was, on the whole, used freely and raised to the plane of fiction by French authors. However, the new handling of the works of the Ancients was indicative of the growth of culture and of the mental habits of twelfth-century men of letters in studying classical material.

The main themes that attracted the attention of our ancestors were those of Troy, Alexander the Great, and Caesar. That of Troy, transmitted from the Classical Age through the *Aeneid* of Virgil, was one of the richest in the lore of the Ancients. Two Latin versions of the Trojan War appeared around the fifth century after Christ. One was the *Ephemeris Belli Trojani* (The Story of the Trojan War), a free rehandling, by an unknown Lucius Septimius, of Greek versions of the war as narrated by Homer in the *Iliad* and the *Odyssey*. In order to give an aura of authenticity to this work, Septimius presented these legendary events as an eye-witness account by a fictitious Ditti of Crete. The other version was the *De Excidio Troiae Historia* (History of the Destruction of Troy) by an unknown author who attributed it to another imaginary eye-witness, Dares from Phrygia. The compiler maintained that he was editing in this work a Latin translation by Cornelius Nepos.

In the twelfth century, these two texts provided the subject matter that Benoît de Sainte-More worked into his *Estoire de Troie* (History of Troy) which he wrote in 1165. Over a century later, in 1267, Guido delle Colonne used this same material for his *Historia Destructionis Troiae* (History of the Destruction of Troy), written in Latin prose. The French text was responsible for the widespread popularity, during the thirteenth and fourteenth centuries, of material taken from classical literature and rewritten in the form of fictional tales.

The theme of Alexander the Great also enjoyed a great vogue. It passed into the West especially with the *Historiae Alexandri Magni* (History of Alexander the Great) by Quintus Curtius Rufus who lived in the first century A.D., and with the *Parallel Lives of the Greeks and Romans* by Plutarch who lived at the end of the same century. The historical material on Alexander had been registered in the fourth century B.C. by contemporaries and close associates of the Emperor. His heroic deeds had also given rise to many fictional accounts. These writings attracted the attention of Julius Valerius who, between the second and fourth centuries of the Christian Era, claimed to have translated from a Greek original his *Res Gestae Alexandri Magni* (Exploits of Alexander the Great). It was very popular in an abridged form that bore the title of *Epitome Juli Valeri* (An Abridgement of Julius Valerius). The Greek text, supposedly registered at the time of the great emperor, was again translated in the tenth century by Leone Arciprete, who lived in the court of the Dukes of Naples and who apprised the reader that he had made his translation during his voyage to Constantinople in 942. His work was known under the title of *Vita Alexandri* (The Life of Alexander) and *Historia de Proeliis* (History of Wars).

The subject matter concerning Alexander the Great, thus transmitted, was rehandled in the twelfth century by two French men of letters: Lambert le Tort, who compiled his *Li romans d'Alexandre* (The Romance of Alexander) and Walter de Chatillon, author of the *Alexandreis* (Epic of Alexander). It is significant that in these books the vernacular was already used. In the following century, Dante made reference to the legend of Alexander to enrich the episodes of his *Divina Commedia* with effective imagery. He placed Alexander among the tyrants and referred to him in several passages of his poem. In later European literature, the translations of Plutarch's *Lives* by Jacques Amyot in 1559 and Sir Thomas North in 1579 served to afford cultural material to Shakespeare, Racine, and Metastasio. The latter two wrote plays on Alexander the Great.

The theme of the Roman Emperor, Julius Caesar, also attracted great attention in the age of the Investitures. An anonymous compilation of the dramatic events of Caesar's life had been made in France, bearing the title of *Les Faits des Romains* (The Deeds of the Romans). It was known in Italy for it was translated into the Italian vernacular in the thirteenth century. Dante was so familiar with the history of Caesar that he repeatedly referred to him in his *Divina Commedia* and looked upon him as the real creator of the Empire.

The intense activity in the twelfth century by the translators and compilers that we have briefly surveyed allows us to understand the wealth of classical culture in the literature of later centuries and the many references to classical themes that appear in most of the books written in Europe during the Renaissance.

CAROLINGIAN LEGENDS

The official attitude toward culture, centering in the recognition of Classicism as the supreme and only representative of learning and civilization, did not prevent inevitable and beneficial contacts with the cultures of the new peoples of Europe that were developing at that time. France and England were the chief contributors. French letters became known in Italy directly, thanks to the closeness of French to Italian and the active religious, commercial, and political ties between the two countries. France gave to Italy cultural material taken from two very important sources: the legends of the Carolingian cycle and the lore of Provençal courtly love. These two currents were couched in two distinct languages, that of the North or language of *oïl*, and that of the South or language of *oc*. The epic strain of the North penetrated into Italy very early and its material was integrated into Italian literature throughout the centuries of the Renaissance. Not less important was the strain of the poetry in the language of *oc*. It determined, or guided, the basic attitude of Italian lyric love poetry from the early thirteenth to the nineteenth century.

The Carolingian legends appealed especially to the masses of the people. From northern France minstrels wandered into Italy and brought with them stories about Charlemagne and his knights: Roland, Renault, Oliver, and the traitor, Ganelon. They recited their tales in the public squares on festival days. So great was their popularity and so lewd was the treatment accorded to the legends by the bards that in 1288 the Commune of Bologna passed a law forbidding minstrels to sing those songs in the squares. Muratori informs us that, long before this, the stories of Roland and Oliver were recited by clowns on the stage of Milan.[3] Echoes of Carolingian legends are to be found even in Dante's *Divina Commedia* where Roland is assigned to Paradise and Ganelon is placed among the traitors. Such great favor did these tales of Charlemagne gain in the hearts of the Italian people that the authors of the mock epic of the fifteenth and sixteenth centuries took their material from the familiar legends.

PROVENCAL LORE

Of equal importance in its influence on Italian literature was the Provençal courtly tradition. In southern France, from the early eleventh century, the courts of noble barons had become renowned as centers of poetry. Troubadours and minstrels had cultivated there a type of lyric, set by them to music and characterized by a Platonic worship of woman. A complex philosophical doctrine on love lifted to a spiritual plane the natural feelings of the poet for his lady. Secrecy veiled their love drama that opened in the ceremonials of court etiquette and rose toward the lyrical height that the poet gave to it in terms of his emotional and artistic capacities.

Courtly poetry in Provence enjoyed its fullest flower in the twelfth century. So great was its popularity that, upon the visit of Provençal poets to the court of the Norman kings at Palermo and to the courts of northern Italy, the fashion was established for Italian poets to use Provençal in writing their lyrics, a custom that endured to the very end of the thirteenth century.

The most famous of the Italian poets who wrote in Provençal was Sordello of Goito. Dante extolled him in his *Purgatorio* as a perfect symbol of noble patriotism. Sordello died around 1270, at a time when Provençal was still used by Italian troubadours, a proof of the deep roots that this cultural strain enjoyed in Italian literature. Sordello owed his fame to a highly lyrical composition (The Plaint of Sir Blacas), in which he, lamenting the death of his noble friend and patron Sir Blacas, invited the rulers of his day to partake of the heart of the most illustrious and noble lord of their time that they might acquire a particle of his generosity and loftiness. It is written in Provençal.

Although another Provençal poet, Lanfranco Cigala of Genoa, who died in 1278, does not enjoy the renown of Sordello, he is superior to Sordello for a greater variety in his psychological musing and a richer gamut of emotions in his love drama. He sang of the radiant smile of a Berlenda Cibo to whom he dedicated his verse, although he also expressed his admiration for other women. Modern criticism has vindicated the significance of his poems and has interrupted the long and unjust oblivion to which Cigala was condemned by the admiration for Sordello.

Italian poets borrowed from Provençal both the ideology of courtly love and the metrical forms used in their lyrics.

There is abundant documentation of the contacts between Provence and Italy during the twelfth century. Alberto Malaspina, a lord of the Lunigiana in the North, known as a lavish patron of poets and well versed in Provençal, exchanged *tenzoni* with Rambaud de Vaqueiras, a poet from Provence who had lived in his court, and Pierre Vidal, another Provençal poet, who visited the courts of northern Italy and lived there at the end of the twelfth century. The Este family, through its patronage, made the court of Ferrara famous for the Provençal poetry cultivated there. In it lived an Italian troubadour referred to as "Maestro Ferrari," who was renowned as a poet in the Provençal manner. He copied with his own hand the works of the famous troubadours of Provence and modestly refused to include his own.

Dante and Petrarch were thoroughly versed in Provençal poetry. Dante mentioned Bertrand de Born, Arnaud Daniel, and Girauld de Borneil in his *Divina Commedia*, while Petrarch laid the foundations of the Romantic legend of Joufrè Rudel and Melisande in his *Trionfi* (Triumphs). Dante looked upon the twelfth century as the golden age of poetry and chivalry in sharp contrast with the gloom that he saw in his own day.

ARTHURIAN LEGENDS

From France came also the Arthurian legends, couched in Anglo-Norman verse. They sang of the new peoples who inhabited the British island. History, religion, and romance are beautifully woven into these legends, poetic creations as meaningful to the British as the Homeric poems had been to the ancient Greeks.

The material of King Arthur and the Round Table went to Italy through French compilations of that fanciful subject matter. In the twelfth century, Beroul (1150) and Thomas (1170) wrote in Anglo-Norman dialect of Tristan and Isolde, of Lancelot and the Holy Grail. However, the greatest contributor to the Arthurian legends was Chrétien de Troyes who died in 1195. These tales crossed the Alps and delighted the courtly circles of northern Italy, whence they spread throughout the country.

Although it was not until the thirteenth century that a vast wealth of manuscripts of translations into the vernacular was available, the Arthurian legends had, nevertheless, already left a deep imprint on the cultural life of the twelfth century. We find the name of King Arthur engraved by an unknown artist on the door of the cathedral of Modena over a warrior sculptured in bas-relief. Likewise, the names of the famous king and his knights echo in many of the historical Latin works written at the end of the century. The references to the Arthurian legends are too many to be here enumerated. The heroes of Britain, especially Tristan, constituted one of the main factors in the cultural background of Italian literature of the thirteenth century. In this century Arthurian legends rival in importance those of Classicism and of Provençal lore.

These brief references to the contacts of Italian men of letters with the material of classical antiquity, the Carolingian tales and the courtly love of Provençal poetry, as well as with the Arthurian legends, constitute the cultural background on which we shall present the rich harvest of creative works in the annals of early Italian literature. Awareness of their deep influence is of inestimable value in explaining the form taken by Italian letters, especially in courtly circles, from the early days until the nineteenth century. The past never died, and the new poets were ever ready to weave its culture into the fabric of their works of imagination.

CHAPTER THREE

Contributions to Culture During the Thirteenth Century

HISTORICAL BACKGROUND

The thirteenth century was one of the most creative ages in Italian history, so powerful and so vivid that the men and events of today often pale in comparison. The narrow and winding streets of the cities were filled with people dedicated to work or with individuals who fought in violent clashes for political and artistic ideals. On festive days, the squares overflowed with human beings listening to storytellers who related the exploits of Roland and of the paladins of Charlemagne. In the churches, the people were admonished to think of the salvation of their souls, and the joys of Paradise were described. The noble and wealthy classes enjoyed the gaiety of the courts and the songs of the poets who awakened a sense of beauty and of harmony in those who listened to their exaltation of feminine charm and love. Intermittently, wars between cities, assassinations, reprisals, and raids broke the normal rhythm of life. Against this turbulent background, noteworthy achievements were made in every phase of intellectual, artistic, and practical activity. A truly amazing energy animated the eight million people who inhabited the peninsula at that time. Of the many whose contributions were great, three outstanding figures emerge: St. Francis of Assisi, Dante, and Giotto.

Political history of the thirteenth century was characterized by the battle between the conservatives and the liberals. Two names echoed: the Guelphs and the Ghibellines, taken from the names of two hostile German families, Welf and Weibelingen. Brought into Italy, Guelph had come to signify faith in the new democracy of the Communes, and Ghibelline represented the attachment to the ideals of the old feudal and imperial aristocracy. Although the people shouted, "Long live the Emperor! Long live the Pope!" the clash was essentially between the conservatives, who were at times reactionaries, and the liberals, who often carried their liberalism to the point of revolution.

From 1220 when Frederick II, the son of Henry VI of Germany and

Costanza, the last descendant of the Normans, ascended the throne of Sicily, the Empire succeeded in stemming the rising tide of the Communes, thanks to the political ability of the emperor. Certain historical facts clearly document the power of the Empire. In 1231, with the *Constitution of Melfi,* Frederick II, who wished to centralize the authority of the state in his own hands, succeeded in limiting the power of both the lay and the ecclesiastic authorities as well as that of the Communes in the kingdom of Sicily. He allied himself with the lords of northern Italy and saw to it that his children contracted marriages favorable to the imperial cause. In 1237, he defeated the militia of the Lombard Communes at Cortenuova.

The beginning of the decline of the Empire was marked in 1239 when Pope Gregory IX launched a crusade against Frederick II, fearing that the imperial authority would consolidate itself in Italy and wreck the dream of the temporal power of the Papacy. In 1241, he convoked the Council of Rome and excommunicated the Emperor, a measure confirmed at the Council of Lyons in 1245. In 1248, Frederick II was defeated at Vittoria by the allied forces of the Communes. His death in 1250 marked the end of the predominance of imperial power in Italy.

The second half of the century saw the triumph of the Communes, especially in Florence where the democratic government succeeded in taking hold and annexing a large part of Tuscany. For long years, the Communes had been fighting continuously, some for the Pope, some for the Empire, but always seeking their own interest and aiming at local supremacy. Pisa had been weakened by the powerful navies of Genoa and Venice in the battle of Meloria in 1284, a preliminary action that was to lead to the final and mortal duel between the two cities in 1298 at Curzola. Genoa crushed Venice and wrested from her the supremacy of the East. However, Genoa herself came out so weakened by the battle that she was unable to prevent the Turks from seizing her possessions in the East. The Communes did not realize that, by an ill-directed concept of freedom, they were paving the way for the servitude of Italy. They lacked a clear consciousness of their future. They did not see that the logic of history carried them toward unity, that their local liberty depended on the vicissitudes in the international sphere, and that Spain, Germany, and France were ready to invade and make of Italy a dependent province.

France, hiding her imperialism under the mask of democracy, was the first to occupy the throne of Sicily and Naples. Charles of Anjou, brother of Louis IX, King of France, in the year 1266, defeated Manfredi, the son of Frederick II, at Benevento. Charles of Anjou had been called to Italy the year before by Pope Clement IV, who had vested in him the authority over the kingdom of Naples and Sicily. In 1268, he conquered Corradino, the last heir of the Swabian throne, at Tagliagozzo in Abruzzi. Thus Charles of Anjou, a French king, became the undisputed master of the realm until 1282, when his tyrannical rule led to the rebellion of the Sicilian Vespers. The Spaniards, who had fomented this rebellion, replaced the French as masters of Sicily by putting Peter III of Aragon on the throne at Palermo. To the French remained the kingdom of Naples, where the Anjou royal family established a splendid court.

In the meantime, there appeared in the various Communes ambitious men who were members of families that had become wealthy by trading with the East and with European countries. These men, with subtle artifice, confused the people and succeeded in having conferred upon themselves lasting authority. Thus was established the rule of the Signoria. At Milan with the Visconti family, at Florence with Giano della Bella, at Mantua with the Este family, at Verona with the Scaligeri, the democratic government was replaced by the rule of despots who, in the name of the people, destroyed the free forms of civil government. They eventually constituted the aristocracy of the fifteenth and sixteenth centuries when the Signoria became hereditary.

However, communal spirit and love for democracy did not die. The autocratic excesses of the demagogue Giano della Bella created such a strong reaction in Florence that the Conservatives or White Party came to power in 1295. It ruled until 1302 when Charles of Valois, the envoy of the theocratic Pope Boniface VIII, decreed that members of the White Party who were in the government should be exiled. After the death of Boniface, through the efforts of Philip the Fair, King of France, Bertrand of Goth, a Frenchman, was elected Pope under the name of Clement V. To the consternation of all Christianity, he moved the seat of the Papacy to Avignon in 1309.

Politically, the regime of the Signoria, supplanting the free Commune, gradually spread throughout the rest of Italy and, both politically and economically, the country slowly fell into a torpor. Liberty remained but a dream, although it was never wiped out from the memory and the soul of the Italian people.

CULTURAL CONTRIBUTIONS

Intellectual and artistic life was very active during the stormy years of the thirteenth century. The records of the cultural history of the time cannot be scanned without a sense of wonder at and admiration for all that was produced while war and civil strife raged in the cities of the Italian peninsula.

Important contributions to political, juridical, philosophic, and theological thought continued to be written in Latin. The work of the early glossators was carried on at Bologna by Francesco di Accorso (1182-1260). To him we owe the *Glossa Magna*, a collection of the works of the glossators who preceded him. It contains one hundred thousand *glossae* or marginal notes in which Roman law was interpreted. The importance of Accorso lies in having shown critically that Roman law did not die during the centuries of the Christian Age and that the laws of the Italian Communes reflected its wisdom and spirit.

In the tumultuous political life of this century, the slow process whereby the lay state was making itself independent of Papacy went on with increasing tempo while thinkers pondered the duties of the new princes towards their subjects. Frederick II was one of the first to put into writing his views on the lay state. To him the lay state and its laws were a definite reality, as proved by his *Constitution of Melfi* in 1231.[1]

One of the earliest contributors to political thought was St. Thomas Aquinas (*ca.* 1225-1274), one of the great philosophers of all time. He was a Dominican monk and a great scholar. He investigated every field of knowledge: the psychology of sensations, the formation of ideas, the nature of concepts, human society, and the culture of his time.[2] He knew Greek, perhaps Hebrew also, and contributed to the spread of Greek culture. He was a pupil of Albert the Great, a famous theologian. He was also a contemporary of Roger Bacon with whom he marked a new phase in the study of philosophy. In addition to being a professor of theology, he had a great interest in political economy. In 1260, he charged William Moerbeke, a Flemish Dominican monk, with the task of translating into Latin the *Politics* of Aristotle, a work that became one of the sources for scholars interested in law.

We owe to Thomas Aquinas the important *De Regimine Principum* (Concerning the Rule of Princes) which marked a departure in the attitude of a churchman toward capitalism and clearly showed the vastness of his mind.[3] *De Regimine Principum* was addressed to the king of Cyprus, Hugh II of Lusignan, to whom he wished to show the best rules for the government of the state. The author stated his belief that authority comes from God, but it resides in the people. He proclaimed that the state exists for the individual and that the importance of the group is subordinate to that of the individuals who compose it. For him the individual was sacred and the citizens the only social reality in the state. The vote should be the privilege of every intelligent and cultured citizen. It is difficult to understand how, having so many new ideas, he could accept the practice of slavery and place slaves on the same level as material possessions owned by the master. He condemned the practice of lending money and of paying interest, but this traditional conclusion was accompanied by a very important distinction between productive capital, invested in a house or landed property, and dead capital, that is, uninvested capital. Those who realize that the traditional attitude of the Church had been hostile to every form of lending money with interest will understand the novelty of such a distinction and the contribution of Thomas Aquinas to the theory of capitalism.

So great was the authority of St. Thomas that one of his pupils, Egidio Romano (*ca.* 1247-1316), known in English history as Giles of Rome, modeled on the book of his teacher the work which he wrote around 1285 for Philip the Fair, who had been a pupil of Egidio in his early youth. The work of Egidio Romano bears the same title as that of St. Thomas and reflects the ideas of both his teacher and Aristotle, on whose writings he composed many commentaries. The book *De Regimine Principum* was published in 1288, and again in 1577.[4] It was translated into French, Spanish, Hebrew, and the Italian vernacular.

Thomas Aquinas also stands out as an important figure in the field of theological and philosophical works written in Latin. In sharp contrast with him is another great churchman, St. Bonaventure of Bagnorea (1221-1274). Although both thinkers moved within the orbit of Christian dogmatism, Thomas Aquinas granted a large role to the intellect in discussing the search for truth. His faith relied on the "understanding" of the object of our beliefs. Bonaventure followed the mystics and relied on intuition since, for him, the object of our faith transcends the capacity of the human mind.

The clash between the two men reflected the bitter struggle waged by their respective orders, intensified by the fact that both Thomas and Bonaventure taught theology at the same time at the University of Paris, the European center of theology. The cultural background of Thomas was Aristotle, who was considered by him the exponent of the scientific approach to religion. Bonaventure relied on Plato, as interpreted by St. Augustine. The split between the two schools of thought continued throughout the Renaissance.

The most important work of Thomas Aquinas in the theological field is the *Summa Theologiae* (Essentials of Theology).[5] The significant feature of this work is the attempt on the part of the author to strengthen the dogma of Christian theology with the conclusions of the pagan thinker, Aristotle. In perusing Aristotle's works, Thomas rejected the strictly scientific interpretation given to them by Averroes in the Arab schools of Toledo. The commentary by Thomas Aquinas constitutes one of the ways through which Greek culture, and especially the scientific thought of Aristotle, became known in the West and blended on a parallel plane with the influence of the works of Plato.

St. Bonaventure was a Franciscan monk. His most important work was the mystic treatise *Iter Mentis ad Deum* (The Journey of the Mind to God).[6] He was a most limpid mirror of the spirit of St. Francis of Assisi, whose life he wrote under the title of *The Legend of St. Francis*. The work is a fervent rendering of the life of the saint in which the deeds of the humble monk are enveloped in an aura of heroic saintliness.

SCHOOLS AND UNIVERSITIES

The condition of schools and universities at this time was a clear confirmation of the rising level of cultural life during the thirteenth century. Children of well-to-do families were still trained in the Trivium and the Quadrivium by teachers of rhetoric. They were taught how to speak well and to write well, according to the rules set forth by the *Artes dictandi*, manuals of rhetoric which explained how to do so correctly, clearly, and effectively, both in Latin and in the Italian vernacular. Interest in the vulgar tongue developed in the same measure as interest in the beautiful Latin form.

By the thirteenth century many, among whom Dante was the greatest, felt that the Italian vernacular was the legitimate medium through which feelings and thoughts could be expressed. We know that in the first decade of the century a famous Florentine, Buoncompagno of Signa, taught at Bologna. He left us a compilation of rules on the epistolary style in the vernacular. Bene of Florence, another teacher, was the author of *Candelabrum*, a book of rhetoric which corresponded to the "trees" or diagrams of the sciences and laws of the time. Guido Fava or Faba (*ca.* 1190-*ca.* 1243) also taught rhetoric at Bologna and wrote a manual that aimed at showing pupils how to develop and present in a dignified form the subject matter of their writings. It bore the title of *Doctrina ad inveniendas, incipiendas et formandas materias* (The Theory of Conceiving, Expressing, and Giving a Beautiful Form to Our Thoughts).[7] He offered both classic and vernacular examples of beautiful style. The examples in the vulgar tongue are of greater interest than the Latin ones since they show that the vernacular was coming into use more and more at the beginning of the century. Guido Fava's text appeared around 1239. He also wrote a *Summa dictaminis* (Summary of Rhetoric) and the *Gemma purpurea* (Examples of Excellent Eloquence).[8]

Many universities were founded in the thirteenth century. The University of Padua had its origin when, in 1222, a group of dissatisfied teachers and students left the excessively Guelph Bologna and established themselves in Padua. Throughout the Renaissance this city was famous as a center of the Averroistic tendency in philosophy and as a scientific center. The University of Naples was founded in 1224 by Frederick II, who imparted on the life of his age a strong cultural impulse toward science as opposed to theology. Other universities of minor importance that were founded in the early decades of the century did not live long. Among these were those of Vicenza (1204), Reggio (1219) and Sienna (1246). The latter two closed after a century, and that of Vicenza ended in 1248. The rising of these centers of learning bears testimony to flourishing economic conditions as well as to the spread of culture, while their closing is a silent testimony of the downward trend of Italian economic and political life that reached a very marked depression in the following century.

TRANSLATIONS INTO THE VERNACULAR

In the over-all character of its civilization, the thirteenth century was infinitely less classical than was the preceding one. From the standpoint of language, Latin remained, to be sure, the language of cultured persons, but French and Provençal were widely studied and even used by Italian authors and poets. Brunetto Latini (1229-1295) wrote his *Trésors* (The Treasure), a sort of encyclopedia on physics and astrology, in French, explaining that he did so because the French language was at that time the most delightful and the most popular. His work was very famous in his day, and Dante looked upon Brunetto as his teacher. *Il Milione* (Millions) of Marco Polo was also first drawn up in French. It has already been pointed out that many poets in northern Italy, although Italian, used Provençal in writing their verse.

A new phenomenon in the culture of the century was the translation and compilation from Latin, French, and Provençal into the vernacular. Since the art of translation as we understand it today did not exist, the dividing line between translation and compilation was not very clear. Authors felt free to add to the text that they translated whatever material they had known in other works. They also adapted it to the conditions of their time, changing Romans into knights and Christianizing pagan authors as the occasion demanded. The vernacular was recognized as the logical medium for the dissemination of learning among those who did not know Latin. It is interesting to note that much of the literature that was being translated into the vernacular during the thirteenth century had been recast into Latin in the preceding century.

Among the important translations of the classics into the vernacular was that of Cicero's *De Inventione* (Concerning Inspiration) by Brunetto Latini. *De Inventione* was freely rehandled by Brunetto and was adapted to the political life of his time in which he took, as a member of the Black Party, a very direct part. The work was done around 1260, the date of the battle of Montaperti, which spelled disaster for the Blacks of Florence.

Toward the middle of the century, Fra Guidotto, a monk from Bologna, translated the *Rhetorica ad Herennium*,[9] a work generally attributed to Cicero, but actually written by an unknown author familiar with Cicero's ideas on rhetoric. Fra Guidotto shows himself fully conscious of the function of eloquence in the society of his time, and he applies its principles to the art of persuading one's listeners.

Bono Giamboni, a Florentine judge, whose name appears frequently in documents of the time between 1261 and 1292, was another important translator of the second half of the century. He translated *Rei Militaris Instituta*, the work of the Roman Vegetius on the art of war, and Paolo Orosio's *History Against the Pagans*, written at the beginning of the fifth century A.D. Giamboni also rendered into the Italian vernacular the *Trésors* by Brunetto Latini during the lifetime of the author, as well as a moral treatise by Pope Innocent III. Worthy of interest is the fact that Paolo Orosio's history was translated into English by King Alfred in the ninth century.

Among the compilations in the vernacular that appeared in this century, there stand out the so-called *Fiori* or anthologies of ethical principles to be found in the works of the Ancients. Toward the middle of the century, there appeared the *Fiori e vite di filosofi ed altri savi ed imperatori* (Flowers and Lives of Philosophers, Wise Men, and Emperors). It was a free translation by an anonymous author of the *Speculum Historiale* (Historical Mirror) by Vincent de Beauvais, with additions of his own. It consists of twenty-nine chapters in which the author also gives an outline of the lives of those whose maxims he quotes.

Around 1300, a monk from Bologna, Brother Tommaso Gozzadini, put together a *Fiore di virtù* (Moral Maxims), collected sayings and tales from the Bible, the classical authors, and the Fathers of the Church, the accepted sources of all knowledge for the men of the time. Taking advantage of the freedom allowed translators, the author presents the theme of virtue, ingenuously and even humorously, as a guide to happy living in our contacts with our fellow men.

Of similar encyclopedic nature were the *Ammaestramenti degli antichi* (Teachings of the Ancients), written toward the end of the century by the Dominican Fra Bartolomeo of San Concordio (1262-1347). He was requested by the wealthy Florentine Geri Spini to translate into the vernacular his own collection of classical maxims which included those culled from writings of Cicero, Seneca, and Ovid. To him we also owe the translation of the works of Sallust, a Latin historian of the first century B.C.

Of great significance also was the use of the vernacular in spreading the knowledge of scientific material. A typical example was the *Composizione del mondo* (The Composition of the World), a treatise in two books written at the end of the century by Ristoro of Arezzo, a monk who possessed a keen sense of observation as well as artistic taste. In it he discussed such natural phenomena as the eclipse, frost, curative waters, the stars and their movement.

Toward the end of the century, side by side with the interest in scientific material, but completely different, was the interest in the legends of the Carolingian cycle, as is evidenced by the free rehandling of the stories of Roland and Charlemagne in poems written in a mixture of French and Venetian dialect. Epic poems taken from French originals about the Carolingian knights appeared especially in Venice. Simultaneously, the *Roman de la Rose* (Romance of the Rose) was translated into two hundred thirty-two often salacious sonnets under the title of *Il fiore* (The Flower). Until recent times, these sonnets were erroneously attributed to Dante.[10]

The compilers of fictional material turned their interest toward the *Roman de Renart* (The Romance of the Fox) as is proved by fragments of translations bearing the Italianized titles of *Reinardo* and *Isengrino* and dealing with the exploits of the dull-witted wolf Ysengrin and the shrewd fox Renart.[11] Although somewhat different from the French text, the Italian version shows that the characteristics of the two animals as given in the French text were kept in the literature of much later periods.

There also exist translations and free handling of other French poems in which the Carolingian legend had vast ramifications, both in the field of history and in that of fantasy. In a codex of the Marciana Library in Venice, there is still unpublished material dealing with such Carolingian characters as Buovo d'Antona, Bertha with the Big Feet, and Ugieri the Dane.

The best known poems in the Franco-Venetian dialect are the *Entrée en Espagne* (Entrance into Spain), by an unknown poet from Padua, and the *Prise de Pampelune* (The Seizure of Pampeluna), written by Niccolò of Verona about a city in Spain of that name. The latter also wrote the last one hundred thirty-one lines of the *Entrée en Espagne* and developed the material of the Carolingian legend more fully than did his predecessor. Although Niccolò of Verona has left occasional glimmers of poetry, his work belongs to the sphere of culture rather than to that of poetry.

The legends of King Arthur and his knights[12] were collected by Rusticiano or Rustichello of Pisa in his *Meliadus,* a title taken from the name of King Arthur's father. Rusticiano used material gathered from the works of the French authors Beroul, Thomas, and Chrétien de Troyes. This compilation is very close to the translations of the time, although the material is rehandled with extreme freedom. Rusticiano also translated into the vernacular the *Lancelot* by Chrétien de Troyes. Another compilation of Arthurian legends, which appeared toward the end of the century, was *La tavola ritonda* (The Round Table).[13] In similar vein was *Les prophecies de Merlin* (The Prophecies of Merlin),[14] published in Venice between 1274 and 1278, a short poem in which events of Italian history are interwoven with the Arthurian legends.

It is interesting to note that there are two versions of the Tristan legends, known as *Tristano Riccardiano* and *Tristano Corsiniano,* from the name of the libraries which own the manuscripts of the two works.[15]

Since the vernacular was especially the language of the people, it is not surprising to find that the legends of the saints, which in the previous century were found in Latin, were written in the vernacular. These are more important from the point of view of the history of the language rather than for any artistic merit that they possess. However, the exception is the *Leggenda Aurea* (Golden Legend) which belongs to the precincts of narrative art. One of the most read books of the time, it was first penned in Latin in 1266 and later frequently translated into the vernacular. It was written by Jacopo of Varazze or Varagine (1230-1298), who was archbishop of this small town near Genoa until 1298, the year of his death.[16] The book is a collection of the lives of the saints in one hundred seventy-seven short chapters and was meant to be read by the faithful on the days when special saints were celebrated by the Church. The author possesses a candor and a simplicity which permit him to envelop his characters in a transparency not different from that often lent by the thirteenth-century artists to the mystic figures of their frescoes.

PRACTICAL ACHIEVEMENTS

The student of the civilization of the thirteenth century finds a perfect harmony between practical and intellectual activities. Side by side with works of great thinkers, distinguished achievements in engineering as well as important discoveries by travelers and explorers were registered.

Many Italian cities made tremendous strides in both engineering and public works. At Milan, the Grand Canal, a vast system of canals joining the city to the Po, was constructed between 1179 and 1258. Genoa improved the conditions of its port by building, between 1176 and 1283, gigantic piers for its protection. In 1295, in the same city, a great aqueduct was brought to completion. Venice developed then the glass industry in which that city held first place until the end of the century.

FAMOUS TRAVELERS

Giovanni del Pian of Carpine (Perugia, 1182-1252), the Flemish William of Rubruquis and the Venetian Marco Polo make up the triad of the great explorers of the time. Del Pian, a Franciscan, went on a diplomatic mission to Mongolia for Pope Innocent IV, leaving Italy in 1245 and returning two years later, after having crossed the Balkans, Russia, and Asia. The fruit of his trip was his book *Historia Mongolorum* (History of the Mongols),[17] a document important for the history and civilization of that people.

Famous and well known are the members of the Venetian family of Polo, Niccolò, Matteo, and Marco, who were partners and traded with the Orient. They owned warehouses in both Constantinople and in Crimea. In 1260, they went to India and traveled as far as the court of Kublai Khan in Mongolia. Marco has completely eclipsed his relatives because of his famous book *Il Milione* (Millions), one of the early original prose works in the vernacular that has come down to us.

Giovanni of Montecorvino (*ca.* 1247-1328) went as a missionary to China and to India where he founded the first Christian mission. One of his letters of 1291 to Bartolomeo of San Concordio shows him to be an acute and precise observer both of the economic life and the geography of India.

Lanzarote Malociclo who lived in the second half of the century discovered, around 1270, the northern Canary Islands and tried to colonize them in the name of Genoa.

The brothers Vivaldi, Ugolino and Vadino, were Genoese navigators who tried to reach India by sailing around Africa. They disappeared without leaving any trace. Leone Vivaldi, son of Ugolino, undertook a similar voyage and landed on the coast of Somaliland at Mogadiscio.

Ascellino was another traveler who lived around 1250. He was a Dominican friar, also sent by Pope Innocent IV to Mongolia. At the end of the century, a Genoese, Buscarello dei Guizolfi, was also active in the Orient. He was in the service of the Khan of Persia from 1284 to 1291.

USE OF ARABIC NUMBERS

Among the cultural accomplishments of the thirteenth century, we must include the introduction into Europe of the practical Arabic numbers which replaced the complicated Roman numerals. This advance was due to the work of Leonardo Fibonacci (*ca.* 1170-*ca.* 1240), the son of a Pisan factory owner on the Barbary Coast, who traveled extensively in the Mediterranean and learned the numerical system of the Arabs from a Moslem teacher. In his book *Liber Abaci*, which appeared in 1202 and again in 1228, he discussed and explained the use of Arabic numbers. The American scholar and his-

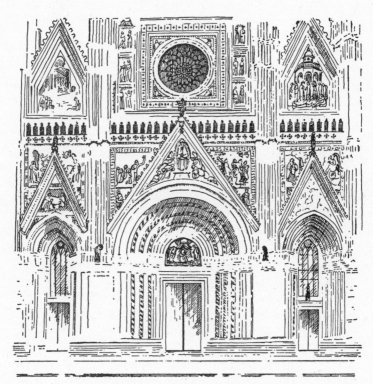

Façade, Cathedral of Orvieto,
by Arnolfo of Cambio and others.

torian, George Sarton, calls Fibonacci the "greatest Christian mathematician of the Middle Ages."[18]

THE STUDY OF MEDICINE

The science of medicine developed tremendously in this century. Dissection of human bodies was begun by physicians at the University of Bologna around 1270. This was a great step forward in the study of anatomy and added greatly

to what was known in this field of science through the charts of the pig transmitted from the Salernitan School and the treatise on the falcon attributed
to Frederick II.

There is a long list of illustrious physicians, among whom Guglielmo of
Saliceto (1210-1280) was the most renowned surgeon of his time. He taught
at the University of Bologna and wrote a treatise on surgery and a book of

Courtyard of Palazzo Vecchio, Florence,
by Arnolfo of Cambio and others.

rules on hygiene, entitled *Summa Conservationis* (Health Rules). His pupil,
Lanfranco of Pavia, who died around 1306, was exiled by the Visconti of
Milan for his democratic ideas and sought refuge in France where he was
known as "Le Grand Alanfranc." He introduced there the innovations in
surgery practiced under his famous teacher and wrote two famous treatises
on that branch of medicine, *Minor Surgery* and *Major Surgery*.

Another illustrious physician was Taddeo degli Alderotti (1229-1295)
who taught at Bologna and was the personal physician of Pope Honorius IV.
His handbook on hygiene was famous, and his work on preventive medicine
anticipated many modern views on keeping fit.

Aldobrandino of Siena was another distinguished physician who wrote a book on hygiene and on diet. It was written for Beatrice of Savoy when she set out to visit her four daughters, all of whom had become queens through marriage.

THE FINE ARTS

The salient point in the history of the arts in the thirteenth century, from Cavallini and Cimabue to Pisano and Giotto, is the deliberate and clear pres-

Madonna, Cathedral of Orvieto,
by Arnolfo of Cambio. Marble.

ence of the personality of the artist in the styles that this century inherited from the past: the Byzantine, the Romanesque, and the Gothic. In the Byzantine works, the artist made every effort to eliminate himself. He was satisfied to execute his work for the glory of the Lord and he conformed as much as possible to the pattern set by tradition. The new artist looked upon his work as an expression of his personality and he constantly sought new forms, whether in architecture, sculpture, or painting. The personal attitude is demonstrated by the fact that most of the specific works bear the names of their creators. The cultural element that is found in all the great works of this century obeyed the creativeness of the artists whether, in their quest for new forms, they used Byzantine, Romanesque, or Classical patterns. It would be a great blunder to assign to the Renaissance only the works, literary or artistic, in which the cultural substratum was classical. The three styles continued

Pulpit, Sant'Andrea Pistoia,
by Giovanni Pisano. Marble.

long after this period and were variously used by artists who revealed in them their personalities.

Architecture continued the traditions of the previous century, but increasingly grafted Gothic elements on the Romanesque. Sant'Andrea at

Vercelli, the Lower and Upper Church of Assisi, the cathedral of Siena planned by Nicola Pisano, that of Orvieto or San Michele by Arnolfo of Cambio, the church of the Frari at Venice, the cemetery at Pisa by Giovanni Pisano, Santa Croce and Santa Maria del Fiore, also by Arnolio, are magnificent examples of the creativeness and inventiveness that add luster to the glory of the Early Renaissance period.

Built at the same time were the communal palaces of Piacenza, Como, Cremona, Siena, San Gimignano, the palace of the Podestà at Florence and that of the Signoria, also at Florence, designed by Arnolfo.

Sculpture was given new life by Nicola Pisano, helped by his son Giovanni and his pupil Arnolfo. Nicola Pisano was both an architect and a sculptor. At Siena, his cathedral, a poem in black and white marble, testifies to what he could do in architecture. His greatness as a sculptor is shown by the pulpit at Pisa, that at Siena, and the fountain at Perugia. The pulpit at Siena, in its massive proportions, in the many scenes sculptured in its five panels, and in the naturalistic themes intertwined on the columns that form its base, is one of the miracles of Italian sculpture. One thinks of Pisano as a simple and unassuming person, completely absorbed by his art, the great calling of his long and peaceful life.

Giovanni Pisano, although not so famous as his father, sculptured the beautiful pulpit in the church of Sant'Andrea at Pistoia and that in the cathedral of Pisa.

In the history of painting, one notices an increasing trend toward Naturalism. This new mode first appeared in Giovanni Cimabue (d. ca. 1302) and Pietro Cavallini (ca. 1250-1339). In Giotto (1266-1337), Naturalism blends most effectively with the religious themes which he illustrated in the frescoes at Assisi, at the chapel of the Arena at Padua, and in his native Florence. His closeness to actual life is so definite and wholesome that the veils of allegory, far from weakening, only soften his figures and add to them the charm that modern artists have felt in his frescoes.

The novelty and vastness of the culture of the thirteenth century justifies the enthusiasm of modern historians and poets who have exalted the greatness of this age.

CHAPTER FOUR

Poetry During the Thirteenth Century

At this time, poetry was considered a more important medium of artistic expression than was prose. Prose was deemed more appropriate for the practical needs of everyday life and for the transmission of knowledge and culture. In fact, poetry antedated prose in the literary history of the thirteenth century. Dante believed that poets preceded prose-writers and prepared the language that the latter used in their writings.[1]

The student is justly surprised at observing at the very beginning of the century a sudden and astonishingly significant literature in the vernacular. It seems hardly short of a miracle that the Italian language should, so early in its life, make its appearance as a polished instrument of expression, capable of communicating even the most subtle thoughts and feelings. The language of today, in both vocabulary and structure, has not changed basically from the language used then.

In studying the literary records of the thirteenth century, one finds two distinct levels or planes: popular literature and courtly literature, a division partly determined by the difference of the social classes to which the two modes of literature were directed. Popular literature aimed at a direct and close-up portrait of man and his passions, and was, therefore, both sensuous and humorous; courtly literature dealt definitely with concepts of reality and was, as a consequence, lofty and idealistic.

Popular poetry, often anonymous, echoed in the squares and in the streets of the various Italian cities or cheered the gatherings of the middle class, while courtly poetry was written in the courts of the princes and in the homes of people of high lineage. Those who wrote courtly poetry were mostly courtiers around Frederick II at Palermo, the supporters of the Empire all over Italy, or members of the White Party in Florence. Since these men of culture relied upon the pittance that powerful lords or wealthy men of the middle class gave them, their verse often reflected political factors and party lines.

On the whole, courtly poetry was related to the conservatism of the Ghibellines and popular poetry to the liberalism of the Guelphs.

It goes without saying that individual temperament also influenced poets in veering toward either popular or courtly poetry. Popular poetry was as spontaneous as the other was reflective and togated. Popular poets looked upon love as an instinctive force, without the veils with which tradition had enveloped it. Courtly poets, in their aggressive exclusiveness, separated very sharply men with a "gentle heart" from the ordinary men whose tastes were uncouth and whose moral habits were vulgar. Only a "gentle heart" could feel love upon gazing on the loveliness of a lady. All the members of their group possessed, of course, a "gentle heart," and all the ladies whom they loved were examples of physical and spiritual perfection. These poets called themselves *servi d'Amore* (servants of Love), an echo of the tradition of Provence and the court of Palermo, and they sang of love by suffusing the longing of their hearts with a Platonic haze.

The two types of poetry were also distinct from each other in their metric form. Popular poetry made use of the *canzonetta*, the *ballata*, originally sung at May Day dances, the Tuscan *rispetto*, the *lauda*, the meter used in the mystery play, and the Sicilian *strambotto*, almost all short compositions. Courtly poetry, on the other hand, preferred as a rule more stately meters. The most frequently used was the *canzone*. The *canzone* consisted of a varying number of stanzas, from five to seven, all patterned on the first as to length of lines and rhyme scheme. Poets often concluded their *canzone* with a shorter stanza called *tornada* or *commiato*, very often used by them to enjoin their *canzone*, variously personified, to seek the company of people of *intendimento* (understanding and refinement) and to avoid undiscriminating persons who would prevent it from reaching the lovely lady to whom it was directed.

Provençal poets brought to Italian lyric the *tenzone*, a composition used to express two contrasting points of view on love, literary art, and politics. Another metrical form cultivated in Italy as a result of Provençal influence was the *sirventese*. It had been used for political content and was characterized by bitter sarcasm and invectives. In Italy, it also expressed a sense of admiration for women, if we are to judge by the testimony of Dante, who tells us in the *Vita Nuova* (The New Life) of having composed a *sirventese*, now lost, in honor of the sixty most beautiful women of Florence, among whom Beatrice occupied ninth place. The *contrasto*, a meter variously used by both popular and courtly poets, was a metrical composition in the form of a dialogue in which two opposite points of view were expressed. Such discussions of the relative merits of a rose and a violet or of the pen and the sword, were handed down from the Latin tradition of the Christian Age. In the thirteenth century, the *contrasto* was used in love poems, in which a suitor pleaded his cause to a cold and indifferent lady.

The division of poetry into the popular and courtly levels is justified by what Dante, a contemporary witness, has written about it in the *Vita Nuova*, composed around 1292, and in the *De Vulgari Eloquentia* (On the Vernacular), a study written a few years later. In both works, he bore witness to the existence of the two modes of poetry by extolling the courtly and vilifying the popular. So violent were his attacks that one feels that his extreme reaction against popular poetry was the result, in part, of his dislike of the populism of the Guelphs. He made a very sharp line of division between the two types of poetry, taking into account their content, vocabulary, and metrical form. He assigned to courtly poetry the task of dealing with ideally viewed human emotions as contrasted with the sensuality of popular poetry.[2] He reserved for courtly poetry "noble" concepts, "noble" words, "noble" because of Latin derivation, and the metrical form of the stately *canzone*. He constantly and unconditionally showed contempt for the language and forms of popular songs. Their bold sensualism, enclosed as a rule in jarring dialectal words, offended his concept of harmonious language and polished form.

Although he restricted his observations to courtly poetry, Dante outlined very clearly the history of poetry in his age. He stated that only in the last one hundred and fifty years had poets written in the vernacular of Provence and Italy, thus assigning the beginning of poetry to 1150 or thereabouts. Before this time poets had written in Latin, but when women no longer understood that language, they expressed their love in Provençal or Italian.[3] According to him, whatever poetry was written in the thirteenth century was called Sicilian, because of the renown that the vernacular of that island had acquired throughout the courts of Italy.[4]

The strains of popular and courtly poetry were unquestionably different and distinct; yet, we must not conclude that these two types were divided by an absolutely fast line. It was not unusual for courtly poets to use modes and forms typical of popular poetry and for popular songsters to refer to the classical and Arthurian traditions. Poets of the court of Frederick II, those of the Florentine group, and Dante himself, abandoned at times the traditional loftiness of the grand style and indulged in the modes and wantonness of popular poets. Conversely, popular poets attempted to ennoble their poems by mentioning legendary characters. These brief deviations confirm rather than deny the historical reality of the two trends.

The intermittent use of the two modes by the same poet is somewhat confusing and one logically wonders which style was natural to the poet. One might even be led to conclude that the predominating form of that time was the one characterized by simplicity and naturalness, the favorite type of the people and the middle class. Viewed from this perspective, the courtly poetry of the time would appear the exception and not the rule, adapted only to a few truly lyrical temperaments, such as Cavalcanti.

We propose to assume as objective an attitude as possible toward the two main art modes found in the literary history of the century. Modern aesthetics has radically departed from the Aristotelian position, accepted by Dante and his friends, that the subject matter determines the noble or low character of art. From the postulate that the history of a king was more poetic than that of a commoner, Aristotle concluded that tragedy was more noble than comedy. However, from the days of Romanticism to our own time the belief has gained ground that the poetic quality of a work of art is determined by the artist and not by the subject matter. The humble kitchen garden can become memorable and lovely under the pen of a true poet, while the most beautiful formal garden can become meaningless if a mediocre poet uses it as his art material. A corollary of this belief is that naturalistic, idealistic, and strictly imaginative themes are not "art," but only the "material" that artists are free to choose and use to reveal their temperament, ideas, and artistic capacity. The greatest of the popular poets of the time, Cecco Angiolieri, reflected a cynical view of human existence in his poems and these are still understandable and significant for us today. Dante, the most outstanding of the courtly poets, embodied in his sonnets his memory of a girl whom he had loved when a mere youth, and the ages have not dimmed the luminous beauty of that image nor the harmony of the lines that he dedicated to her. Both men were different and both poets used different media to make enduring the anguish of their hearts, one through a scoffing cynicism whose poignancy has seldom been equaled, the other through an inimitable devotion to the memory of a pearl-like countenance.

In the context of these conclusions, the naturalism of popular poetry and the idealism of the courtly school are on the same footing. Neither popular nor courtly poetry will be evaluated in terms of the naturalistic or idealistic elements that it contains, but rather through the common denominator of the significance achieved, the measure of human feelings revealed, and the beauty of form and melodiousness found therein. To study poetry is to discover the common ground where all types and varieties meet.

CHAPTER FIVE

Popular Poetry

The first real attempts at poetry in the Italian vernacular belong to the thirteenth century. It is difficult at times to ascertain whether some of the poems belong to this century or to the preceding one, for it is only logical to believe that many of the songs to be found in its chronicles and manuscripts came from an earlier time.[1] Giosuè Carducci[2] discovered in 1276 a great number of poems in the records of the Archives of the Notaries at Bologna that registered deeds executed by them. In these official documents unknown notaries had interspersed popular songs, many of them composed at an earlier date. However, on the whole, little actually remains of poetry written before the thirteenth century.

THE LOVE THEME

The basic theme of popular poetry was love, expressed in its varying aspects. There was in it a strong vein of naturalism, the only form of art known to the people. Poetry composed of sensations, laughter, and tears, without transposition of any kind, had always been heard, but the obscene songs and wanton dances attributed to previous centuries document realism in life rather than realism in art.

We have a *contrasto*, written around 1190, by Rambaud de Vaqueiras, a Provençal troubadour who lived in Italy. In it, he offers his love to a Genoese woman of the people, using his own vernacular, and she rejects his passionate protestations, using her own dialect. Whether Rambaud himself wrote the answers of the woman or whether he borrowed them from a popular song is hard to say and not of great importance, but whoever did compose them showed himself a master of the new language.

There also remains, transmitted from the twelfth century, a very beautiful Sicilian couplet, of extreme simplicity, in which the poet addresses his beloved with the following words:

Vorrei saper dov'abiti l'inverno
Per stare così fresca nella state.

Pray tell me where you spend your winter
To be so fresh in summertime.

Carducci[3] quotes some *strambotti* in various dialects which he calls very old. A fine example is that which begins *Sonno fu che me ruppe, donna mia* (It was sleep, oh my beloved, that ruined me). It is a dialogue between a lover and his mistress who has forsaken him. She had defied convention to visit him, but had been unable to rouse him from a deep sleep. He protests his love for his lady and laments the ensuing solitude in which she has left him. With these words the poet expresses his regret and great disappointment:

Non me lamento tanto dello sonno,
Quanto faccio di voi, patrona mia,
Che n'ci venisti a l'alba dello giorno
Quando lo dolce sonno me tenia.

I do not complain so much of sleep
As I do of you, oh mistress mine,
For you came at the dawn of day
When sweet sleep held me.

Aglow with passion is the *strambotto, Gimene al letto della donna mia* (I went to the bed of my lady) in which an unknown poet has treated the love theme in a very naturalistic manner.

There are many lines of exquisite beauty in these *strambotti*. We find true poetic charm in the one expressing a lover's admiration for the beauty of his beloved. Another refers to the admonition of a woman to her clandestine lover to be prudent while she offers her rosy lips to him, lips left unkissed by a neglectful husband. In still another, thus sang a romantic lover to his lady:

Brunetta ch'ai le ruose alle mascelle,
Le labbra dello zucchero rosato;
Garofolate porti le mammelle.
....
Tu se' la fiore: s'io n'amassi mille,
Non t'abbandono mentre ch'aggio il fiato.[4]

Oh my Brunette, you who have roses on your cheeks,
And pinkish lips covered with sugar;
And whose breasts are sweetly perfumed,

....

You are the flower: and if I should love a thousand women,
I shall not abandon you as long as I have breath in my body.

In the following *strambotto*, likewise, the poet expresses admiration for his love:

Più che lo mele, 'ai dolce la parola.

Saggia e onesta, nobile e insegnata,
Ai le bellezza della Camiola,[5]
Isotta la bionda e Morgana la fata.
Se Biancifiori ci fossi ancora,
Delle bellezze la giunta è passata.
Sotto le ciglia porti cinque cuose,
Amore e foco e fiamma e gigli e rose.[6]

More than honey are sweet your words.
Wise and stately, noble and sage,
You possess the beauty of Camiola,
Isolde the blond and Morgana the fairy.
If Blanchefleur were still living,
Her beauty would already have been surpassed by you.
Under your brow you carry five things,
Love and fire and flame and lilies and roses.

One of the earliest popular poets was Cielo (or Ciullo) of Alcamo, probably of Sicily, who wrote around 1235, and about whom nothing specific is known. Using his southern dialect, he projected a short but vivid love drama in his *Rosa fresca, aulentissima* (Fresh rose, most perfumed). It is written somewhat in the form of a *contrasto* in which the man asks for love and the woman at first repulses him and then yields, carried away by the violence of her own passion. The significance of the poem lies in the rich psychological substratum that runs through the composition.

The action is taken from actual life and remains amazingly close to it. The unveiled desire of the man constitutes an ever-present undertone to the varying reactions of the girl as she passes from an attitude of indifference, even hostility, to one of curiosity in this bold lover who so relentlessly woos her. As he persists, her curiosity deepens into interest in marriage, but when the man declares that he is not interested in marriage, she, now unable to resist him further, beseeches him at least to swear loyalty to her on the Bible, which he so opportunely has brought with him. After this formal promise, she yields completely, inviting the man to follow her to her bed where, as she tells him, unexpected joys await them.

These character developments give to the poem a complexity unsuspected under the rough dialect in which the *contrasto*, with the exception of the harmonious and charming first line, is written.

Near Cielo of Alcamo, we find other poets who present life and love at close range. Compagnetto of Prato, a juggler, also succeeded in infusing a rich psychological vein in his poem *Per lo marito c'o rio* (On account of my wicked husband),[7] which sings of the grief of an unhappily married woman. In it, the wife blames the unjust accusations and beatings of her husband for having awakened love in her heart for her lover, to whom she yielded in order to avenge herself on the uncouth and hated husband.

The theme of the *malmaritata* (unhappily married woman) echoes frequently in popular poetry. The unhappy wife speaks with vehemence and sincerity in an anonymous poem found in the Vatican Codex 3793, *L'altrieri fui in parlamento* (The other day I met my lover).[8] Married through her father's arrangement to a man other than the one she loves, the girl laments to her beloved:

> *Tu se' in terra il mio dio:*
> *Ne le tuo' mani sono arenduta;*
> *Per te collui non voglio io.*
> *Ciertto bene degio morire,*
> *Ch'lo chuore del corpo m'è tratto.*

> You are my god here on earth,
> In your hands I have placed myself;
> Because of you, I do not want him.
> A sure death is awaiting me,
> For my heart from my body has been wrenched.

The man is incapable of accepting his responsibility and tells her philosophically that arranged marriages are a common occurrence. He offers her a clandestine love which will repay her for the monotony of marriage.

There are also several examples of a theme close to the motif of the *malmaritata*, that of a girl who openly reveals to her mother her desire for a husband, while the mother rebukes her bitterly for her lack of modesty.

We also find many *lamenti* in which the betrayed woman gives outlet to her grief and anger. Odo delle Colonne, generally considered one of the poets of the Sicilian school, has left us a very beautiful poem in which the woman grieves over her loneliness now that another woman has stolen the heart of her lover. She asks her song to transform itself into a shining dagger and transfix the heart of her rival, for then her lover will return to her and, with him, light to her life and joy to her heart.[9]

Rinaldo of Aquino, another member of the Sicilian group, has likewise left us a *lamento* which reveals the grief of a woman whose fiancé has left for the Crusade and who cannot understand why the Cross has brought her so much sorrow.[10]

One occasionally finds themes in popular poetry other than love. A very beautiful poem tells of a boy who has lost his nightingale and laments his loss with tender desolation.[11] It is a tenuous poetic motif in which stand out the attachment of the boy to the tiny bird and the song of the latter who has regained his freedom. The same motif is to be found in another poem in the Vatican Codex 3793 which reveals the grief of a girl who has lost her falcon. The falcon is molded with a force and a clarity attainable only by a poet of discriminating and sensitive artistry.[12]

In the second half of the century, popular poetry increased and echoed in various parts of Italy. There are short compositions, in the middle of the century, by the Florentine Ciacco of Anguillara, and sonnets by La Compiuta Donzella Fiorentina. These two poets stand out among the popular songsters of their time for their ability to convey greater elevation of feeling and for their power of expression.

Ciacco wrote a *villanella*, a dialogue between a gentleman of high station and a peasant lass. The girl at first repulses him scornfully, but then yields, won by the sincerity and gentleness of her lover. In the insistence of the man, there is a delicate strain of melancholy which beautifully envelops the song and tempers its sensual note.[13]

Two very charming sonnets are attributed to La Compiuta Donzella, a poet known only by the flattering name of "The Accomplished Damsel of Florence." In the first sonnet, a girl confesses that the joy that spring engenders in the hearts of all men is unknown to her, for she is destined by her father to marry a man she does not love. The first and last lines

A la stagion che il mondo foglia e fiora[14]

In the season when the world grows green and flowers

are identical, and they reveal a clear sense of form in the author who encloses in them the grief of the girl, as a goldsmith would enclose a precious stone in a finely wrought setting. The second sonnet tells of the indecision that besets a girl who must decide between going into a convent or marrying a man chosen by her father. The inference that she would not abandon the world if she could marry the man of her choice injects a note of mischief.[15]

Realistically, but with greater complexity, everyday life echoes in the verse of a large group of Tuscan poets. Folgore of San Gimignano, Cenne della Chitarra, Rustico di Filippo, and many others, the greatest of whom was Cecco Angiolieri of Siena, lived and wrote approximately at the end of the thirteenth century and the beginning of the fourteenth. They distinguished themselves by the spontaneity of their expression and by modeling the emotions and thoughts in their poems on their actual experience. Hate and love, admiration and scorn are their own passions without transposition in accordance with patterns offered by tradition. At the same time that Guinizelli and Dante were discussing the mysterious nature of love and of the gentle heart, these poets were attesting, in their realistic poetry, to the fact that they found no unity nor uniformity in the life they lived and portrayed.

Folgore of San Gimignano (ca. 1250-ca. 1317), an amiable minstrel with strong Guelph leanings, cheered with his poems the gay parties in which the wealthy Florentine and Sienese delighted. He wrote two collections of sonnets in which echoes the joyous and refined life that he depicted for his listeners of the upper middle class. One, *Sonetti de' mesi* (Sonnets for Each Month),[16] dedicated to Niccolò de'Nisi, to whose gracious generosity he entrusted himself, sings of the amusements of the various seasons and months. In the other collection, *Sonetti de la semana* (Sonnets of the Week), dedicated to a Guelph nobleman, he described a life of gay gatherings and tournaments such as was customary in the Tuscany of the last part of the thirteenth century.[17]

Closer to the popular poetic mode was Cenne della Chitarra, a minstrel from Arezzo who died around 1336.[18] This musical entertainer kept the scheme followed by the more refined Folgore in his sonnets, but mockingly changed the joys enumerated by the poet of San Gimignano into the unpleasant experiences that his *brigata avara* (miserly group) found in the various months of the year.

Rustico di Filippo (ca. 1230-ca. 1292), a Florentine, was a poet endowed with real personality. His short collection of *canzoni* written in the courtly mode concerning his love for a woman is rather boring, but the poetry in which he humorously sketched figures observed in his own day assigns him to an important place as a caricaturist in the literature of this time. The sonnets in which he satirized the ugliness of Messerino or flayed the haughtiness of a boastful man are poems which remain fresh to this day.[19]

With this group can also be considered the sonnets and *canzoni* of Bindo Bonichi (1260-1338).[20] He was a Sienese merchant who took time from his work to gratify the vein of genuine poetry that he possessed. His sonnets, like those of Rustico, were written while the observing eyes of the merchant-poet were focused on the society of his time and on his contemporaries. His *canzoni* reflect, in a more sustained style than the sonnets, the philosophy of a middle-class man, possessed of a deep sense of measure, a strong attachment to his republic, love for freedom, and honesty. In both sonnets and *canzoni*, he gives his reactions to the changing conditions of the social life of his time, reactions reflecting pessimism about the present and glorifying the past.

The true poet of the Tuscan group, Cecco Angiolieri, died in 1321. He was born of a noble Sienese family, but he allowed himself to be drawn into the mud of a plebeian and disorderly life because of his love for Becchina, the daughter of a shoemaker. His *canzoniere* reflects the various moments of this love and the degrees of degradation to which the poet sank.[21] Cecco ends the story of his life with the celebrated sonnet *S'i' fosse foco, arderei 'l mondo* (If I were fire, I would burn the world). It is one of the most original and effective renderings of hatred that one finds in the history of poetry.

> *S'i' fosse foco, arderei 'l mondo*
> *s'i' fosse vento, lo tempesterei;*
> *s'i' fosse acqua, l'annegherei;*
> *s'i' fosse Dio, mandarei 'l en profondo:*
>
> *S'i' fosse papa, sare' allor giocondo*
> *che' tutti i cristiani imbrigherei;*
> *s'i' fosse 'mperator, sa' che farei?*
> *A tutti mozzarei lo capo a tondo.*
>
> *S'i' fosse morte, andarei da mio padre;*
> *s'i' fosse vita, fuggirei da lui:*
> *similemente faria da mi' madre.*
>
> *S'i' fosse Cecco, come i' sono e fui,*
> *torrei le donne giovani e leggiadre*
> *e vecchie e laide lasserei altrui.*

If I were fire, I would burn the world
If I were wind, I would blast it;
If I were water, I would drown it;
If I were God, I would send it to deep Hell.

If I were pope, indeed then I would be happy,
For I would make trouble for all the Christians.
If I were emperor, do you know what I would do?
I would cut off the heads of all men.

If I were death, I would go to my father,
If I were life, I would flee from him.
Similarly would I do to my stepmother.

If I were Cecco, as I am and once was,
I would pick for myself the young and pretty women
And leave for others the old and ugly.

Cecco is a worthy forerunner of the poets of hate: Villon, Heine, Stecchetti, and Baudelaire.

Among the many varieties assumed by the popular genre, we should not fail to mention the poetry written in a satirical vein. The great mass of such poems testifies to the interest that citizens had in literature and also to the attachment they had for their republic. There were a great many *tenzoni* or debates throughout the century that were characterized by an ironical spirit. They dealt at first with questions of love and poetry, but, as the century progressed, the political theme became predominant. Satirical attitudes and verses are found in many popular poets. The most pronounced trait of the poetry of Rustico di Filippo is satire. This is also true of Bindo Bonichi's sonnets in which humor assumes a satirical character as he sketches his contemporaries. In most popular poets, satire and humor were closely mingled and led them to laugh at the human weaknesses and foibles that aroused their interest and indignation.[22]

Grossly satirical, too, is the *Acerba* (Bitter Truths) by Cecco Stabili of Ascoli (1269-1327), a contemporary of Dante. This book is still read largely because in it the author attacked Dante's *Divina Commedia* by calling unscientific many ideas therein contained. His own version of these truths constitutes an ill-digested encyclopedia of the scientific lore of his time. The references in the book to science are now of little importance. Indeed, the satirical vein with which it ripples is the only element still alive for the reader of today.

An anonymous poem, composed in 1315, deserves special mention because of the human qualities reflected in it by the author. It was written under the painful impact of the rout of Montecatini in 1315, inflicted on the Guelph forces of Tuscany by Uguccione della Faggiuola, the ambitious lord of Pisa and Lucca. In the form of a ballad, the poet imagines a dialogue between the mother of King Robert, whose younger son was killed in that battle, and a common soldier who survived the onslaught and went to break the sad news to the royal mother. Through the heart-rending words of the stately queen as expressed in the ballad, the author has clearly revealed his own deeply sensitive qualities. He depicts in natural and human fashion the deep tenderness of a loving and bereaved mother.[23]

THE RELIGIOUS THEME

Religion occupied an important part in the life of the century, both as a personal feeling and as a factor in the culture of the time. It is not surprising, therefore, to find the religious theme echoing in a large section of the popular poetry.

The *Chronicle* of Salimbene of Parma (1221-1287), that reflects vividly and faithfully the monastic and social life of the century, bears testimony to the "Alleluiah" in the year 1233, when the roads of Italy resounded with voices imploring the Lord to send peace to men weary of endless wars. The heart of the people had been touched by the gospel of love that Giacchino of Fiore had preached at the end of the twelfth century and that St. Francis of Assisi had revived in his day. Documents of the time also present Fra Benedetto, the monk with the cornet, who used to gather large crowds around him with his music and then speak to them of God with ardor and eloquence. A more ascetic form of religious fervor was that of Ranieri Fasani who appeared at Perugia in 1258 and spoke of the futility of the love for material things, exhorting all to a life of mortification and even to self-scourging. The order of the *Disciplinati*, referred to in English as the Flagellants, was founded by Fasani. Grouping together for study and worship, the *Disciplinati* founded organizations in Venice which were known as *Scole* (Schools).

The followers of Fasani composed *laude*, short poems in the form of a dialogue, often presenting an imaginary conversation between the Virgin and Christ. Under this religious form, the feelings expressed were deeply human, consonant with the relationship of mother and child. The following is an example of the poetry composed by the *Disciplinati*:

Anema de Cristo, sanctificami,
Sangue de Cristo, imbevami,
Aqua de lo lado de Cristo, lavami.

Soul of Christ, sanctify me,
Blood of Christ, enter into every part of me,
Water from the side of Christ, wash me.

In studying the large body of religious poetry of this century, coldly didactic works should not be confused with the poetry that, in Latin or in the vernacular, possesses genuine lyric quality and a beauty that the passing of six centuries has not dimmed. The works of Uguccione of Lodi, Patecchio, Giacomino of Verona, Bonvesìn of Riva, Pietro of Barsegapè, whether moralistic or religious, hardly belong to the history of literature, for, by common consent, they lack artistic value.[24] They served the practical purpose for which they were meant, but they possess only linguistic and historical value as documents of the social conditions of the time.

To the history of literature belong the hymns sung under the immense ceilings of the cathedrals. Latin works like the *Dies Irae*, that rang out with terrifying effect, and the *Stabat Mater* that, singing of the anguish of Mary the Mother for the loss of her Child, moved the hearts of our ancestors, will be forever enthroned in the annals of true poetry. Of equal importance and beauty are the poetic utterances of two religious men of the century: Francis of Assisi and Jacopone of Todi.

Francis of Assisi (1182-1226) was the son of a wealthy merchant who made his fortune by trading with France. It was in memory of his life in that country that he named his son Francesco. Young Francesco had a turbulent and fiery youth that led him to partake of the pleasures of life with an expectation that was never satisfied. In his middle twenties, in a moment of religious crisis, he abandoned the world and dedicated himself to a life of devotion to Christ and service to his fellow men. He patterned his existence on Christ's precepts to a measure that was beyond the comprehension of the average man of his day. He renounced wealth and worldliness, and dedicated himself to poverty. The people called him *Il Pazzo* (the Crazy One). He agreed with a faint smile and called his madness "holy madness." Using the picturesque and courtly imagery of the time, he spoke of Lady Poverty and Lady Chastity to signify that he espoused these virtues. Giotto immortalized the symbolic language of the Saint in his frescoes in the cathedral of Assisi by depicting him in the act of giving a wedding ring to three beautiful maidens who represent Poverty, Chastity, and Obedience. St. Francis called his companions the Knights of a New Round Table and himself a minstrel of the Lord. He founded a religious order, the Franciscan, based on the virtues that he admired and exemplified in his own life. Although Pope Honorius III had some misgivings concerning the extreme mysticism of the precepts of the movement, he nevertheless gave to it official recognition in 1216.

St. Francis of Assisi was both a mystic and a poet. He loved all aspects of creation and all men. Both the social and artistic life of his time bear the mark of his influence. The glorious cathedral of Assisi and many other beautiful churches and monasteries bear witness to the religious fervor that he aroused in the hearts of his contemporaries. Many works of sculpture and painting are also due to his spiritual influence. His was a true poetic instinct, for only a poet could find so much beauty as did he in a life of poverty and sacrifice. The Franciscan movement which developed around him is responsible to a large extent for the part that the religious theme played in the popular poetry of the century.

The famous *Inno delle creature* (Hymn of God's Creatures)[25] is, in its elemental simplicity, the first voice of genuinely poetic resonance heard in the new vernacular. The title does not properly fit the poem, for the central theme is the praise of the Lord not on the part of his creatures, but rather on the part of St. Francis himself who gives thanks to the Lord for the wonders of creation. The hymn reflects one of those rare and fleeting moments of complete harmony in which the human soul feels attuned to God, the universe, its fellow men, and itself.

It is written in an Umbrian dialect that reminds one of an unpolished diamond, rough and unformed, but beautiful. It is enclosed in couplets linked by assonance and not by rhyme. Yet, the poem possesses perfect form. It is like a perfect triptych, an altar piece that a painter of that time could have executed, carried away by his love and admiration for Francis of Assisi. Perhaps the analogy of a self-portrait in three poses is more accurate. In the first part of the poem, the Saint appears closed within himself, humble in the presence of the Lord, "Whose name no man is worthy of mentioning." In the second part, he slowly raises his eyes toward the sky and then looks all around him. He is lost in bliss before the beauty of what the Lord has created: Brother Sun and Sister Moon, the Stars, Brother Wind and Brother Fire, and Sister Water. How wonderful is the universe and how wonderful the soul of man! The humble monk muses on how beautiful it is to pardon our enemies, to bear infirmities, and suffer tribulations for love of the Lord.

Even death holds no awe for those who love the Lord. In a moment of perfect harmony and bliss the Saint gives ardent thanks to the Almighty Father. In the last mood, he slowly withdraws within himself, closed again in his customary humility.

The poem is made unforgettable by the use of images that in their elemental simplicity possess extraordinary power and beauty. Before the gentle friar stands the sun in all its glory as lord of all creation, surrounded by Sister Moon, the stars "clear and beautiful," the fire "beautiful, jocund, robust and strong," and Sister Water "chaste and humble." A rapt amazement allows him to repeat the word "beautiful" without danger of monotony. The description of the water as chaste and humble is rich in a mysterious charm and imagery that evokes in the reader a vision of limpid brooks and clear streams silently flowing between green banks. The *Inno delle creature* is truly a poem created for the joy of man.

The annals of the poetry of this century closed with another voice, different but equally powerful, that of Jacopone of Todi (1230-1306). His poetry was likewise characterized by its elemental quality. Under its brevity, obscurity, and simplicity, one gradually becomes aware of an unsuspected power.

Like St. Francis of Assisi, Jacopone, a notary by profession, turned to meditation and godliness after a carefree life filled with gaiety. He was approaching fifty when the death of his wife who had always been his faithful companion in his worldly life, yielding to all his whims, revealed to him a strange and moving drama. She had met her death when the floor on which they were dancing one night collapsed. The inner tragedy of his wife's soul became known to Jacopone when, in preparation for burial, it was discovered by those who bathed her that she had worn close to her flesh a hair shirt with nails that tore her skin at the slightest movement. The realization that his wife had punished herself in such a manner in order to atone for the wantonness of the life she had led with him was an overwhelming and terrible revelation to Jacopone. He renounced this life and joined the *Disciplinati*. His love of God awakened his poetic genius. In one of his poems, fired by mystic enthusiasm, he invited all diseases to come to him and make him suffer.

> O Signor, per cortesia, mandame la malsania.
> A me la fevre quartana — la contina e la terzana,
> la doppia cotidiana — colla grave idropesia.
> A me venga mal de dente, — mal de capo e mal de ventre,
> a lo stomaco dolor pungente, — en canna la quinantia,
> mal de occhi e doglia de fianco — e l'apostema al lato manco.

O Lord, be merciful and send me ill health.
Send me all kinds of fever: the quartan, the tertian,
    and the continuous,
The one that comes twice daily, and punish me
    with heavy dropsy.
Let toothache come to me, headache and bellyache,
Acute pain in my stomach, in my throat inflammation;
Pain in my eyes and pain in my side,
Even a tumor in my left side.

One would expect this listing of human ailments to be highly prosaic; on the contrary, Jacopone communicates astounding fervor to these lyrics.

Jacopone was a man who never ceased to struggle against the world and himself. He called the irrational state in which he lived "holy madness," echoing the words of St. Francis, although he was the very opposite of the gentle and mystic Saint. The directness of his poetry, mostly in the form of the *lauda,* suited his uncompromising nature. With feverish wrath he attacked the world's wickedness and especially the unholy political game played by Pope Boniface VIII, his most hated enemy, against whom he boldly thundered:

Lucifero novello — a sedere en papato;
lengua de blasfemia — che 'l mondo hai envenenato,
che non se trova spetia, bruttura de peccato,
Là 've tu se' enfamato. Vergogna è a proferire:
    Ponisti la tua lingua — e scontra la religione
    a diciare blasfemia — senza nulla rascione;
    e Dio sì t'ha sormesso — en tanta confusione
    che onom ne fa canzone — tuo nome a malidire.

New Lucifer sitting on the throne of the Papacy;
Blasphemous tongue, that has poisoned the world,
There is no kind of ugly sin
In which you have not become infamous.
It is a shame to have to acknowledge it:
    You used your tongue against religion
    By uttering blasphemies without any reason.
    God has led you to such a confusion
    That everyone makes a song out of it in order to curse
        your name.

He warns Boniface:

> *O papa Bonifazio, — molt'ày jocato al mondo.*
> *penso che jocundo — non te ne porrai partire.*
> *Como la salamandra — sempre vive nel fuoco,*
> *cusì par che lo scandolo — te sia solazzo e juoco.*

> O Pope Boniface, much have you played in this world.
> I believe that you will not be very happy in leaving it.
> Just as the salamander lives constantly in the fire,
> So it seems that scandal is entertainment and play for you.

Boniface retaliated by excommunicating him and sending him to prison for six years. Not daunted, Jacopone continued to attack him from his prison cell.

There were other sides to Jacopone's soul and poetry. The remembrance of a beautiful woman invaded the solitude of the cloister, and he confessed that the thought of her, in spite of himself, tormented him. To atone, he promised to wear no cloak nor socks in the cold of winter and to scourge himself until there was no skin left on his body.

The most beautiful of Jacopone's poetry is that which sings of the grief and love of the Virgin. In her sorrow, one feels the sorrow of a mother and of all mothers, and in the infant Jesus there is the touching image of the charm and innocence of childhood. In the *lauda* on the Crucifixion, Jacopone, offering a rudimentary dramatic form, addresses himself to the Madonna

> *Donna del paradiso*
> *lo tuo figliolo è priso,*
> *Jesu Cristo beato.*
> > *Accurre, donna e vide*
> > *che la gente l'allide!*
> > *Credo che lo s'occide,*
> > *tanto l'an flagellato.*

> Woman of Paradise
> Your son has been imprisoned,
> Jesus the blessed.
> > Hasten, woman, and see
> > How he is being tied!
> > I believe that they will kill him,
> > So much have they scourged him.

The Madonna speaks to her son as he lies dead before her:

> *Figlio, l'alma t'è uscita,*
> *Figlio de la smarrita,*
> *Figlio de la sparita,*
> *Figlio mio attossecato!*
> *Figlio bianco e vermiglio,*
> *Figlio senza somiglio,*
> *Figlio, a chi m'appoglio?*
> *Figlio, pur m'hai lassato.*
> *O figlio, bianco e biondo,*
> *Figlio, volto iocondo.*
> *Figlio perchè t'ha el mondo,*
> *Figlio, cussì sprezzato?*

> Son, your soul has deserted you,
> Son of a woman who has lost her mind,
> Son of a woman who lives no longer.
> Son of mine, whom men have poisoned.
> Son white and vermilion,
> Son who had no peer,
> Son, on whom shall I lean?
> Son, you have now left me,
> Son white and blond,
> Son whose countenance was jocund,
> Son, why has the world
> Spurned you to such a degree?

The soul of Jacopone was capable of great tenderness as he contemplated the infant Jesus. In a strange jargon of the Italian vernacular, he described very touchingly the Child as he lay on the hay in the stable of Bethlehem and nursed at his mother's breast.

Jacopone was a born poet. His unfinished and unpolished poetry makes one think of a huge block of marble that, though barely touched by the chisel of a great sculptor, nevertheless clearly reveals the power and beauty that the artist has evoked in it, a sort of Rondanini Pietà, the last of the three famous renderings of this theme, sculptured by Michelangelo when he was too old to wield his hammer with the strength of his younger days.[26]

CHAPTER SIX

Courtly Poetry

THE SICILIAN SCHOOL

Throughout the thirteenth century, courtly and popular poetry developed along parallel lines. Although during the last decades of the twelfth century courts in most Italian cities had cultivated poetry and much had been written in Provençal, the greatest center of culture and art was at Palermo in the splendid court of Frederick II. Because of his generosity and his dream of becoming the successor to the Empire, his court became a haven for poets from every part of Italy who had left their own cities because of the hostility of the Guelphs. It was at Palermo that the first poetic school was founded, referred to as the Sicilian school. Among those who lived in the court of Frederick at Palermo were Jacopo of Lentini, Pier of Vigna, both from the southern part of Calabria; Jacopo Mostacci, probably from Pisa; Giacomino Pugliese, from Puglia as his name indicates; Guido delle Colonne, perhaps from Rome; Rinaldo and Jacopo, both from Aquino; Percivalle Doria, from Genoa; Folco Ruffo from Calabria; and Odo delle Colonne, probably from Rome.

It is of importance to note that the poets of the Sicilian school occupied political posts in the court of the Emperor. Pier of Vigna was the Chancellor of the court and was famous for the beautiful Latin style that he used in writing about the political questions of the Imperial Chancery. Jacopo Mostacci was the official falconer. Guido delle Colonne was a judge at Messina. Jacopo of Lentini was a notary in the court. The appellative "Il Notaro" that constantly accompanies his name no doubt bears testimony to his position. The reference to the official duties of these poets is here stressed as proof that poetry represented only a small part of their activities. Poetry was, in fact, a part of the court etiquette and epitomized the role of poets as courtiers in the entourage of the Emperor. Frederick II himself, his father-in-law, and his two sons Enzo and Frederick of Antioch, composed sonnets and *canzoni* whose generic character testifies more to a social custom than to genuine inspiration.

In the light of these facts, it is not surprising to find that the poems written at the court of Palermo and associated with the Sicilian school were highly uniform and conventional. They were couched in the traditional form of the *canzone*, although that of the sonnet was added, first used, it is generally believed, by Jacopo of Lentini. The basic ideas enclosed in these metric forms were borrowed from the Provençal courtly love code, with the result that the poetry of the Sicilian school was rich in concepts, but sadly lacking in sentiment. Poets did not sing what stirred their hearts, but repeated, in an involved and clumsy manner, what tradition had transmitted to them. The convention of keeping secret the love that existed between the poet and the lady of the court also contributed to the impersonal and lifeless quality of the poetry of the time.

The negative opinion expressed above concerning the poetic value of the Sicilian School is confirmed by Dante's testimony in his *Divina Commedia*. In a dramatic encounter in Purgatory with Bonagiunta Urbiciani, Dante causes him to confess that Notaro Jacopo of Lentini, Guittone of Arezzo, and he himself had not succeeded in reaching a lyric height in their poems because, unlike Dante and his friends, they had failed to listen to the voice of their hearts, a poetical way of stating that they lacked the gift of inspiration and sentiment. Modern critics, notably Francesco De Sanctis,[1] have not departed from this negative conclusion.

Nevertheless, here and there, one finds beautiful images and well turned-out verse that leads one to lament all the more the monotonous wasteland of the poetry of the Sicilian school. King Enzo wrote a *canzone* to his lady from Bologna, where he was imprisoned after the battle of Fossalta in 1249, until his death in 1272. The poem opens with the expression of feelings common to most poets of the Sicilian school, voiced in an involved and heavy form:

> *Amor mi fa sovente lo meo core pensare,*
> *dami pene e sospire,*
> *E son forte temente per lungo adimorare*
> *ciò che poria avenire.*[2]

> Love often causes me to think of my beloved.
> It makes me suffer and sigh,
> And I entertain great fear, on account of my long stay,
> Of what might happen.

But quite different is the *commiato* in which the poet-lover enjoins his *canzone* to go to Puglia where he has left his beloved and where his heart abides:

> *E vanne in Puglia piana,*
> *la magna Capitana,*
> *la dov'è lo mio core notte e dia.*[3]

> And go to the boundless plains of Puglia,
> To the great capital city,
> There where my heart abides, night and day.

In Jacopo of Lentini, one notices a slightly more pronounced poetic personality than in the rest of the group.

> *Rimembrati a la fiata*
> *Quando te ebbi abrazata*
> *A li dolzi basciari.*
> *Ed io basciando stava*
> *In gran diletamento*
> *Con quella che m'aveva,*
> *Bionda, viso d'argento.*[4]

> Remember the time
> When I held you in my arms
> Sweetly kissing you,
> And I stood kissing
> With great delight
> The lady who had enslaved me,
> Blond, a countenance of shining silver.

Occasionally one finds in his poems musical lines in which he evokes the image of his lady, such as the *Bionda, viso d'argento* that has just been quoted. In spite of this, one must conclude that his poetry shares the conventional character of the Sicilian school. He shows more cultural traces than do his fellow courtiers in his references in his poems to the perfect love of Tristan and Isolde, of Pyramus and Thisbe, but the bloom of real poetry is lacking.

Small fragments of genuine poetic value have been handed down under the name of Giacomino Pugliese. In one of his love dialogues, he portrays the drama of two lovers who, at first, almost with hatred, reproach each other with reciprocal wrongs and, in the end, slowly yield to the love which returns to them.[5]

Rinaldo of Aquino rises above the poets of the Sicilian group through a poetry that is not constantly weighed down by abstract concepts, but, indeed, often reveals a deep sentiment. Among the more vital compositions of the Sicilian school is his *Amorosa donna fina* (Lady, gentle and love-giving)[6] where convention is destroyed by violent passion which breaks through with a force unequaled in the courtly verse of this school.

> *E quello bascio m'infiamao*
> *che dal corpo mi levao*
> *lo core e diello a voi.*

> And that kiss inflamed me so
> that from my body it took away my heart
> and gave it to you.

Graceful and original also is his poem enclosing a moment of doubt in a woman who asks herself whether her love may not be a passing whim due to the effects of spring. It must be added that the enthusiasm of Rinaldo as he describes nature awakening from the sleep of winter is sincere and has been rendered with simplicity and effectiveness:

> *Ormai quando flore e mostrano verdura*
> *le prata e la rivera,*
> *li auselli fanno isbaldore dentro da la frondura*
> *cantando in lor manera,*
> *infra la primavera che ven presente,*
> *frescamente così frondita,*
> *ciascun invita d'aver gioia intera.*[7]

> When meadows and rivers
> Show flowers and green grass as at present,
> The gentle birds within the leafy trees singing
> In their wont manner
> Make their loud and confused warbling.
> The spring which advances
> So fresh and full of leaves
> Invites everyone to have complete joy.

While the Sicilian school contributed but little to true poetry, it exercised a deep and lasting influence on the culture of the thirteenth century by keeping alive the Provençal traditions and transmitting them to the poets of the second half of the century. Dante, as a historian of poetry, never failed to exalt the contribution of Palermo to the poetry of his time. The later poets took the *canzone*, the sonnet, and the *commiato* from the Sicilian tradition. They borrowed ideas from the doctrinal background of that school and recast them in poems of genuine lyrical significance.

THE TUSCAN POETS

After the death of Frederick II in 1250, Tuscany became the principal center of culture in Italy. This does not mean that poetry died out completely in southern Italy[8] nor that the art was not cultivated in other parts of the country and written in other dialects. Venetian songsters, as we have seen, translated the Carolingian and Arthurian legends very freely. For the most part, however, courtly poetry, as well as popular, was written in the Tuscan vernacular with variations due to local differences in the language. Italian, a language above all dialects, partaking of each of them and yet separate and distinct, as Dante later envisaged it, did not yet exist. Centuries elapsed before the Tuscan vernacular, in which Dante, Boccaccio, and Petrarch wrote their works, was recognized as the literary language of Italy. As a rule, courtly poetry recorded in history after 1250 followed the patterns of courtly love, in the form of the *canzone* and the sonnet.[9]

Guittone of Arezzo (*ca.* 1230-1294), although not a great poet, is the first arresting figure that one meets among the Tuscan poets who wrote around 1250. After a rather carefree and thoughtless youth, he turned to religion, at about the age of thirty, and became a member of an order called *Servi di Maria* (Servants of Mary) or *Serviti*. His large contribution to poetry (two hundred sonnets, forty-four *canzoni*, six ballads, and eight epistles in metric prose) is highly conceptual and obscure. One is fully conscious that the poet was struggling to give expression to ideas not different from those of the Sicilian poets, but made more ponderous because of a doctrinal content. The confusion in Guittone between doctrine and poetry was very great. He covered the doctrinal content of his *canzoni* with rhyme schemes on which he had labored long without succeeding in awakening in them the spark of poetry. This is true of his love poems as well as of his didactic and political verse. His *canzone, Ai lasso or è stagion de doler tanto* (Alas! now is the time to really grieve),[10] written when Florence suffered a crushing defeat by the united forces of the White Florentines and the Sienese at Montaperti (1260), is, in part, a powerful dirge; but, on the whole, it is weighed down by moralistic concepts and political allusions to the history of the time. Dante, displeased that Guittone, who in his opinion wrote in such a rough and unfinished style, should enjoy great fame among his contemporaries, attacked him with his customary violence. Critics, to a large extent, have agreed with Dante.

The words of contempt that Dante addressed to Guittone were also directed against other poets of the older generation: Chiaro Davanzati, Bonagiunta Urbiciani, Gallo Pisano, Mino Senese, and others.[11] We should take Dante's judgment with reservations, since he looked upon the older poets as his competitors in the field of poetry and as his antagonists in his effort to give a stately and new form to the Italian poetry of his day.

In modifying the judgment of Dante concerning many of these poets, we should be, above all, very circumspect concerning his criticism of Chiaro Davanzati. Davanzati was a member of the White Party and among those exiled from Florence who took part in the battle of Montaperti in 1260. Judging by the documents of the time, he was already dead by 1280. During his lifetime he enjoyed a certain amount of popularity, as is evidenced by the fact that the Vatican Codex 3793 contains ninety of his *canzoni* and sonnets. In all, he has left us sixty-one *canzoni* and one hundred and fifty sonnets in which he sings of love and of the political events of his time.

Chiaro Davanzati possessed a genuine sense of poetic form, as one can judge from his sonnet on Narcissus in which Narcissus finds sweet the death that he meets in trying to reach his own image. Davanzati gives voice to his own feelings when he writes that he, too, is attracted toward death when he gazes on the beauty of his lady. Resuming the theme developed in the first lines of his poem, he concludes:

> *Com a Narcisi parami piagente,*
> *Vegiendo voi, la morte soferire.*[12]

> Like Narcissus, I find it delectable,
> Upon seeing you, to suffer death.

The sonnet *La splendida luce quando apare* (The bright light when it appears) has feelings and ideas which were later echoed by Dante in describing the qualities of Beatrice and the effects that she produced on him. The luminous quality of her countenance, her power to give joy to a sorrowing heart, the recognition of her perfection by other women, are all characteristics that Dante has echoed in refined form in his sonnets praising Beatrice.

In the sonnet *Adimorando 'n istrano paese* (While living in a strange country),[13] Davanzati describes with beautiful effect his constant passing from sadness to joy and from joy again to sorrow as he thinks of his beloved. When he thinks of the day when he will return to her, rather than feeling joy, he sinks into gloom as he realizes the uncertainty of the future.

It cannot be said that the conventions of courtly poetry are absent in the works of Chiaro Davanzati, but it must be admitted that his verse, nevertheless, throbs with sentiment, often breaking through the atmosphere of impersonality and allowing the ideas and images of the poet to emerge in a clear and musical form.

Bonagiunta Urbiciani (*ca.* 1220-1290) does not owe his literary fame to his own abstruse poetry, but rather to Dante who made of him the prototype of the traditional poet. This is also true of another poet of the older generation, Dante of Maiano. His name has come down to us because of a sonnet written in anything but a courtly vein in reply to a request by Dante Alighieri. Dante, using a symbolism inherited from the poets of Provence, had sent to the poets of his time a sonnet asking them to interpret a dream in which Beatrice had appeared to him, clad in a diaphanous, vermilion gown, and asleep in the arms of Love. Love, personified as a lord of frightening countenance, offered her the heart of Dante to eat, but she refused. Three poets replied to Dante: Guido Cavalcanti, Cino of Pistoia, and Dante of Maiano. Not one understood the true meaning of the sonnet that only wished to imply the refusal of Beatrice to reciprocate Dante's love. The three replies have come down to us together with Dante's sonnet to Beatrice, and only because of this episode do we know of Dante of Maiano.[14] Cavalcanti and Cino of Pistoia, in their attempts to interpret the sonnet, lost themselves in the abstractions characteristic of the time. Dante of Maiano heaped insults on Dante in his inability to understand the great poet.

We have dwelt on this episode in order to document the conditions of the literary life of the Tuscan poets at the end of the century. Only a few succeeded in renewing the courtly material of the Provençal tradition and in withdrawing it from the mire of the commonplace and the conventional.

One of these was Guido Guinizelli of Bologna (*ca.* 1240-1276). Chronologically, he belonged to the older generation of Chiaro Davanzati, Bonagiunta Urbiciani, Folcacchiero dei Folcacchieri, Dante of Maiano, and Brunetto Latini, but he distinguished himself through a poetic gift greater than that of his contemporaries. Dante, in his *Purgatorio,* acknowledged him to be the originator of the new poetic manner referred to by him as the *Dolce Stil Nuovo* (Sweet New Style).[15]

Guido Guinizelli belonged to the noble family Principi, and he followed his father in the practice of law, becoming a judge at Bologna. He was exiled in 1274 in the antidemocratic reaction headed by the Lambertazzi family. He died in exile at Monselice in 1276. During his own time he won fame as the author of a doctrinal *canzone* beginning *Al cor gentil repara sempre amore* (Love always finds shelter in a gentle heart).[16] Guinizelli expressed in it the motif of love as a natural and positive force. The *canzone* is a justification of human love, a goal that courtly poets set for themselves from the Provençal troubadours to Dante and even later. Guinizelli speaks through varied images of the part that love plays in the heart of a noble man. It seeks shelter there as naturally as a bird flies to the green of the forest, as a magnet attracts iron, as a precious stone is of inestimable value. All this conforms to the plan of God as Creator of the universe. To woman, the *bella donna* (beautiful lady) is given the task of revealing *il vero* (the truth) to her lover. When the poet's soul, after death, is in the presence of the Lord and must give an account of his love, Guinizelli will answer thus:

> *tenea d'angel sembianza*
> *che fosse del tu' regno;*
> *non mi fu fallo s'eo li posi amanza.*

> She had the countenance of an angel
> Which belonged to your kingdom;
> It was not a sin if I put my love in her.

Today this *canzone* does not represent for us the best that Guinizelli wrote although it rises above the many doctrinal poems written in the second half of the century.

To our modern taste, the most beautiful of Guinizelli's poems are the sonnets in which he sings of the beauty of his lady, likening her to the lily, the rose, the morning star, and to all that which is beautiful on earth and in the heavens. Such is the sonnet *I' vo' del ver la mia donna laudare* (I want truly to praise my lady)[17] in which the beauty of his lady is perfectly blended with her spiritual perfection and sweetness. Vivid colors and harmonious lines distinguish it. Dante echoed Guinizelli's sonnet in the most perfect of his own sonnets in the *Vita Nuova*, *Tanto gentile e tanto onesta pare* (So gentle and so stately she appears), and he reached in it a perfection that renders it one of the sparkling jewels among the vast wealth of Italian lyric poetry.

To make more complete this brief sketch of Guido Guinizelli as a poet, it is well to dwell on two sonnets[18] of strongly popular character that are in sharp contrast with the lofty tone of his *canzoni*. One is against an irascible old woman whom he hates and for whom he wishes every evil. It begins in a manner far from courtly — *Diavol te levi, vecchia rabbiosa* (May the devil carry you away, wrathful old woman) — and it ends with the conclusion that if vultures, ravens, and hawks do not eat her it is because her flesh is too dried up and hard. The other sonnet, *Chi vedesse a Lucia un var cappuzzo* (Who-

"*May the devil carry you away, wrathful old woman.*"

ever would see Lucia in her small hood), is a well-turned out sketch of a pretty girl wearing a grey bonnet with many-colored stripes. The poet sees her and the desire to kiss her overpowers him:

> *Ah, prender lei a forza, oltra su' grato,*
> *e baciarli la bocca, e 'l bel visaggio*
> *e li occhi suoi ch'èn due fiamme di fuoco.*

> Oh, if I could only seize her, even if she resisted me,
> And kiss her mouth and her beautiful face,
> And her eyes that are aglow with two flames of fire.

The parallel existence of these diverse compositions is a proof of the sincerity of the poet who, near the ecstatic mood prescribed by the Provençal poetic tradition, suddenly reveals an entirely different mood and reaction.

Guinizelli is acknowledged by other poets, contemporaries of his, to have brought new form into courtly poetry. Although Bonagiunta Urbiciani, in a sonnet addressed to Guinizelli, considered him *oscuro* (obscure), he added that the poet from Bologna had

> *mutata la manera*
> *di li plagenti detti de l'amore,*
> *de la forma e de l'esser.*

> Changed the manner
> Of the pleasing verse of love,
> Of its form and of its essence.

Bonagiunta felt that Guinizelli was like one who lights the way for those who follow him, but who cannot see the way himself. The lack of distinction between doctrine and poetry prevented Bonagiunta from seeing in Guinizelli the poet we admire today.

Not even Dante clearly distinguished, in his youth, between doctrine and poetry. It was only in the intimacy of his mature years, while writing the *Divina Commedia*, that he became aware that true poetry was born only of sentiment. It was then that he called the poetry of his youth, his own as well as that of his friends, the poetry of the *Dolce Stil Nuovo*.

THE FLORENTINE POETS

During the last decades of the thirteenth century, there appeared in Florence a group of young poets united by similarity of political and literary ideals. Most of them were members of the White Party, and their conservatism in politics was reflected in their exclusiveness in art. They disdained populism and held in contempt the sensuous character of popular poetry and, especially, its jarring and unmusical rhythms.

The most important of these poets were Guido Cavalcanti, Dante Alighieri, Cino of Pistoia, Lapo Gianni, Gianni Alfani, and Dino Frescobaldi. They looked on Guido Guinizelli, if we accept Dante's testimony, as the forerunner of their school of poetry, and they chose his famous *canzone, Al cor gentil repara sempre amore* as the pattern on which to model their verse.

There was no direct declaration by these poets of their theories concerning the art of poetry. Judging by the type of poems that they wrote, one would conclude that they aimed at producing a philosophical poetry characterized by a very polished form. Each of the major poets of the group wrote, in fact, a *canzone* in which, through long and involved arguments, he delved into the nature of love, concluding that love was a definite and positive force in the life of man.[19]

These poets were strongly united by bonds of friendship, and they communicated with each other by writing in verse.[20] They often referred with warmth and admiration to the loveliness of the ladies of their friends. It was to members of this group that Dante, the greatest of them all, in 1283, addressed his sonnet *a tutti i fedeli d'Amore* (to all servants of Love). In it he asked his friends to interpret his dream about Beatrice and to which, as we have already stated, three of the poets replied. He also wrote a sonnet, a perfect pattern of romantic verse, in which he expressed the vague longing to be wafted over the sea in a small vessel in the company of two friends, who were poets, and their ladies, with whom they would happily discourse on love. He mentioned by name the other two poets: Guido Cavalcanti and Lapo Gianni. He also referred by name to Monna Vanna, Guido's love, and Monna Lagia, Lapo's beloved, but he left the name of his own lady veiled in secrecy.[21] Following a custom that has many parallel examples, Cino of Pistoia, upon the death of Beatrice, wrote a *canzone* addressed to Dante, mourning with him the loss of such a lovely person.[22] Very intimate, indeed, was the friendship of these poets.

The love drama in the *canzoni* of the Florentine group was made to begin at the moment that the luminous eyes of a beautiful woman (as in all conventional poetry, all women were beautiful) met the eyes of the poet and dealt him a mortal blow. From that time on, all his faculties (referred to as *spiriti* and *spiritelli*) were absorbed by his love. A very fanciful psychology was established to reveal the state of the poet. His eyes, heart, mind, and intellect were personified and brought into play in order to discourse on the loveliness of the woman. She was endowed by the Lord with perfection of soul and body so that she might show men the pattern of an ideal form. She radiated love as she walked through the streets and made men with a "gentle heart" rejoice, while those of a debased nature became frightened. So powerful was her virtue that if an unbeliever were to gaze upon her, he would become converted. Other women were not jealous of her beauty because she honored them all by her perfection. Through her, men were lifted to a moral plane so high that only noble feelings and acts were possible to them. Suspended in such an atmosphere of paradise-like clarity, the poet happily sang of his beloved's comeliness and virtues. Not much can be perceived of the personal traits of the women loved by these poets, in spite of the fact that they were usually named, a departure from the secrecy of the Sicilian school.

The woman's eyes, smile, and gait, if mentioned, only show her ethical perfection and give no clue to her actual qualities. Dante's reference to the pearl-like forehead of Beatrice is an exception and not the rule.

Although the theoretical aim of the Florentine school was to produce a *canzone* made significant by doctrine, the genius and greatness of soul of the poets often forced them to recount their personal experiences, thus creating an entirely different type of poetry from that of the Provençal poets and the court of Palermo. The psychological study of their love experience was carried out through a vaster and deeper range of thought. The truth is that, in spite of the theoretical positions that still confused poetry and doctrine, the love theme in these poets flowered into beautiful images and expressed exquisite feelings. It is this that constitutes their enduring quality. They renounced their interest in the forms of social life and the hidden sensuality expressed by their predecessors at Palermo, and they focused their attention on the psychological effect that love had on them, revealing love as an obscure and awe-inspiring experience.

In discussing the poets individually, we begin with Guido Cavalcanti (*ca.* 1255-1300) because he was, most likely, the oldest, and he exercised great influence over the entire group.[23] Dante considered him superior to Guinizelli, and Lapo Gianni referred to him as *sol colui che vede Amore* (the only one who really sees Love). Guido was probably born in 1255 in Florence of a Black family, although he allied himself with the White Party against Corso Donati. He took a direct and active part in the political life of Florence, as one would expect of a man endowed with a passionate and even violent nature. To avenge himself against Corso Donati because of a plot to kill him on his pilgrimage to the shrine of Santiago of Compostela in northern Spain, Guido, upon his return to Florence, spurred his horse against that of his political opponent, bringing about a bloody clash between the Blacks and the Whites. This occurred on May Day in 1300. As a result, Guido was exiled to Sarzana. His banishment was sanctioned by his best friend, Dante Alighieri, then one of the city officers whose task it was to keep peace in the city. Guido contracted malaria in the swamps of Sarzana and returned to Florence to die in the month of August of the same year.

Contemporary authors present Guido as a man given to deep thoughts. He had the reputation of being an unbeliever, a charge often made against the members of the White Party. Dino Compagni in his *Chronicle* stated that Guido was often seen in the streets of Florence, wrapped in a long cloak, lost in meditation, wondering whether or not it could be proved that God does not exist.

During his lifetime, Guido was known especially for his *canzone, Donna mi prega perch'io voglio dire* (A lady requests me and I am eager to say),[24] a composition bristling with deep and involved definitions and arguments concerning Love and its attributes. In it, he conformed to the custom of courtly poets of writing doctrinal *canzoni*, and this conformance to fashion brought him renown. Today, we admire him for the other poetic forms to which he dedicated his genius.

Guido was married, when still very young, to Beatrice degli Uberti, daughter of Farinata, the famous leader of the White Party, but in his poems he sang especially of his love for a girl named Giovanna, who was so beautiful that she received the charming nickname of Primavera (Spring). She also appeared in one of Dante's sonnets in the company of Beatrice Portinari, and the two beautiful girls are referred to as *meraviglie* (wonders of loveliness and charm). Guido's ballad *Fresca rosa novella, piacente Primavera* (New fresh rose, sweet-faced Primavera)[25] is one of the best of his lyrical compositions. The joy of the poet is rendered by the short, tripping lines in which he invites nature to spread its colors before his Primavera, the birds to sing, and men, old and young, to extol her praises, for she has truly an angelic form. On his visit to Toulouse, France, Guido saw Mandetta, a young girl of that city, whose features reminded him of Giovanna, and to her he dedicated exquisitely beautiful sonnets, possessed of a light and delicate, yet passionate character. The remembrance of other loves passes like a shadow over his sonnets.

Guido's inventiveness and interest in new forms led him farther than the other poets from the conventions of courtly love. He recast in his own way the French *pastourelle,* and the finished product has a charm and melodiousness that are unforgettable. The ballad *Era in pensier d'amor* (My thoughts were all of love)[26] beautifully interweaves his interest in Mandetta of Toulouse with his being attracted by two country girls whom he chances to meet. Action and feelings are barely sketched, but the lightness of touch fits perfectly the poetic mood of the poet.

So resonant is the theme of Death in him that it succeeds in overshadowing and almost eclipsing the erotic element. It superinduces in his verse a sense of tragedy that is so real as to bring the reader very poignantly within the circle of the poet's experience.

The full measure of Guido's lyrical power is found in his ballad *Perch'io no spero di tornar giammai, ballatetta, in Toscana* (Since I never hope to return to Tuscany, my little ballad).[27] In it, Guido, ill with malaria, asks his ballad to go back to Florence and to take his soul into the presence of his lady, to whom it will say: I came to abide with you, having departed from him who is a servant of Love. The ballad translates most beautifully the distressed state of body and soul of one who felt life ebbing away from him.

Guido Cavalcanti shared with Dante Alighieri the honor of having set new modes of courtly poetry. One is tempted to say that, in the field of lyric poetry written before 1300, Guido deserved this honor even more than did the epic spirit of Dante.

Lapo Gianni (*ca.* 1250-*ca.* 1328) was a less gifted poet than Cavalcanti. He, too, shared in the close friendship of Dante. He was a notary by profession and added to his practical activity the habit of jotting down ballads that followed rather closely the pattern set by the Florentine School.[28]

Even less original was another contemporary poet, Gianni Alfani, about whose life very little is known. Like Guido, he wrote from his place of exile. His lack of creativeness led him to echo the ideas and forms of Guido's poetry. However, some of these versions and echoes are well executed. His ballad *Ballatetta dolente* (Sorrowing little ballad)[29] is quite obviously patterned on Guido's composition. Yet, the work expressed with renewed grace the loneliness of the poet. The similarity between the poems of Gianni Alfani and those of Cavalcanti is not casual. In specific cases the less gifted poet has knowingly used the modes of Guido. Thus, in the ballad *De la mia donna vo' cantar con voi* (I wish to sing with you about my lady),[30] in referring to himself as *l'anima sbigottita* (my frightened soul), he consciously employed the same effective phrase used by Guido in his ballad written in exile to express the state of his whole being.

Such intimate friends were the two poets that Alfani addressed a sonnet to Guido[31] in which he communicated to him the offer of love on the part of a lady who had not been very careful in hiding her feeling for the poet.

Cino of Pistoia (*ca.* 1270-*ca.* 1337) was very famous in his own day as a student of law. His writing of poetry must be viewed against the background of his activity as a celebrated jurist and judge. He studied in France at the University of Orléans and at Bologna, and taught law at Siena, Florence, Perugia, and Naples, from 1321 to 1331. He wrote a comment on the first nine books of the Justinian code. He defended the independence of the Empire from the Church and even went so far as to declare the Empire superior to the Church as a political institution.

He wrote poetry very extensively, but with very little inspiration.[32] The study of law seemed to have made heavy the wings of his verse. He sang of a woman to whom he referred as Selvaggia. His poems are most faithful in expressing the theories of the love code as accepted by the Florentine group, but they are weighed down by obscure thoughts, not illumined by the freshness of expression and musicality of his friends.

Cino was the poet from whom Petrarch learned the art of poetry. At Dante's death, the younger poet penned a sonnet in which he imagined that the Muses were grieving very piteously over the death of such a great master of verse. He also grieved in verse over the death of Beatrice, as previously stated.

The most respectful of the theoretical aspects of the Florentine school was Dino Frescobaldi (*ca.* 1270-*ca.* 1316), remembered as a handsome man for whom rhymes were an integral part of his art of love. Not much is known of him except that he came of a family in which the cultivation of poetry was a tradition. His father, Lambertuccio, wrote poetry and so did his son. Dino left a collection of twenty-two poems.[33] His poetry is rather prosaic, although not involved. One feels that he lacks the poetic afflatus and veers unduly toward a realistic approach of the love theme. In one of his sonnets[34] he even inquires whether a perfect love can be more readily obtained from a young girl (*pulzella*) or from a mature woman (*donna*). He concludes in favor of the maiden.

In the final evaluation of these poets, one realizes that the background of the school was rather conventional and, at times, monotonous. Yet, because of individual inventiveness, the Florentine group wrote sonnets and *canzoni* that enriched the treasure of perfect poetry of all times.

From their midst, a gigantic figure, Dante Alighieri, arose. He merits a chapter apart because, although in his youth he wrote as a member of the group, in his mature age he went beyond the boundaries of the Florentine school in learning, artistic ability, and, especially, in the cosmic resonance of his poetic inspiration.

THE ALLEGORICAL POETS

Allegorical poetry played an important part in the literary life of this period. Clerks, throughout the Christian Age, departed from a literal reading of pagan authors, notably Virgil, and even Ovid, and sought, through a figurative interpretation, to find adumbrated therein Christian truths, thus making the classical works acceptable to Christian readers. In the thirteenth century, vernacular poets who aimed at the grand style, reacting against the literalness of popular poets, used this allegorical device to ennoble poetry. They were able to achieve this end by adding to their poetry a supersense through the personification of human traits and the use of a very rich imagery.

Particularly representative of this style of poetry was the famous French allegory *Le Roman de la Rose*, written toward the middle of the century by Guillaume de Lorris (who lived around 1230), and completed by Jean de Meung (*ca.* 1250-*ca.* 1305). In it, the love drama is described in a highly symbolical manner. The Lover seeks his Rose, his sweetheart, in a high-walled garden and reaches it only after many trials and tribulations. At first,

The Lover seeks his Rose.

he is hindered by such personified human forces as Chastity, Slander, Jealousy, Envy, and Modesty, but he is then helped by the lovely ladies, Compassion and Courtesy. The popularity that the book enjoyed in Italy a century before Geoffrey Chaucer made it known to the English public in his translation is attested to by two well-known free versions in the Italian vernacular.

The Florentine Brunetto Latini patterned his *Tesoretto*[35] on *Le Roman de la Rose*. The poem, written around 1262, in rhyming couplets of seven syllables, reveals the gloomy mood of the author, saddened and depressed by the outcome of the battle of Montaperti. Latini allegorically described his passing from a dark forest, as life seemed to him upon hearing of the defeat of his Guelph Party, to the realm of knowledge. He seeks solace in Nature, that, symbolically represented as a magnificently gowned Lady, instructs him in matters of science while the personified human qualities of Courtesy and Prowess instruct him in moral matters. The work has no poetic atmosphere. Its chief merit lies in having aimed at spreading in the vernacular scientific and philosophical knowledge. Dante admired it so much that he transferred to the *Divina Commedia* the image of the forest in order to convey his own intellectual bewilderment.

Also typically allegorical is the *Intelligenza* (Intelligence)[36] in which an anonymous Tuscan author, once believed to be the historian Dino Compagni, tells a love story in which love is identified with knowledge rather than with sentiment and passion. In the poem, the author sees a most beautiful lady in the springtime and falls victim to her charm. She wears a diadem studded with precious stones and lives in a princely palace, the walls of which are adorned with frescoes representing the legendary deeds of Alexander the Great, Caesar, the Greek and Trojan heroes as well as those of the Round Table. Seven queens are the attendants of the extraordinary Lady with whom they live a life made beautiful by music and dancing. Starting from the premise that Love leads to Truth, the poet discusses the nature and the beauty of the stones in the Lady's diadem and concludes that, symbolically, the Lady represents Intellect. There is a quaint beauty in the lines that describe spring but, on the whole, the breath of poetry is lacking in the work.

Francesco of Barberino (1264-1348) also used the allegorical style in two didactic works that are interesting documents of customs and social life around 1300. He was a notary and a student of law, having received a degree in canon and civil law from the University of Florence. During a visit to Provence which lasted four years, he wrote *Documenti d'amore* (Teachings of Love) which deals with what Love itself dictates to twelve ladies, representing the various beneficent effects that love produces in man. Only through Love does man acquire such qualities as, among others, Courtesy, Prudence, Justice, Goodness, and Nobility. The book is in verse and is a sort of epitome of the point of view on Love expressed by the Florentine poets in their *canzoni*. It is written in the vernacular and is accompanied by a commentary in Latin.

The other work by Francesco of Barberino, *Del Reggimento e costume di donna* (Of the Education and Manners of Woman), is more original. The poet has given allegorical form to Eloquence and Initiative, the two qualities that prescribe the proper manners and customs that a woman should follow in life, whether she be a nun or a girl destined to become a mother, whether a lady or a person of the people, whether a married woman or a widow. The author illustrates his doctrinal points with anecdotes, some of which are true short stories, rich in humor and a keen sense of observation.

Dante Alighieri, too, made use of allegory in many parts of his *Divina Commedia* and in his *canzoni*. These will be studied in the chapters dedicated to the great poet.

The lily, the rose, the morning star. . . .

CHAPTER SEVEN

Dante Alighieri: His Minor Works

Dante Alighieri was born in Florence in 1265 of an old and noble Black family whose financial condition was not very prosperous at the time of his birth. Dante's father, Bellincione Alighieri, remarried after the death of his wife Bella, Dante's mother; but he, too, died when Dante was only eighteen. This may have been one of the causes that contributed to making Dante's adolescence thoughtful and lonely, as he presents it in *La Vita Nuova* (The New Life).

Not much is known about the early education of Dante. He was probably trained in the Trivium and Quadrivium in the manner of the children of well-to-do families. His affectionate tribute to Brunetto Latini as his teacher testifies to the influence that the author of the *Tesoretto* had on him in instilling in his mind the love for knowledge and poetry. The Latin classics, and especially Virgil, delighted him and shaped his future as a lover of poetry. The mind of Dante was molded by Classicism, the Bible, and the Provençal lore, judging from the reflection of these three cultures in *La Vita Nuova*, the book of his youth.

Around 1285, Dante married Gemma Donati to whom he had been betrothed since 1277 when he was but twelve years of age. They had three sons, Giovanni, Jacopo, and Piero, and a daughter, Antonia, identified with a Suor Beatrice who died in a convent at Ravenna in 1350. The family became extinct with the death of the poet's grandchildren.

Nothing is known of the actual relationship between Gemma Donati and Dante in their family life. The love theme expounded in his poems rested on an imaginative plane, unrelated to marital love and duties. Personal life was deemed unworthy of treatment in poetry. The speculations of the curious on this score are groundless and unwarranted.

The love, *fino amore* (perfect love), that illumined the works and undoubtedly the life of Dante was that which he had for Beatrice, daughter of

Folco Portinari, a distinguished and well-to-do Florentine citizen. She married Simone de' Bardi and died when very young on June 8, 1290. These data pertain only to the historical reality of Beatrice, which is no longer doubted today. We do not know much about the actual life of the young woman who bore that name. We know much more about the Beatrice who was reborn in the mind and soul of the poet, especially after her death, and who lives in the *Vita Nuova* and in the *Divina Commedia*.

After the death of Beatrice, Dante sought consolation in the study of philosophy. We are told by him in one of his later works that for thirty months he frequented with such assiduity the religious schools where philosophy was discussed that even his eyesight was affected, and that this study drove out of his life any other interest. If we take literally the testimony of the poet, he spent the time between Beatrice's death and his political career, which began in 1295, in acquiring the very accurate and vast doctrine that made of him one of the most learned men of his time.

In 1289, Dante fought as a private at Campaldino in the war that Florence waged against the Ghibelline city of Arezzo. Soon after, he took part in the encounter in which Florence wrested the fortress of Caprona from Pisa.

In 1295, Dante turned to practical thoughts and decided to enter politics. Disillusioned and even embittered by the policies of Giano della Bella, the nobleman who had consorted with the proletariat in order to attain power and destroy the democratic laws that the city had previously enjoyed, Dante ran for office as a candidate of the White Party. His change of party allegiance came on the crest of a violent reaction against Giano della Bella's policies. The latter had decreed in 1293 that only members of the guilds could aspire to offices in the administration of the Commune. This ordinance had been very hard on Dante and other young men who had hoped to serve in the administration of Florence and earn their livelihood by this coveted activity. The law was modified in 1295, thus making it possible to seek public service by simply enrolling in one of the guilds, without actually practicing a trade or profession. Dante enrolled in the guild of druggists and physicians, and thus the door to public office was opened to him. In the election of 1295, he won a place in the administration of his city. He became a member of the office of the Captain of the people, one of the *Savi* or Elders, one of the Council of the One Hundred, and finally, in 1300, a *Prior*, a post which he held until 1302 when he was forced into exile.

The political situation of the city was very tense at this time because of the hostility between the Blacks and the Whites. It was in May of the year 1300 that he was called upon to pass judgment on the bloody clash between the two parties, provoked by Guido Cavalcanti. Dante voted for the expulsion of the leaders of both sides, although he knew that this would mean that his best friend would be banished from Florence, so unswerving was the poet's sense of justice.

The most ominous factor in the political situation of the city was the interference of Boniface VIII in the internal affairs of Florence. Following his theocratic policy, he was interested in elevating the Blacks to power and in removing those who opposed his policies. Taking advantage of the bloody disturbance just mentioned, he sent Charles of Valois to Florence as a peace-maker. This was an excuse to put the Blacks in power and, upon Charles of Valois' arrival in the city, the White government fell. The victorious Black Party began a series of reprisals that culminated in the exile of the White Leaders.

At this time Dante was in Rome as an envoy in order to present the case of the Florentine government to Boniface. It was a hopeless task and, while he was still in Rome, the Blacks were placed in power by Boniface's envoy. The new podestà of Florence, Conte dei Gabrielli of Gubbio, preferred charges against Dante in which the poet was accused of fraud and of having embezzled public funds. He was sentenced to pay the enormous fine of five thousand florins, to be banished from Tuscany for two years, and to be excluded from seeking public office for the rest of his life. Should the fine not be paid, Dante's possessions were to be confiscated, and if he himself were apprehended he was to be burned alive. Party spirit was at such a high pitch that men were heartless to an incredible degree. Even Dante's children were condemned to follow their father into exile upon reaching the age of fourteen.

The charges preferred against Dante were, of course, false. The poet did not deign to answer them nor did he return to Florence. Thus began the painful peregrinations that lasted until his death.

His exile was made more grievous by the unworthy character of his own political associates. He discovered this when, in June, 1302, the exiled Whites tried to organize a military alliance against Florence with the Ubaldini, a Ghibelline family, and, in 1310, when Heinrich VII, the incumbent Emperor, beseiged Florence at the exhortations of the enemies of Guelphism. Dante himself addressed an epistle to the Emperor, begging him to re-establish the White Party in Florence. Both plans failed because the exiled Whites were actuated by self-seeking motives, with not even a shadow of love of justice and decency.

In his writings, Dante proclaimed with pride that he had created his own party, the common fate of intellectual men when they fall into the company of crafty politicians.

During his exile, the poet struggled against want, for the only means of livelihood open to him was the service that he could render to political leaders. He served first the lord of Forlì, Scarpetta Ordelaffi, in 1303; then, the master of Verona, Bartolomeo della Scala, in 1304; then, Franceschino and Moroello Malaspina in the Lunigiana region; and, finally, in 1318, Guido Novello of Polenta, at whose court he and his children found gracious hospitality until the poet's death on September 14, 1321. Dante was buried with great honor in Ravenna, near the church of San Francesco, where his ashes still rest.

THE *VITA NUOVA*

The *Vita Nuova* was written about 1292, two years after the death of Beatrice. It was a book of memories that related primarily the effects of Beatrice's love on the poet. She had brought a new life to him; hence the title, signifying a higher life than that which he had hitherto known.

Dante gathered in his book the poems that he had penned between 1283, the date of the first sonnet, and the year 1292, when he decided to write the prose that served as an introduction and commentary to them.

The life experience of the poet, as actually lived and as recast through his imagination, is projected in the *Vita Nuova* on three planes: the plane of real life, that is, the connections that Dante actually had with Beatrice and other women; the plane reflected in the poems written at a relative distance of time after the actual experience; and the plane of the prose that reveals how the poet looked at those experiences under the impact of the death of Beatrice.

The story related in the *Vita Nuova* is very simple. Dante saw Beatrice for the first time at the age of nine and love kindled his heart. She was beautifully dressed in red, as befitting her age. Love glowed with greater intensity when, nine years later, he saw her again as she passed through the streets of Florence in the company of two ladies, and she greeted him in a voice and manner worthy of the noble maiden that she was. Young Dante touched the highest points of bliss at her salutation. His love for Beatrice, however, did not prevent him from being sensitive to the charms of other young women. People began to speak of him as a wanton youth, and Beatrice denied him her greeting.

The poet sought the seclusion of his room and dedicated himself to writing poems in which he described the unhappy state in which he lived. There came a moment when he grew weary of this subject matter, and, breaking away from his self-pitying egocentricity, he sought "new material" in exalting the beauty and virtues of Beatrice.

It was at this point that he wrote the famous *canzone, Donne ch'avete intelletto d'amore* (Women who have an understanding of love), which was meant to be the most perfect eulogy of the nobility of Beatrice. The scene is laid in Heaven. The poet imagines that an angel complains to the Lord that Beatrice is not in Paradise. It is Paradise's only imperfection. The Lord, in the guise of Divine Compassion, replies that Beatrice has been allowed to remain on earth in order to spare her lover unbearable sorrow. There follows an exaltation of Beatrice as a woman possessed of all the qualities that courtly poets had lent to their ladies. The *canzone* ends with a *commiato* in which the poet enjoins his *canzone* to go to his beloved by seeking the company of courtly persons and avoiding that of villainous ones. It will find Love in the company of Beatrice, to such an extent are the two one and the same. The *canzone* will entrust itself to Love in quest of pity for the poet.

The new subject matter chosen by Dante led him to write two very beautiful sonnets: the one that begins *Ne gli occhi porta la mia donna Amore* (My lady carries Love in her eyes) and the even more enchanting *Tanto gentile e tanto onesta pare la donna mia* (So gentle and so stately appears my lady). These two sonnets seem to be the sublimation, in terms of artistic perfection, of all that previous poets had written in extolling the perfection of a woman. Many of the ideas therein expressed echo those of Guinizelli and the Florentine poets, but the musicality and luminosity that they received in their new form and setting make these sonnets stand out far above the works of Dante's friends.

At this point, the story of the *Vita Nuova* resembles a novel even more than in the first part. The reader finds detailed accounts of personal events in the life of the poet. Dante appears sick in bed, attended by his half-sister, and he becomes deeply disturbed, because the thought of the death of Beatrice has darkened his mind in a dream. So vivid is his dream that he actually cries and sobs, much to the consternation of his sister and of some friends of hers who happen to be in the house. The dream is followed by another in which the poet sees himself dead.

Another chapter tells us of the day that Dante sees Giovanna, Cavalcanti's lady, and Beatrice pass by him. He feels that they are approaching, for he sees Love advancing joyously toward him. The two girls are beautifully portrayed as objects of perfect loveliness.

The story moves toward its climax with the death of Beatrice that darkens the whole universe for the poet. No words are adequate to describe his state.

About a year after her death, Dante tells us that while he was seated in his garden, steeped in grievous thoughts concerning the loss of Beatrice, he saw a young and comely woman who, from her window, was looking at him with infinite sweetness and compassion. The poet fell in love with her and wrote several sonnets in which he gave expression to his feelings for her. Dante was fully conscious that in being interested in the *Donna Gentile*, as he euphemistically referred to her, he betrayed his love for Beatrice, but this realization did not appear in all its naked truth until he was writing the prose of the *Vita Nuova* and he remembered that passing fancy. The victory of Beatrice and his return to her memory and love receive a final and beautiful acknowledgment through the words with which the *Vita Nuova* closes, words in which the poet, foreshadowing his writing of the *Divina Commedia*, promised that he would say of her what had never been said of any other woman.

Dante has expressed his love for Beatrice in the *Vita Nuova* through the forms of the Provençal tradition. Among the many conventional elements therein contained, there stands out the recurrent use of the number nine, the mystic symbol related to the Trinity, when referring to events that concern Beatrice and Dante's love. These conventional elements, however, constitute an unimportant part of the book. They only concern the culture of the poet as it is reflected in his work. The living and vital part is found where the torment of the poet has been so deep and powerful as to break the fetters of convention and to emerge in all its human pathos. It is here that Dante, the man, goes beyond the scholar and doctrinaire.

The *Vita Nuova* was written in the light of the literary creed of the poet at the time that he began his work. His creed is couched in very clear terms: *E però che soprastare a le passioni e atti di tanta gioventudine pare alcuno parlare fabuloso, mi partirò da esse; e trapassando molte cose le quali si potrebbero trarre de l'essemplo onde nascono queste, verrò a quelle parole le quali sono scritte ne la mia memoria sotto maggiori paragrafi.*[1] (And since to dwell on passions and on acts of extreme youthfulness seems to be a kind of speech worthy of the fabula,[2] I shall depart from them [passions]; and, passing over many things that could be taken from the pattern of which they are a part, I shall come to those words that are written in my memory under more important headings.) Dante believed that it was unworthy of true art to deal with passions that were indicative of the man in him. True art should deal with those actions that expressed the deep, absolute, and divine part of his being. His love for Beatrice belonged to this high plane and constituted the "more important headings" in his memory, as in his youth it had represented life at its best, above the vagaries and superficialities of his natural self.

In writing the *Vita Nuova*, his program led the poet to transpose the actual events, first through the filter of the poems, and then through the finer one of the prose. "To filter" for Dante meant "to idealize" his love for Beatrice; and "to idealize" was to remove elements of passion from his love experience, as the code of courtly love prescribed. This process is most visible in the sonnet in which the poet described Giovanna and Beatrice as they passed by him. In it, the two lovely women are seen in an atmosphere of beauty and enchantment, but in the prose, written years later, Giovanna becomes St. John, Christ's precursor, and Beatrice, by implication, Christ himself. Giovanna was lifted to this plane of symbol by deforming her lovely name of "Primavera" and interpreting it as *prima verrà* (she will come first), as did St. John. Likewise, through the ethical preoccupation of the courtly love code, Dante transformed into the women of the foil[3] the young women who had attracted him in his youth and for whom he had written sonnets later included in the *Vita Nuova*. If one reads them independently of the prose, one discovers many contradictions.[4] The reality felt at the writing of the prose does not conform to the actual feelings conveyed by the sonnets.

The *Vita Nuova*, as a whole, far from losing value and beauty because of these contrasts, is enhanced by them and lifted to the honor of being the first psychological novel in the history of Italian literature. This is particularly true of the episode of the *Donna Gentile* in which the struggle between the passion for the young woman who charmed him and the pale image of the dead Beatrice is most dramatically developed. Who will reproach the poet for having varied the idealistic material of the *Vita Nuova* with bits of actual experience that refused to be obscured by literary preoccupations?

It is certainly true that the most beautiful sonnets are those in praise of Beatrice and that these are rooted in Provençal lore, but it is equally true that the book of Dante's youth acquires a new value by the presence of those elements that the poet planned to repress.

Dante, when a mature man, referred to the *Vita Nuova* and the poems written by the members of the Florentine group as belonging to the *Dolce Stil Nuovo* (Sweet New Style). He considered Guido Guinizelli, as we have already stated, the "father" of those who *rime d'amor usar dolci e leggiadre* (made use of verse melodious and charming in singing of love). He reserved for himself the title of initiator of this new style of poetry.

In his famous encounter with Bonagiunta Urbiciani on the slopes of Purgatory,[5] he stated that he marked the beginning of the new style with his *canzone*, *Donne ch'avete intelletto d'Amore*. Guinizelli used the basic concepts and metrical forms of the new style, but Dante brought to it beautiful verse and undying renown.

Bonagiunta, who was of the generation that preceded that of Dante, was made to admit that with Dante's *canzone* there dawned a new poetic era. Dante, with false modesty or sincere conviction of his merits, accepted the praise of Bonagiunta by revealing to him the basic tenet of his poetic creed:

> *Io mi son un che, quando*
> *Amor mi spira, noto, ed a quel modo*
> *che detta dentro, vo significando.*[6]

> I am one who, when
> Love passes by me like a wind, I harken, and in that manner
> That he dictates within me, I signify.

Dante's answer made clear to Bonagiunta why the poetry before Dante had failed to achieve artistic significance. Bonagiunta spoke in the episode of two styles, the old and the new: that of the Sicilian poets and that of Dante and his friends. The subject matter of the two schools was the same, but poets like Jacopo of Lentini, Guittone, and himself had not listened to the voices of their hearts as had the poets of the Florentine group.

The problem that we pose at this point is an important one. Can it be said that, at the time in which Dante wrote the *Vita Nuova*, that is to say, around 1292, the theory followed by the poets of the Florentine group was based on the belief that only spontaneity of feelings engendered true poetry? Is it not more logical to believe that Dante attributed to the poetry penned in his youth, his own as well as that of his friends, an aesthetic idea that he had reached only in the years of his thoughtful maturity? When, in the *Divina Commedia*, Dante wrote his imaginary conversation with Bonagiunta, his youth and the poetry written then were only a vague, though dear, memory. Actually, in the *Vita Nuova*, Dante had followed the theory of the doctrinal character of art, the principle shared by the poets of the Florentine group. The term *Dolce Stil Nuovo* was not used around 1292. That beautiful name echoed in the soul of Dante as he looked at a past that was gone forever. As a matter of fact, the new idea that Dante revealed to Bonagiunta had not entered his mind even when he wrote his *De Vulgari Eloquentia*

(On the Vernacular), about ten years before the *Purgatorio*. Had the idea of the identification of sentiment and poetry guided the writing of the *Vita Nuova*, most probably he would have included it in Chapter XXV of the book of his youth, a chapter reserved for matters pertaining to the art of poetry. His sonnet

> *Amore e cor gentil sono una cosa*
> *Siccome il Saggio in suo dittato pone*

> Love and the gentle heart are one and the same thing
> As the Sage says in his poem

by referring to Guinizelli as the Sage, "the man who knows," shows that Dante adhered to the poetics of the school and to the belief that doctrine was the chief component of poetry. The *canzone, Donne ch'avete intelletto d'amore*, was, in fact, developed within the circle of the doctrinal position accepted by the courtly poets of his time. It was not characterized by senti- ment nor by sweet-sounding verse and rhymes. In spite of a few beautiful lines, doctrine still guided him in writing this famous *canzone*. If lyrical gems stud the old gold of the *Vita Nuova*, they came into being independently of the theory that was shared by the poets of the Florentine School and Dante.

THE MINOR POEMS

At the same time that Dante wrote the poems that he included in the *Vita Nuova*, he penned others of a different inspiration and character.

To this section that embraces compositions written before and soon after his exile belong the sonnets that he exchanged with Forese Donati.[7] Dante reflected in them that part of his life that, using his own terminology, can be called "the smaller headings" of his existence. They show the poet at close range as he abandoned himself to satire and to irony, even resorting to remarks in bad taste implicating Forese's wife. A proof of the fact that these sonnets were a true reflection of the poet's feelings is to be found in the *Divina Commedia* when, in the encounter with Forese in Purgatory,[8] Dante ex- presses his deep regret for the levity that had characterized the actions of his youth. He atones for his crude references in those sonnets to Forese's wife, Nella, by proclaiming her to be the only virtuous woman who was left in Florence.

Dante also exchanged satirical sonnets with Cecco Angiolieri. These are not extant, but we can surmise their nature from the caustic answers that the scoffing Cecco sent to the poet.[9]

To the same emotional level belong the *Rime Pietrose* (Stony Rhymes),[10] *canzoni* about a mysterious woman called Pietra (Stone), a name or harsh nickname which Dante bestowed upon a heartless woman who had spurned his love. The name admirably portrays the passionate mood of the poet. The use of *pietra*[11] as a rhyme scheme is original with Dante. It echoes continuously throughout the *canzone* and is used to convey the hardness of the woman and the distraught state of mind of the poet. Unlike the sonnets written to Forese, that are couched in a form very close to the popular one, the compositions addressed to Pietra follow, in vocabulary and terminology, the form of courtly poetry, but they bring out in sharp relief the theme of resentment, hatred, and violence therein expressed.

As in the case of the sonnets written to Forese, one must accept the reality of Dante's feelings here projected, for, in the *Divina Commedia*, when he meets Beatrice at the top of the mountain of Purgatory,[12] he confesses to her the sinful life that he had led after her death. Here the poet reveals, in a most human way, the actual truth of his love affairs, casting aside the Provençal convention of the oneness of love that had led him to deny in the *Vita Nuova* that he had ever been unfaithful to the memory of Beatrice.

A wider range of natural elements is found in these lyrics than in those destined to express the ecstatic mood of Dante when he speaks of Beatrice. In the *commiato*, his *canzone* is referred to as *montanina* (coming from the mountains of Casentino) and bits of natural scenery are used to reflect the love drama of the poet. He portrays the woman with a bundle of grass on her head, even if the bundle is ennobled into a *ghirlanda* (garland), and he avows that his love for the woman has caught him *più forte assai che la calcina pietra* (more firmly than mortar binds a stone).

These characteristics sharply differentiate the *Rime Pietrose* from the *Vita Nuova* and show how faithfully Dante reflected his life in his poetry.

Besides the love poems included in the *Vita Nuova*, Dante wrote others[13] addressed to persons of unknown identity. They are couched in poetic modes that follow very closely Plato's idea of love as expressed in the *Symposium*: an aspiration to the ideal forms of life in order to reach happiness. Although these poems are both allegorical and doctrinal, they are, nevertheless, basically love poems written in different moods. Some of them express the love theme with overtones of doctrine and of ethical preoccupations; others are melodious and charming, comparable to the most beautiful sonnets of the *Vita Nuova*.

The *canzone*, *Tre donne intorno al cor mi son venute* (Three ladies have come and are standing around my heart), is typical of the philosophical genre. It was written shortly after the beginning of the poet's exile. It is the expression of the poet's longing for the justice that had been denied him. Justice and two of her handmaidens are represented by the three ladies who surround his heart where Love abides. Interweaving the theme of justice with that of love, Dante claims that one who is capable of perfect love must, of necessity, be capable of perfect justice. It is here that we find his famous comment:

> L'esilio che m'è dato onor mi tegno.

I hold as an honor the exile that has been meted out to me.

and, he continues,

> Cader tra' buoni è pur di lode degno.

To fall among worthy people is indeed worthy of praise.

Likewise, in the sonnet

> Due donne in cima de la mente
> Venute sono a ragionar d'amore,[14]

Two ladies, abiding above any other thought in my mind,
Have come to discourse about love,

the poet presents two aspects of love: love as wisdom and love as the embodiment of beauty and charm, concluding that there is no contrast between them.

Among the most important *canzoni* of philosophical motivation are those that he commented upon in his *Convivio*. These are penetrating soundings of his own heart as he reflects on the nature of love and tries desperately to keep it on a high level while experience is challenging his idealism.

A perfect example of melodious verse is the ballad

> Per una ghirlandetta
> Ch'io vidi, mi farà
> Sospirare ogni fiore.[15]

For a small garland
That I saw, every flower
Will cause me to sigh.

It has a lightness of touch and a simplicity that assign to it a place of honor near the best compositions of the poet.

The same musicality and resonance of intense intimacy are found in the ballad

> *Deh! Violetta, che in ombra d'amore*
> *M'apparisti.*[16]

> Please, gentle Violet, who in the delicate guise of love
> Appeared to me.

It is a passionate plea for compassion on the part of the poet to the woman whose loveliness has awakened an irresistible love in his heart.

A great variety of moods, each expressed with originality, is found in these lyrics. They are variations on the basic theme of the positive character of love. From this consideration stem the philosophical *canzoni* and the more personal compositions in which he reveals his own experiences as a lover.

Also to be included among the minor works of Dante that tradition has carefully collected are two Latin eclogues,[17] written during the last two years of the poet's life. They are addressed to Giovanni del Virgilio, a professor of Latin at the University of Bologna, who wrote to Dante in 1319 inviting him to sing of some important contemporary event in Latin verse. Only so, he wrote, might the poet become known to intellectual persons, rather than to the plebeian readers of his *Commedia*, that is couched in the vernacular. Giovanni del Virgilio stated that he would then be proud to present the poet to the illustrious persons of Bologna, wearing a garland of laurel, as befitting the great poet that he was.

Dante's answer was couched in the bucolic modes that Virgil had used in his eclogues. He presented himself as an Arcadian shepherd, Tityrus, living happily in Sicily, the original cradle of bucolic poetry, and intent only on cultivating poetry while tending his sheep. He confided to his admirer and friend that the fervid desire of his heart was to be crowned poet in his Florence as the author of the *Commedia*.

Giovanni del Virgilio sent a second letter to Dante reiterating his invitation to go to Bologna, but the poet, in a second eclogue, expressed his fear of going to that city because his enemy Poliphemous lived there. Dante wrote that he would remain in his rustic abode and would continue to dedicate himself to the cult of the Muses.

Tradition has also kept several of Dante's epistles,[18] written during his exile. They are in Latin and discuss political and philosophical questions.

The most important of these epistles are the three addressed to Heinrich VII of Luxemburg, and the one to Can Grande della Scala accompanying a copy of a few cantos of the *Paradiso* that the poet had dedicated to him. The three epistles to Heinrich VII reveal the anxiety of the poet in exile concerning the peace and dignity of his Florence to which he fervently hoped to return after Heinrich's victory over the Blacks. They are also a clear and living document of Dante's political ideas on the Empire as a system capable of achieving the unity of the whole world and especially of Italy. The epistle to Can Grande is the most authoritative introduction to the *Divina Commedia*, whether one believes that it was penned by Dante or by an anonymous author, as many hold. It presents the central ideas that guided the poet in writing his poem, and it stresses the symbolical undertone that he meant to assign to the events narrated in it.

To round out this brief presentation of Dante's works, it is well to mention a scientific discussion that he held in the church of St. Elena at Verona in 1320. In the presence of the clergy, he maintained the thesis that in no place can water be higher than the earth, as many believed at that time. The title of his short essay is *Quaestio de aqua et terra*.[19] It is very illuminating as to the ideas of the time and it reveals Dante's passionate interest in the investigation of truth during the years of his exile.

From Giotto's portrait of Dante.

CHAPTER EIGHT

Dante as a Thinker

The theoretical power of Dante's mind is reflected and diffused in all his works, but his reputation as a thinker rests especially on three books written during his exile: the *Convivio* (The Banquet), the *De Vulgari Eloquentia* (On the Vernacular) and the *De Monarchia* (On the Universal State).

THE *CONVIVIO*

The *Convivio* was composed in the early years of the poet's exile, between 1304 and 1307. Dante had envisaged it as a long commentary on fourteen of his *canzoni*, a commentary that would be an epitome of all the knowledge of his time. Actually, he wrote only the introduction and the commentaries on three of his important *canzoni*; in all, four books.

In his introduction, the poet stated that he would offer a "banquet" consisting of the "meat" of wisdom contained in his *canzoni*. It would be served on the "bread" of the Italian vernacular, the new language that, in his opinion, was capable of expressing *altissimi e novissimi concetti convenevolmente, sufficientemente e acconciamente* (most lofty and new concepts in a manner that is proper, adequate, and becoming).

The *canzoni* that Dante chose dealt with Love as a universal and absolute concept, and they were enclosed in a form that metrically and in vocabulary reflected the loftiness of the theme expressed in them. His *canzoni* must have been well known in the courtly circles of Florence, for at least one of them was set to music by Casella, a gifted friend of the poet. Dante informs us of this in his *Purgatorio*[1] when he meets there his dear friend Casella. The three *canzoni* commented upon in the *Convivio* are: *Voi che 'ntendendo il terzo ciel movete* (You who through understanding move the third Heaven [the sphere of Venus]), *Amor che nella mente mi ragiona* (Love that discourses with me in my mind), and *Le dolci rime d'amor ch'i' solia* (The sweet rhymes of love that I was wont to use).

The subject matter treated in the *Convivio* referred especially to ethics, as is borne out by the lengthy discussion in Book IV on what constitutes true nobility. However, other topics were also discussed: the four senses of poetry that a critic should seek in verse (literal, allegorical, moral, and anagogical); the ten heavens and their relation to the liberal arts; such basic questions as, among others, the nature of the universe, man's relation to it as an individual and as a citizen, the nature of the problem of evil, and the immortality of the soul.

The doctrinal part of the *Convivio* was written primarily under the influence of Aristotle and Ptolemy, but it also shows strong contacts with Plato, the Neo-Platonists, and the Latin masters of ethics, Cicero and Seneca. The *Convivio* is a book of philosophy and science.

Although the modern reader feels that he is constantly in the presence of a vast and profound mind and that the work is a great encyclopedia of the knowledge of Dante's day, the *Convivio* only comes to life when it is placed in the setting of the poet's exile. It must be read in the context of those unhappy days when Dante, penniless and without a home, was forced to defend himself against those who accused him of being a worthless and profligate man. Although doctrine enters into the *Convivio* as a predominating element, it actually remains on a secondary plane, for the book was written for practical reasons. Dante informs the reader that he wrote it to put an end to "a great, infamous accusation or danger."

The danger was a real one: that of being deprived of earning his daily bread because of the accusation of his enemies that he was a man of loose moral habits. They had documented their accusations by quoting from Dante's own *Vita Nuova*, at the end of which he had revealed that he had strayed from the love of Beatrice to that of the *Donna Gentile*. They pointed out that Dante himself had called that love *vilissimo* in his book. Because his livelihood depended on whether his accusers would be believed or not, the poet addressed the *Convivio* to the powerful men and women of Italy, fervently hoping that he could convince them of his innocence and receive from them the post of ambassador or envoy, a post to which his learning gave him the right to aspire.

Dante's hurt and humiliation are vividly portrayed to the reader in his constantly recurring plea that his love had never been dissociated from virtue. He promised to show that the *canzoni* which his enemies had used to pillory him would appear *sì d'amore che di vertù materiate* (possessed of both love and virtue). He likened himself to Boethius who was accused of treachery by King Theodoric and who, under the pretext of writing of the consolation of philosophy, wrote in reality in order to remove "the eternal infamy of his exile." Even more clearly did Dante declare: "I fear the infamy of having followed such a great passion, as he who reads the above-mentioned *canzoni* concludes that it enslaved me."

He was eager to remove even the suspicion that his "love was directed toward sensuous pleasure." Hence, he repudiated completely, in his *Convivio*, his love for the *Donna Gentile* by putting Philosophy in her place. In commenting upon the sonnet to her

> *Chi veder vuol la salute*
> *Faccia che li occhi d'esta donna miri,*

> He who wishes to know salvation
> Let him look at the eyes of this woman,

the poet wrote that "the eyes of this woman are her demonstrations, which, shining in the eyes of the intellect, move the soul to love, once the soul is freed of its contradictions." Philosophy is made, in the *Convivio*, the supreme ruler of his soul, even to the point of putting it above his love for Beatrice.

The pages of the *Convivio* flame with indignation and with ill-repressed wrath against the enemies of the poet. Their greatest beauty lies in the vividness with which the actual existence of the exiled poet is rendered. Unforgettable is the passage in which Dante describes his life in exile: *Veramente io sono stato legno sanza vela e sanza governo, portato a diversi porti e foci e liti dal vento secco che vapora la dolorosa povertade* (Truly I have been a ship without sail and helm, tossed to different ports, river mouths and shores by the dry wind that rises from painful poverty). Coldly cynical are the vivid remarks concerning fame or discredit that grow or wane in direct ratio to the friendship or hostility of those who mete them out. Equally stirring and revealing are his attacks against the literati of his days, those very persons with whom he had to compete in his quest for work. He bitterly denied to them the right of calling themselves by that name. For him they had no more right to be so called than a man who rented a harp for monetary gain had the right to be called a harpist. He accused them, to their undying shame, of praising the vernacular of other peoples while spurning their own. He singled out those who extolled Latin without actually knowing it. He scornfully stated that if he had written the commentary to his *canzoni* in that noble language, they would not have been able to understand it. In later centuries, none of the defenders of the Italian vernacular has attained Dante's fervid enthusiasm for his mother tongue. All of Dante's bitterness, attacks, and humiliations are woven around the two practical pleas of the *Convivio*: that he might be recalled to Florence and that his ability as a man of learning be recognized by persons of distinction.

One should not attempt to remove arbitrarily the contradictions that exist between the *Vita Nuova* itself and the idealistic and abstract version of it given in the *Convivio*. These contradictions, however, should not lead one to accuse Dante of insincerity. Responsibility for these inconsistencies rests with the enemies of the poet who compelled him to give a political answer to a political accusation. Knowledge of the presence of the weaknesses of human nature in illustrious men of the past, rather than dwarfing them, gives a fuller measure of their greatness.

THE DE VULGARI ELOQUENTIA

The *De Vulgari Eloquentia*,[2] in two books, is an essay on language and poetry. Like the *Convivio*, it was written by Dante during the first years of his exile. Although left unfinished, it possesses a unity of its own in that it stands as the first official recognition of the Italian vernacular as a medium of expression. It is written in Latin as befitting a work destined to be read by the intellectual class of Dante's day.

For those who are interested in studying the birth of the vernacular and the appearance of its conscious use as an instrument of art, the *De Vulgari Eloquentia* is a milestone in the history of culture.

As one would expect especially in an age of transition, side by side with traditional and even conventional points of view, one finds in the *De Vulgari Eloquentia* vivid flashes of originality and unexpected intuitions and conclusions, worthy of the poet of the *Commedia*.

Dante's explanation in Book One of the origin of the various languages is traditional: the multiplicity of tongues goes back to the tower of Babel. Yet, at the same time, he possessed a historical consciousness of the evolution of languages. He had a full awareness of the interdependence of the three languages that were spoken on the European continent: the Germanic languages, Greek, and the Neo-Latin languages. It is also to his merit that he felt the unity of the Neo-Latin languages in their vernacular forms of French, Spanish, Provençal, and the language of *sì* (Italy), and that he followed their growth in the field of literary history. He assigned to the language of *oïl* (northern France) the glory of having attained distinction in prose works. To the language of *oc* (Provence), he conceded the glory of having sung of courtly love. He reserved to the language of *sì* the honor of being the nearest to Latin and of having served two poets, Cino da Pistoia and himself. To Cino, he granted primacy in singing of love; for himself, he retained primacy as a poet of rectitude.

Dante was firmly convinced that the vernacular should be the language used in writing poetry of the "grand style," as Lord Saintsbury calls it. In the *Convivio,* as we have seen, he inveighed, with foresight and courage, against his contemporaries who spurned their Italian vernacular. In the *De Vulgari Eloquentia,* he proclaimed the rules of perfect poetry.

As we know, Dante saw poetry in the light of two diametrically opposed styles: the courtly and the popular. They differed in content, vocabulary, and meter. Content was the chief dividing line between the two poetic modes. Although at the very opening of Book Two of the *De Vulgari Eloquentia* this distinction is couched in the Aristotelian terms of "tragic" and "comic" verse, the core of the question bears every trait of a rigorously ethical distinction.

Starting from his belief that all human conditions are either good or bad, he concluded that it was imperative for a courtly poet to rise above the crudities of the popular songster. He spurned those who wrote *casualiter,* that is, at random, and he enjoined courtly poets to compose *regulariter,* that is, with full consciousness of the mastery of their art. He also established a perfect correspondence between ethics and art, and he claimed that "what is good is befitting worthy men, what is better is befitting those who are worthier, and what is excellent is befitting the most worthy ones."

In his desire to separate the noble poetry to which he aspired from the drab verse of the populists of his age, he urged courtly poets to sing of three subjects only: the useful (*Salus*), the pleasurable (*Venus*), and the ethical (*Virtus*). Since a courtly poet must aim at excellence in all things, he added a significant warning: *dum nullo accidente vilescant* (provided these human conditions are not made ignoble by any accidental trait). A courtly poet should deal only with life envisaged as a universal entity, a pure concept, free from the whims and contradictions of what is "accidental." A courtly genre accordingly should possess depth of thought (*gravitas sententiae*), lofty style (*superbia carminum*), a winged metrical form (*constructionis elatio*), and nobility of vocabulary (*eccelentia vocabulorum*). Only so can a poet be a poet of rectitude, the highest qualification of the art of poetry.

Within the framework of his "perfect poetry," he outlined his theory of the "illustrious vernacular." Persuaded as he was that everything human was subject to constant change, he did not wish to entrust language to the individual, local, and arbitrary character of the various dialects. His noble poet should conform to the noble speech that the tradition of courtly poetry had established from the poets of Sicily to those of his own group in Florence. He claimed thus that in Italy there already existed a language that shared the traits of local speeches, but was above them all. This was the "illustrious vernacular," the language of refined persons, that his ideal poet was to use.

Dante's principal merit consists in having given a psychological foundation to the study of speech. He attributed a social function to it by linking it to the final goal of human life. Language was the means through which man could communicate his thoughts to his own kind with whom he lived in society, and he could thus reach the plane of rationality in civil life. For Dante, man occupied a middle position between angels who were pure rationality and animals that were pure instinct. Animals did not possess thoughts to communicate to others; angels saw reflected in the mind of God the thoughts of others without the aid of the senses. Neither angels nor animals had any need of speech. Only man being both angel and animal had need of language to reach the goal in civil life that God had assigned to him.

In establishing the basic traits of the grand style that he advocated, Dante went beyond the goals and scopes of the rhetoricians of his time through his consideration of content. Rhetoricians had considered only form. Dante's significance rests on having realized the unity of content and form in art and on having stated that in poetry content determined artistic form.

This sense of unity between content and form was derived by Dante from his mental habit of seeing all parts in the light of the whole. He lived in a universe which rested for him on eternal and unchanging principles. Whether he considered language or government, art or theology, he always argued from these principles, both religious and ethical, to which he gave unswerving allegiance. For this reason, Dante stands in the history of Western culture as one of the greatest moral masters and poets.

THE *DE MONARCHIA*

This most important treatise on government[3] was written later than the *Convivio* and the *De Vulgari Eloquentia*, perhaps around 1310 or 1312. Since it dealt with a universal problem — the question of peace, at a moment in history when Italy was ravaged by war — Dante wrote it in Latin, the universal language of the time. He stated at the very outset of the book that he felt it was a moral duty for a man of doctrine to use his knowledge for the good of all. Although possessed of a classical mentality resting on immutable concepts, unbreakable moorings of his philosophy of life and history, he never lost sight of the world in which he lived nor of his personal experiences.

The *De Monarchia* contains a most complete presentation of Dante's political thought. It is a stately structure with deep foundations that rises to encompass the whole of man and his history, his life on this earth and in the world to come. In the theoretical field, it is to the other works of Dante what the *Divina Commedia* is to his verse.

The *De Monarchia* is in three sections, and it proposes a way by which universal peace can be achieved among the states by making them a part of the system of the Empire. Although Dante referred to the Empire of his day, from which he expected the salvation of Italy, basically his thesis contains the idea of the "one world" that has echoed in our own time. The firm, subtle logic of the work makes one constantly aware of the presence of Dante, the honest and fearless thinker who was fully conscious that the evil in the life and history of his time was due to human greed and to the lack of a rational basis of conduct in individuals as well as in the relations among the various states.

The *De Monarchia* was written as an indictment of the theocratic policies of Boniface VIII by a deeply religious man, who saw with agonizing concern the seat of Papacy moved from Rome to Avignon in France. In his heart, Dante scored Philip the Fair for the change, but he blamed Boniface VIII for the plight of the Church and of Italy. He had hoped that the Empire, represented by Heinrich VII of Luxemburg, might bring order to the chaotic conditions of Italy and Florence. The death of that sovereign in 1312 must have struck a cruel blow to the hopes of the poet. Concern over the political situation of Italy had never left him from the very beginning of his exile. What he felt and thought had been voiced in the pages of the *Convivio* and in several of his epistles. But the dismay of the thinker before the sad spectacle of Italian political life, and the vanishing dream of a universal state that he had always cherished, took a powerful and final form in the pages of the *De Monarchia*.

The treatise is projected against the vast canvas of the poet's philosophy of life and history. Two concepts, that of "liberty" and of "rationality," stand out in it like two beacons that shine above the murky night of the chaotic history of Dante's day. Liberty was the goal that the poet assigned to man on earth; rationality was concerned with the means whereby man can attain that liberty.

The thought of Dante is majestically universal. For Dante, rationality was God, the Good and the *Jus* (Law). The *Jus* represented for him an equitable proportion of personal good in the relation of man with man and of state with state. It followed that if universal rationality guided the deeds of men and states, peace would be a logical consequence, and both men and states would fulfill their task of achieving happiness on this earth and eternal bliss in the life to come. Liberty, in his mind, was closely woven with moral life, individually and collectively, in the ratio of cause and effect. To be free was to live ethically: men, by mastering the natural passions; states, by eliminating the desire to expand into neighboring territories. Men and the states could achieve freedom only within the framework of the Empire. This high moral level could be realized only through rationality, the harmony between the vision of the intellect and the individual and collective actions. Only then would the world know peace. The concept of liberty thus projected in the *De Monarchia* is one of the many debts that Dante, through St. Thomas Aquinas, owes to Aristotle. It remained the pivot of the poet's thought in all his works and throughout his life.

Dante clearly saw the unity of law in God, and looked upon God as the only dispenser of authority. From Him, since the beginning of history, has emanated the temporal power granted to the Emperor and the spiritual authority given to the Pope. To these two pivotal agencies God has respectively entrusted the task of ministering to the physical requirements and spiritual needs of man.

In discussing man, his nature and his duties, Dante gives clear recognition to the temporal goal of man on this earth. In the history of ideas of the Western world, this recognition marks a milestone. It is Dante's chief contribution to the thought of the Renaissance. His predecessors in the field of ethics had spoken mainly of the spiritual goal of man in the life to come. The temporal goal was only a means of attaining the spiritual. Dante established a very harmonious parallelism that placed the two goals on an even plane. He believed that the goal of man in the life to come was that of contemplating God, but he recognized the legitimacy of practical action during man's life on this planet.

So great was the stress that he placed upon the temporal aspects of man's life that he divided them into three categories: the speculative, the artistic, and the practical. He assigned to the intellect the task of integrating the artistic and the practical activities by lifting the instinctive forces of man to the plane of rationality.

Dante passionately believed that moral unity was the only basis on which individual and collective life could rest and freedom and peace be attained. This dream of a good and happy life, he maintained, could only be realized within the Empire, divinely instituted by God through the establishment of the Roman Empire, its victories and its greatness. The Empire would minister to the states and the states would serve the material needs of man. To the Church he reserved the task of serving mankind's spiritual needs.

Writing in defense of the Empire, Dante used very fervently the argument of the historical precedence of Rome over the appearance of the Christian Church. If this be true, he argued, most assuredly the Emperor received his authority directly from God. The power of the Pope and that of the Emperor were separate and distinct. These powers should be kept as such, if humankind was to reach the goal assigned to it by God.

Dante showed more clearly than any other thinker of his time the changes that his age was undergoing in every field. In his works, old attitudes are side by side with new and daring ones. In his reasoning, he followed the strictest scholasticism; yet so great was he that one readily perceives through coldly assembled syllogisms the presence of a powerful mind and of a vision that makes him one of our contemporaries.

In the *De Monarchia*, Dante gave to the world one of the best balanced pictures of individual and collective existence by reducing both to the common denominator of rational living. For this reason, he marked a significant moment in the history of modern thought.

CHAPTER NINE

The Divine Comedy

The *Commedia*, to which posterity has reserved the qualification of "divine," was written during the long and painful years of Dante's exile, probably from 1307 until the last years of his life. Following the Aristotelian definition, Dante called it *Commedia*, since the protagonist, the poet's very self, survived the journey related therein. The complete title, couched in Latin words, was *Incipit Comedia Dantis Alagherii, Florentini Natione, Non Moribus.*[1] An unknown editor who greatly admired the poet's work added the word "divine" to its title in 1555.

Dante wrote the *Convivio* and his Latin works for the intelligentsia of his time. He penned the *Commedia* for himself. It was the intimate book to which he entrusted his innermost thoughts and feelings. He distilled in it, day by day, the bitterness of his existence and expressed therein his pride in not having lost his faith in life and in God. The poem was not released during the poet's lifetime. It was better so, for the opinions and feelings that it contained of the man who boasted of having formed his own party would have offended both the Guelphs and the Ghibellines.

The *Commedia* is projected against the background of the world of the Beyond. Following the Christian belief in Hell, Purgatory, and Paradise, the poet has grafted the three kingdoms on the framework of the Ptolemaic system. The three panels are very different in basic structure and character.

Hell is an enormous, conic-shaped chasm, wedged in the Northern Hemisphere between Jerusalem, one of the fixed points of Dante's world, and the center of the earth. It is divided into nine circles. In the first circle, Dante has located the Limbus where he has placed those who have not received baptism and whose lot is that, although not subjected to any suffering, they will be forever denied the vision of God. In the Limbus, he has assigned a special place to the great spirits of Antiquity. They live in a castle surrounded by seven walls, the symbols of the seven liberal arts. The first four of the eight remaining circles constitute the Upper Hell and are reserved for the sins of nature: lust, gluttony, avarice, and wrath; the last four, constituting the Lower Hell, are reserved for the sins of malice: heresy, violence, fraud, and betrayal. The seventh circle, that of violence, is subdivided into three smaller circles enclosing those who have used violence against their neighbor (tyrants), against themselves (suicides), and against God and nature (blas-

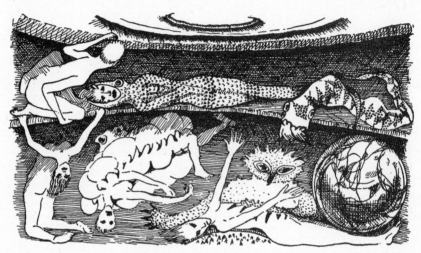

The circles of Dante's Hell.

phemers, homosexuals and usurers). With subtle irony, as if to signify the great variety of fraud, Dante has divided the eighth circle into ten subdivisions. He has reserved the four sections of the last circle, that of betrayal, for those who have broken faith with their kinsmen, their fatherland, guests, and benefactors. This last and ninth circle is formed by the lake of Cocytus. To signify his contempt for traitors, Dante has imagined that the waters of Cocytus flow down the slopes of Hell, carrying with them the filth of all other sins. Lucifer, who stands in its center, half of his body in the Northern Hemisphere and half in the Southern, flaps his six gigantic wings and causes the waters of Cocytus to freeze. In that ice are caught the sinners who have offended the basic loyalties of social life.

Purgatory, in the form of a very high mountain, is situated in the Southern Hemisphere where, according to tradition, the Earthly Paradise was believed to have been located.[2] Here a serene atmosphere prevails, befitting the theme of forgiveness, hope, and purification. There are nine ledges on the mountain of Purgatory: the first two, or the Antepurgatory, are reserved for those who have died while excommunicated by the Church or who have delayed until the very end their change of heart; the remaining seven are for those who have committed the seven mortal sins.

Paradise is circular in shape and is formed by the celestial spheres of the Moon, Mercury, Venus, the Sun, Mars, Jupiter, Saturn, all of which enclose Hell and Purgatory in their circular motion. The starry Heaven, the Crystalline Heaven, and the Empyrean are placed horizontally over them. Here the spirits of the blessed are visible, and divine harmonies fill the air.

Dante's poem is, basically, a vast tale in which an imaginary journey through the three kingdoms of the world of the Beyond is dramatically related. The central and essential theme therein developed is the passing of the poet from the state of man as pure instinct to that of one who feels the impact of spiritual and intellectual values. Dante begins his journey in a dark forest, the symbol of the poet's life when he was absorbed by his political activities and concerned with practical life. Here he wanders blindly in a pathless maze, but he never loses consciousness of what is good. From the gloom of the forest, he sees a light at the top of a hill, the symbol of absolute Truth identified with God, and he eagerly begins to climb toward it. But three beasts stand in his way: a leopard, a lion, and a she-wolf, which represent, in turn, lust, pride, and avarice. Frightened, Dante descends again into the forest and realizes that to overcome these qualities, inherent in all humanity, and to reach the ultimate truth, he needs a help that transcends nature. Beatrice, in her seat in Paradise, is informed by Lucia of the plight of her lover and sends Virgil to help him.

Virgil, as befitting the courtly person he is, hastens to the forest and leads Dante to the very door of Hell where a forbidding inscription forces him to ponder over the tragic problem of evil and its consequences. The poet has reflected his awe in words that echo with ominous force in the mind of every reader:

> Per me si va nella citta dolente,
> Per me si val nell'eterno dolore,
> Per me si va tra la perduta gente.
> Giustizia mosse 'l mio alto Fattore,
> Fecemi la divina Potestate,
> La somma Sapienza, e 'l primo Amore.
> Dinanzi a me non fur cose create,
> Se non eterne, ed io eterna duro:
> Lasciate ogni speranza, voi che 'ntrate.

Through me one goes into the dolorous city,
Through me one goes into eternal woe,
Through me one goes among the lost people.
Justice moved my eternal Maker,
Divine Power made me,
The Highest Wisdom and the First Love.
Before me there were not things created,
Except eternal, and I endure in eternity:
Leave every hope, ye who enter.

At the gate of Dis.

The poet fully understands that Hell has been created by God in His attributes of Justice and Omnipotence, but he finds it difficult to reconcile God as Love with God as the dispenser of eternal punishment. Encouraged by

Virgil, Dante enters the gates of Hell and, ferried by the ancient Charon across the River Acheron, he passes through the ghastly nine circles of the infernal chasm. He is aware that his heart will be deeply stirred and touched by the destiny of the sinners whom he will meet. He becomes greatly troubled, for he knows that as a believer in God he should not have pity for them. The struggle between his intellect and his heart is constantly with Dante, even though Virgil repeatedly tells him that compassion for the plight of the sinners should not move his heart.

Purgatory is a high mountain in the Southern Hemisphere.

Under the continued guidance of the Roman poet, through a subterranean passage, Dante emerges from Hell into the Southern Hemisphere and his tired eyes gaze on the beautiful and refreshing sight of the sea whence the mountain of Purgatory rises. The quivering of the waters in the morning light gives relief and joy to the poet. At the foot of the mountain, Dante and his guide meet the Roman Cato, the guardian of Purgatory and the symbol of freedom from human passions that Dante sought in his journey. From him they receive permission to enter his kingdom. On their way to the portals of Purgatory, the poet and Virgil meet the spirits of some of the personages who were contemporaries of Dante: Casella, a musician and friend of Dante; Manfredi, the son of Frederick II, who was excommunicated by the Church; Belacqua, still as indifferent and apathetic as he was on earth and still too sluggish to climb the rocky slopes of Purgatory.

The wayfarers reach a beautiful valley where princes and famous rulers are gathered and, from there, while lost in a deep sleep, the poet reaches the gate of Purgatory, carried in the arms of Lucia, the embodiment of the memory of one of Beatrice's friends.[3] An angel invites Dante and Virgil to enter, after using his sword to engrave on the poet's forehead seven p's, which stand for the seven *peccati* or mortal sins. The sight of the successive torments meted out to the sinners by divine justice for the purification of their souls causes the p's to disappear one after the other from Dante's forehead and he is thus restored to the original pure state of his intellect. It is now that Virgil, in the last act of his mission, tells the poet:

> *Libero, dritto e sano è tuo arbitrio,*
> *E fallo fora non fare a suo senno,*
> *Per ch'io te sopra te corono e mitrio.*

> Free, straight, and healed is your will,
> And it would·be wrong not to act according to its bidding;
> For which reason I crown and miter you master over yourself.

Dante and Virgil enter the leafy and green forest of the Earthly Paradise, the beauty of which is in perfect harmony with one whose intellect has reacquired full rationality. Here they witness a most amazing procession, composed of the great spirits of the Old and New Testaments, a symbol of the Christian Church, and Dante receives illumination from them. He is helped in passing through the Earthly Paradise by Matelda, a friend of Beatrice in the now distant days of their youth, who plunges him into the waters of the Lethe, where all memory of evil-doing is destroyed, and into the Eunoè, where the memory of good deeds is renewed. At this point Beatrice appears and Virgil leaves Dante, for the poet no longer needs his guidance. In a very human way, Dante confesses to Beatrice his sinful life after her death. She forgives him and they rise together through the spheres where the spirits of the blessed appear to the poet in terms of the effect that each sphere has exercised over them while on this earth. After having risen through all the spheres, Beatrice, her mission as a lady moved by love accomplished, entrusts Dante to the famous French mystic, St. Bernard of Clairvaux. It is St. Bernard who leads him to the Empyrean where God abides.

They rise together through the spheres.

Here, Dante gazes into a luminous point, a symbol of God. In Him, the poet reaches the goal toward which he has striven in vain on earth: harmony between his instinct and his will, and a complete understanding of the oneness of phenomena and essence. His attainment of this supreme goal is identified with a sudden and revealing light that strikes and illumines his mind.

The poet describes thus his experience:

> *Nel suo profondo vidi che s'interna,*
> *Legato con amore in un volume,*
> *Ciò che per l'universo si squaderna;*
>
> *Sustanze ed accidenti e lor costume*
> *Quasi conflati insieme, per tal modo*
> *Che ciò ch'io dico è un semplice lume.*

I saw that in its depths penetrates,
Bound with love in one volume,
What through the universe is unfolded
In multiplicity of forms:

Substances and accidents and their ways,
Almost perfectly blended together, in such a manner
That what I write gives but a feeble glimmer of its actual unity.

The simultaneous mention of "substances" and "accidents" is not casual. It shows that the poet sought his truth in the maze of the contradictions of everyday life. The new truth shining before him encompasses and unifies both the spiritual world and the world of phenomena. The *Commedia* is primarily a book of faith.

In the very last lines of the poem, by comparing his inner life to a wheel that revolves with perfect rhythm among all its parts, the poet shows the perfect harmony that he has achieved:

All'alta fantasia qui mancò possa;
Ma già volgeva il mio disio e 'l velle,
Sì come rota ch'igualmente è mossa,
L'amor che move il sole e l'altre stelle.

Here power failed my fancy,
But already my longings and my will,
In the guise of a wheel which is moved with an even rhythm,
Were moved by the love which sets in motion the sun
        and the other stars.

Now the universe has become for him truly "a boundless sea of being," pure spirit, as Beatrice has taught him. Through her love every clash between his instinct and his intellect has been destroyed. He has reached the state of rationality.

In perusing the *Commedia*, the reader should respect Dante's admonition[4] to seek its literal meaning first, and then to see in it an allegorical significance. The Inferno is the reflection of the world of nature with all the tendencies that lead man to evil and perdition. Purgatory is the world of purification. Paradise is the world of freedom as a means of reaching perfect happiness in God.

The three animals that bar the way of the poet to the mountain are not only three beautifully etched beasts, but also the symbols of natural tendencies that lead men astray into the jungle of everyday existence. In the literal sense, Beatrice is the girl whom Dante met in Florence and for whom his love con-

Virgil assists Dante past the three beasts: a leopard, a lion, and a she-wolf.

tinued to grow after her death. On the plane of allegory, Dante unquestionably meant for the reader to add symbolic meaning to his characterization of Beatrice, a poetic shadow of his love-dream that acquired greater religious and philosophical depth without ever losing its romantic afflatus.

Who are the three guides in the light of allegory? Dante does not reveal their symbolical meaning, but it is certain that they are three persons whom the poet loved and deeply revered and whom he contrasted with the three natural forces represented by the three beasts. It seems logical, therefore, to see in the three guides the three aspects or degrees of transcendentalism in which he placed his faith: Virgil, poetry; Beatrice, love of woman; and St. Bernard, cosmic love, the love of God. Since the poet has reserved for St. Bernard the mission of leading him to the vision of God, he has evidently assigned to cosmic love an even vaster and deeper significance than he has given to his love for Beatrice.

In its lofty symbolism, the *Commedia* contains a revision of the love concept as fashioned by the poets of Provence, and as treated by those of Sicily and Tuscany.[5] These poets, as well as Dante himself in the *Vita Nuova*, basically speaking, had not been able to go beyond the coldly theoretical meaning of love. In the thoughtful days of his manhood, the poet became aware that he had given only lip-service to the creed of perfect love. In the *Vita Nuova*, he had to suppress the literal truth in order to prove that Beatrice was the only woman that he had ever loved.

The love concept was resumed in the *Commedia* in a totally different manner. The poet, now in the full flowering of his mind, with a knowledge of life that a mere youth could not have possessed, rededicated himself to the task of telling anew what the memory of Beatrice had indeed meant in his life. The *Commedia* thus became an epitome of Dante's whole life, the inventory of all that had been meaningful or meaningless in his human experience. It reflects, though in new forms and heightened to a superlative degree, the ideas that had been diffused in all his other works.

The pivot of the poet's revision of the love-concept is the Provençal tenet that the function of a woman's love is to lead man to God. As he grew older, Dante was fired with the desire to transform this formula into a living reality. He had promised this task to himself when he penned the last words of the *Vita Nuova*: "I hope to tell of her what has never been said of any other woman." He kept his promise and wrote the most exalting glorification of woman that has ever been made.

Stamped on nearly every page of the *Commedia* is the reflection of the poet's character. Among the most arresting lines are those in which the poet has enclosed his life philosophy with a directness and sincerity unknown to the poets of previous centuries. It would not be too bold to say that one finds in his poem statements that Dante would have hesitated to express in a philosophical treatise. His tercet revealing his concept of evil is one such case. In it, at the very opening of his *Inferno*, he confides:

Temer si dee di sole quelle cose
Ch'hanno potenza di fare altrui male;
Dell'altre, no, chè non son paurose.

We must fear only those things that
Are capable of doing harm to our fellow men;
Not others, for they are not fearful.

This confession, in intimacy and directness, is not dissimilar from his statement concerning the necessity of acting once we have decided on a definite course. In both the *Inferno* and *Purgatorio*,[6] he causes Virgil to chide him for indulging in thinking and hesitating rather than boldly carrying out his resolutions. In *Purgatorio* where he repeats in a more polished form the thought already expressed in the *Inferno*, he makes Virgil utter the famous words:

Sta come torre ferma che non crolla
Giammai la cima per soffiar de' venti.

Stand like a powerful tower that never
Moves its summit under the fury of blasting winds.

These are words befitting a man who lived alone and did not fear to tell his friends and foes what he saw as the truth. His repeated statements concerning his relying on his conscience only and his standing like a "tetragonal tower" against the blows of fortune are eloquent commentary on his ethical code.

Dante was a man who never knew what it was to compromise. For this reason, in his *Inferno*, the "lukewarm" are relegated outside of Hell. For him, they are unworthy of being even in the infernal circles. In repeated attacks, the poet declares that the heavens chase them out in order not to be less beautiful, and deep Hell does not receive them for fear that the damned ones would find some glory in their presence. The damned would declare themselves to be not so bad if those featureless persons were near them. By compromising with good and evil, the lukewarm have forfeited both justice and compassion from God. Their reward can be only absolute contempt.

Because of the nobility of his character, Dante considered betrayal the gravest of all sins. He reserves the last circles of the Inferno for the traitors and he depicts them steeped in varying measure in the ice of Cocytus, cold as their unfeeling hearts. He inveighs against them with cruel irony and, at the moment of betrayal, he assigns them the lot of continued life on this earth without a soul. He imagines that as soon as one betrays, his soul swoops down into Hell and a devil takes its place in the body of the sinner. This is the lot that the poet has assigned to Branca d'Oria, whom he had recently seen on earth. Dante, upon learning from one of the sinners that d'Oria was already in the circle of the traitors, locked in the ice of Cocytus, feigned surprise and, with unmatched sarcasm, describes the traitor's life on earth in the famous line

E mangia e bee e dorme e veste panni

He eats, drinks, sleeps, and wears clothes,

a most damaging restriction, indeed, of human existence.

In the consideration of sins, Dante departs from the strictly ecclesiastical attitude toward evil. One of the deepest impressions of the reader is the realization that, for Dante, evil is our punishment. The underlying characteristic of the *contrappasso*, the relation between the evil perpetrated and the punishment meted out by God to each of the sinners, is the unbreakable relationship of sin and punishment.

Dante's fertile imagination has exploited this analogy to produce amazing situations. The lustful ones are whirled by a terrific storm, similar to the fury of the passion to which they have yielded on this earth. The soothsayers, for having dared to gaze into the future, have their heads turned backward and must look backward as they walk forward. Such is their retribution for not having been satisfied in life with the knowledge of the present. Those who in their earthly life have caused divisions and have brought schisms into the Church have their heads and bodies slashed by a sword. One of them, Bertrand de Born, walks carrying his head in his hand in the guise of a lantern. Tyrants are steeped in a lake of boiling blood, the blood they have spilled on earth. Evil counselors have been transformed into flames reminiscent of the destruction which they have wrought by their wicked counsel.

In writing the *Commedia*, Dante was fully conscious of the difficult task that he had assigned to himself. In the *Inferno*, he has invoked only the Muses, for, according to his theory of content discussed in the *De Vulgari Eloquentia*, the subject matter of the first *cantica* was of the lowest and did not require, therefore, a lofty poetic form. The gloom of the realm of the damned has been rendered through the jarring rhymes that the poet wished for before attempting to describe the horrors of the last circle. His language is direct and strong, for he is primarily concerned with what he wants to tell the reader. There is no conscious attempt to embellish and polish his form.

For this reason, he often uses words that cause embarrassment to a prudish person. Theoretically, in the *De Vulgari Eloquentia*, he had excluded such words from the vocabulary of a poet who sought the grand style, leaving them for popular songsters. He should not be criticized if his loathing for human degradation and his resentment against his enemies forced him to depart from his theory by using terms that he had forbidden to courtly poets. The poetry of the *Purgatorio* and the *Paradiso* is characterized by an unforgettable musical quality perfectly attuned to his theory of the correspondence of poetic form and content. In the *Purgatorio*, he has invoked Calliope as well as the Muses, for, having left behind the "dead poetry" of evil of the *Inferno*, the nature of the world of Purgatory calls for a higher type of art. Here he employs harmonious rhymes, especially when he enters the Earthly Paradise. In the *Paradiso*, feeling totally incapable of supplying the proper form to such a sublime topic, he has invoked the aid of Apollo himself. The beginning of Canto II in the *Paradiso* is one of the most vivid expressions of the consciousness of beauty and power ever penned by a poet. Dante likens his poetry to a stately ship that proudly rides the waves of the sea. Minerva, in the guise of a strong wind, swells the sails of his ship, and Apollo is his helmsman. The subject matter of the spiritual world through which he ascends under the guidance of Beatrice calls for a lofty diction that befits the treatment of the vision of God and absolute Truth.[7]

The *Commedia* is executed with infinite care and sense of harmony. The interest of the poet in the number three, so widely evidenced in the *Vita Nuova*, is carried over to the major poem. The three worlds are sung in three *cantiche: Inferno, Purgatorio*, and *Paradiso*. Each *cantica* has thirty-three cantos with an extra canto in the *Inferno* that serves as an introduction. Each stanza has three lines, the first and the third of which are bound by the same rhyme, while the middle line links the first stanza to the following one. This is Dante's own rhyme scheme, referred to as the *terza rima*. A multiple of three, the number nine, is the guiding measure for the architecture of the *Inferno* with nine circles, the *Purgatorio* with nine ledges, and the *Paradiso* with nine heavens. Dante ends each *cantica* with the word *stella* (star), as if to signify a memory of the consolation that he found in contemplating the heavens when men had forsaken him.

Dante's journey is made varied and dramatic by the introduction of episodes that bring into relief outstanding individuals singled out among the incredibly large multitude of the sinners and the blessed. The episodes are enhanced by the revelation of the unexpected concerning the characters with whom the poet talks. The reader is constantly taken by surprise as the various characters present their lives in a light totally different from that known to their contemporaries. This happens most visibly in the episodes of Francesca of Rimini, Pier of Vigna, Ulysses, and Count Ugolino, the most dramatic of the *Inferno*.

In contrast with the common belief that Francesca was an adulteress, killed by her husband Gianciotto in the moment that her brother-in-law Paolo kissed her, she is made to picture her love in the light of courtly love.[8] The poet is so struck by this revelation that he falls in a swoon. Pier of Vigna, known to all to have been imprisoned by the Emperor Frederick II as a traitor, proclaims his innocence and swears that he never broke faith with his beloved master. Ulysses relates how he died in a shipwreck after he had crossed the Strait of Gibraltar and had ventured southward in the Atlantic. After leaving Troy, he explains, he had not returned to Ithaca because a burning desire for knowledge goaded him to undertake a perilous voyage into the unexplored and mysterious world that lay beyond the columns of Hercules. Thus, Ulysses is no longer the embodiment of slyness, but rather the new man that Dante felt in himself, as revealed by the beautiful words that the poet places on his lips:

> Considerate la vostra semenza;
> Fatti non foste a viver come bruti,
> Ma per seguir virtute e conoscenza.

> Consider your origin;
> You were not made to live like brutes,
> But to follow virtue and knowledge.

The meeting with Count Ugolino in the pit of the traitors of one's country offers a striking contrast between the beastly hate that the Count evidences by gnawing at the brain of his enemy, the Archbishop Ruggeri, and his tender feelings as a father who has seen his children starve at his feet when condemned by Pisa to die of starvation in the city-prison called Muda.

In other episodes found scattered in the three *cantiche*, Dante dramatically refers to the history of his time in its various aspects, expressing his admiration for the Florentine life of the past and the sadness, even hatred, engendered in him by the baseness of the present. Ciacco, a Florentine of the poet's time, is described in the circle of gluttony, meditating on the internal strife of their city. Filippo Argenti, placed among the wrathful in the muddy pool of the Styx, awakens in the poet an uncontrollable desire for vengeance. Farinata, even in the fiery tomb of the heretics, is tormented by the thought of the difficulties of his White Party, suffering under the unjust laws imposed on it by the Blacks. Brunetto Latini makes the poet conscious again of his love for poetic glory, as in the days when they were together in Florence. It was the author of the *Tesoro* who had urged Dante to follow the way of philosophy and poetry. The episodes of Count Ugolino and of Manfredi, the latter found in the *Purgatorio* and presented as a victim of the pitiless policy of the Papacy, are moving pages torn from the political history of the time, as are the lesser episodes of Maestro Adamo, Fra Alberigo, Bocca degli Abati, and others. In the *Paradiso*, Piccarda, Forese's sister, Romeo, Cunizza, and Carlo Martello, the stern and strong men of the old Florence, reveal variously the historical vicissitudes of the era.

The *Commedia* displays amazing technical procedures. The poet often uses the simplest words with the most surprising effect. When he sees Celestine V,[9] whom he does not deign to mention by name, but to whom he refers as "he who through cowardliness made the great refusal," the poet breaks forth with

> *Incontanente intesi e certo fui*
> *Che quest'era la setta dei malnati*
> *A Dio spiacente ed ai nemici sui.*

> Immediately I understood and became certain
> That this was the sect of the ill-fated ones
> Displeasing to God and to His enemies.

We know of no other use of irony more subtle, more bitter, and more contemptuous than this. Through that "immediately" the poet conveys to the reader the idea that the presence alone of the ineffectual Pope had made him instantly realize the type of sinner in that place. The same can be said of the effect that he produces with the very trite word "all" in the case of Farinata. Virgil, who shouts to his pupil

> *Vedi là Farinata che s'è dritto;*
> *Dalla cintola in su, tutto, il vedrai*

> See Farinata who is standing there,
> From his waist up you will see him — all,

reveals to us with that simple word the gigantic proportions of the hero. With the same force "all" is used in describing the souls of the sinners before Minos, the judge in Hell. The evil that they have perpetrated forces them to confess their guilt, just as it compels them to run desperately toward their torment, "so that fear turns into longing." As soon as they reach the presence of Minos, they confess "all," revealing the innermost recesses of their hearts. In this expression the *tutta* refers to the soul and allows the reader to surmise all that his imagination is capable of seeing and feeling in the vaguest word in any language.

The extraordinary achievement of the *Commedia* lies in the success of the poet in transforming material, by its very nature abstract, into vivid and intensely human poetry. One of the devices repeatedly used is that of interspersing the poem with beautifully etched landscapes. Though gloom predominates in the timeless atmosphere of the *Inferno*, picturesque nooks of Italy are constantly evoked in the description of the world of the Beyond and are beautifully blended with it. Nature poetry touches the highest point of perfection in the description of the sea at dawn as Virgil and Dante prepare to climb the mountain of Purgatory and when they enter the divine forest at its top. So beautiful are the three cantos dedicated to the latter scene that Chaucer, in the *Knight's Tale,* patterned on Dante's Matelda his charming Emily as she gathered flowers in her garden while sweetly singing.

The *Purgatorio* also offers a great variety of beautiful and, at the same time, familiar images. By way of an example, in the first ledge where the sinners of pride are weighed down by enormous stones that they carry on their backs, the poet describes himself and the proud Oderisi, as they walk side by side, in the likeness of two yoked oxen slowly moving along a road. On the ledge of envy, those guilty of this sin have their eyes sewn together by a wire and hold each other up by leaning against one another in the manner of beggars often seen grouped together in front of churches on festival days, their heads close to one another.

The task of humanizing the content of the *Commedia* and making it accessible to the reader is most visible in the *Paradiso*. Even such abstract questions therein discussed, as the spots on the moon, free will, the responsibility of the Jews in the death of Christ, the reason why children are often unlike their parents, the wisdom of Solomon, and the inscrutability of divine justice, become meaningful and human when explained by Beatrice to her lover-poet.

Although the *Paradiso* is the realm of the blessed, the poet has not relinquished, even in the uppermost of the eternal spheres, his interest in and memory of this earth. Italy, Florence, and the history of his time are ever-present in his thought. When Dante meets Cacciaguida, his ancestor recalls to him the noble Florence of his own time, in contrast with the upstarts and clownish villains who, in Dante's opinion, crowded within the precincts of the enlarged city of his day. The announcement of the poet's exile by Caccia-guida creates one of the most moving sections of the whole poem. Equally moving is his encounter with Piccarda, Forese Donati's sister, who brings back to Dante's mind the memory of the years of his stormy youth. His praise of Piccarda's loveliness parallels the praise that he lavishes in the *Purgatorio* on Forese's wife, Nella.

The soul disappears as a heavy object sinks into the darkness of deep waters.

Dante also makes the *Paradiso* comprehensible to the reader by the use of similes taken from the world of nature: birds, flowers, light, water. Dante introduces them at any time that his unerring sense of art makes him aware that the sustained loftiness of his verse should be broken. By way of example, the presence of the souls in the sphere of the Moon is described by comparing them to images reflected in a mirror. So complete is the illusion of the poet that he actually turns backward as if to look for the tangible persons of the spirits that he has noticed in the clarity of the sphere. Equally vivid is the simile used by Dante when he likens the disappearance of a soul after it talks to him to the sinking of a heavy object into the darkness of deep waters.

Various, yet uniformly beautiful, are the ways in which the poet renders the smile of Beatrice.[10] It is a smile in which the love of a mother is woven into that of a lover. Dante keeps her on the same human plane on which he placed her when he met her at the top of the mountain of Purgatory. Here he tells the reader that upon seeing her again, he has gratified his "ten-year-old thirst" for her. Beatrice remains in Paradise as the highest exemplification of perfect love, lofty yet human — of a superior humanity consonant with the memory of a beloved woman now dead. Even in her symbolism, Beatrice is human to the degree that, at one point, she admonishes her lover not to gaze into her eyes so intently, for Paradise is "not only in my eyes." The overtone of her superior humanity is perfectly conveyed by her smile as well as her luminous eyes.

The cultural influences in the *Commedia* are many and deep. They are used with the unerring wisdom that only great poets possess. Classical lore, the Bible, Provençal culture, the philosophy of the time, all have been used by the poet to enrich the topography and the variety of his world. The infernal rivers, Acheron, Styx, Phlegeton, are of classical origin as is also the frozen lake of Cocytus. Cato of Utica, although a pagan and a suicide, is the keeper of the mountain of Purgatory. The infernal monsters, Charon, Minos, Cerberus, Pluto, Flegiàs, Gerion, some of the giants as well as Brutus and Cassius, have been taken from the classical cycle. The latter two are placed in the mouths of the three-faced Lucifer, together with Judas Iscariot. They are the arch-traitors in the history of humanity: Brutus and Cassius, the betrayers of Caesar, the symbol of the Empire; Judas, the betrayer of Christ, the symbol of the spiritual world. Many other classical characters appear in the *Commedia*: Achilles, Paris, Dido, Cleopatra, Ulysses, Diomedes, Sinon, Cato, and the Emperor Trajan. Statius appears in Purgatory in a revealing episode in which the Latin poet is made to express his reverence and love for Virgil.

Classical also is the division of sins into sins of nature and sins of malice. Dante has taken this division from the Ethics of Aristotle and has used it to give a perfect architectural form to the huge chasm of the Inferno.

From the Bible, which Dante knew most intimately, he has taken the gigantic figure of Lucifer with a flight of the imagination which does not fail to achieve sublimity in the primitive and almost grotesque qualities attributed to the fallen angel. Dante imagines that Lucifer has been hurled down from God's world into the earth, remaining fixed in its very center, while the earth that he has displaced when he passed through it has risen skyward into the Southern Hemisphere to form the mountain of Purgatory. Now the upper part of the gigantic figure of Lucifer rises into the last circle of Hell. He has three faces, which symbolize the trinity of evil in contrast with the trinity of good. Hairy and revolting is his huge body with six wings at the top of his shoulders. At the fringe of the frozen lake, there is a rim out of which rise the giants of antiquity, both classical and Biblical: Nimrod, Antheus, Phialtes, and others. They are chained and, as Dante draws near them in passing from the eighth circle to the ninth, they loom in the distance like gigantic towers. The poet imagines that one of them, Antheus, lowers

Lucifer has three faces. Hairy and revolting
is his huge body. . . .

Virgil and him into the ninth circle at the pit of which is seen Lucifer in awesome grandeur.

Although scholars have held that Dante did not know Plato directly, since only the *Timaeus* (in the version of Chalcidius) was mentioned by him in his writings,[11] it must not be concluded that the poet was unaware of the idealism of Plato in the specific forms that it took in his *Symposium* and other dialogues. Since Plato's ideas penetrated the West with Plotinus and the Fathers of the Church, the *compendia* and commentaries of his day must have been the means through which Dante became acquainted with Platonism. There is also no doubt that St. Augustine, one of the early admirers of Plato who had a deep and lasting influence on Dante, served as a link between the poet and the Greek thinker. Moreover, there is a strong possibility that Dante perused the translation of *Meno and Phaedon* by Aristippo of Catania which, as we have seen, was executed at the court of William the Norman in 1156 at Palermo. The *Purgatorio* cannot be read without realizing that Platonism was the pattern on which Dante modeled the laws governing that section of his poetic world.

When Dante imagines that as soon as Virgil plucked the rush he was to tie at the bidding of Cato around the poet's waist, another rush grew in its place, he must have had in mind the Platonic law of *negatio,* a law that inexorably governs the world of nature, but could not exist in the perfect state of Purgatory, a part of the supernatural world. Platonic also is the behavior of the leaves responding to the caress of the wind in the divine forest and the origin of the wind that Dante feels on the summit of Purgatory. To have thought that the Angel in carrying the souls of the sinners in a small vessel from the Tiber to the foot of the mountain does so without moving its wings, bespeaks the Platonic concept of the exclusion of effort in the supernatural sphere. Another example of Platonism is visible in Dante's placing in the plants of the Earthly Paradise the seminal powers transmitted to all vegetation on earth by the breeze that the celestial spheres create in their circular motion.

The *Commedia* is one of the great books of world literature. It belongs to all humanity. More than a book, it is a world in itself, in which the poet has succeeded in assembling and harmonizing the most varying elements: tradition and poetry, science and art, philosophy and religion, world history and that of his time, God, the epitome of good, and the brutal forces of nature identified with evil. The *Commedia* exalts man and keeps alive in the reader the feeling of the nobility of human life, history, and civilization through the same faith that Dante preserved untarnished despite vicissitudes and trials that would have bent and broken any other man.

CHAPTER TEN

Prose Writing in the Thirteenth Century

One of the salient facts in the intellectual life of the thirteenth century was the use of the vernacular in the fields of fiction, history, and drama. These new works show that cultural life was gradually penetrating into parts of the social body other than the courts and the official centers of learning to which, to a large extent, it had been previously confined.

EARLY ATTEMPTS AT FICTION

The early and largely anonymous authors of fiction took their subject matter from Latin and French originals, modifying it in terms of their own cultural level and temperament. Although their works were very elementary from a psychological point of view as well as in the language used, their child-like simplicity and spontaneity often gave them a charm peculiarly their own.

France contributed greatly to the establishment of the Italian tradition in fiction. From that country was transmitted to Italy the material of the *Thousand and One Nights* together with, as we have already seen, the classical stories of Greece and Rome, the Carolingian tales and the stories of the Arthurian knights.

The *Libro dei sette savi* (The Book of the Seven Sages), a collection of tales taken from the *Thousand and One Nights,* but greatly modified, had its model in the French *Roman des Sept Sages.* Basically, it was the version of the *Book of Sindbad* that reached Italy through a French translation and was variously adapted to the Italian environment and taste. The original setting is changed into that of Christian Rome. A Roman emperor and his son take the place of the two main characters who appeared in the *Thousand and One Nights.* Other numerous anachronistic details are found in the background against which the action is projected. The plot deals with the postponement of the execution of the emperor's son, wrongly accused by his stepmother of having attempted to seduce her. In the end, while the seven sages entertain the emperor with their tales, the young prince proves his innocence and is restored to his father's favor, while the stepmother is condemned to death.

Similarly derived was the *Conti di antichi cavalieri* (Tales of Ancient Knights)[1] whose anonymous author took the subject matter of his twenty tales from French translations of various traditions: the tale of Saladin, from Eastern history; that of Tebaldo (Thibauld), from France; those of Agamemnon, Hector, Scipio, Caesar, Pompey, Regulus, and Brutus, from the classical cycle.

Another collection, *Dodici conti morali* (Twelve Moral Tales), derived its material from the French *Fabliaux*. They depict in a satirical vein ludicrous situations in which persons of the Church find themselves. The general tone of the collection, contrary to what the title implies, is far from moral.

Toward the end of the century the *Roman de la Rose* was also recast in a series of two hundred and thirty-two sonnets under the title of *Il fiore* (The Flower). Although the work had been attributed to Dante, modern criticism now rejects this theory. Equally in doubt is the authorship of the *Detto d'amore* (A Motto of Love) in which a Ser Durante is said to have used the material of the French allegorical novel at the end of the century. The poem is both fictional and allegorical, the two basic traits of the French original.

From the French was also translated and freely rehandled the charming tale of *Floire and Blanceflor*, written by an unknown author around 1160. The work was executed toward the end of the century and was given the title of *Cantare di Florio e Biancofiore* (Romance of Floire and Blanceflor).

On a different plane is an early example of allegorical fiction in prose that appeared in the second half of the thirteenth century — the *Introduzione alle virtù* (Introduction to Virtues) by Bono Giamboni, the Florentine judge whom we have seen as the translator of Brunetto Latini's *Tresors* and other works. It is the story of a journey from the valley of vice to the summit of spiritual perfection under the guidance of philosophy. The book adumbrates the central idea of the *Divine Comedy* without the poetic afflatus with which Dante vivified and made immortal his journey. More than to art, Giamboni's work belongs to the history of culture, in that it illustrates the high place that the new generation of scholars assigned to knowledge and ethical living.

From the large mass of translations, cultural contacts, and free rehandling of former works, there stand out three works of fiction that very clearly bear artistic traits: the *Novellino* (The Book of Short Stories), the *Fioretti di San Francesco* (The Little Flowers of St. Francis), and the *Milione* (Millions) of Marco Polo.

The *Novellino*, written around 1300, was the first collection of short stories that we may legitimately call art. It is a book still alive for us in its simplicity and charm. It was first printed in Florence in 1525 by Carlo Gualteruzzi and again in the same city, in 1527, by Vincenzo Borghini. These early editions bear the title of *Le cento novelle antiche* (One Hundred Ancient Tales), a number that recalls the one hundred cantos of Dante's *Divine Comedy* and the one hundred short stories of Boccaccio's *Decameron*. Originally, there were probably one hundred and fifty stories, for that is the number found in earlier manuscript editions of the charming booklet. This larger collection bears the subtitle of *Libro di bel parlar gientile* (Book of Beautiful and Genteel Language) in which there is an echo of the denomination of *Dolce Stil Nuovo* that Dante gave to the poetry of his youth.

Nothing specific is known of the author who was, very likely, a Tuscan and a cultivated man. He states thus the aim pursued in his collection: *Questo libro tratta d'alquanti fiori di parlare, di belle cortesie, e di be' risposi e di belle valentie e di doni, secondo che per lo tempo passato hanno fatto molti valenti uomini.*[2] (This book deals with a few beautiful examples of beautiful diction, beautiful courtly acts, beautiful answers, beautiful gifts, which are known to have been accomplished in the past by many gallant men.) The author used oriental and classical sources as well as contemporary material, but he left on it the imprint of his naïve character. He delights in wit and reveals a marked taste for opulence, good taste, beautiful clothing, and clever sayings. He has an aristocratic sense of life which he manifests through his admiration for illustrious men and for those who enjoy a luxurious mode of living. He presents in his stories the Classical Hector and Aeneas, the Romantic Lancelot, the Oriental Saladin, and the contemporary figures of Prester John, Frederick II, and Azzolino.

Most beautiful is the story of the three rings that reappeared in the *Decameron* and was used by Gotthold Ephraim Lessing in a rather heavy version in his *Nathan der Weise*. Witty is the tale of the Saracen cook and the poor man who stole the steam from the cook's kitchen and was enjoined by the sultan to pay the miserly Fabrac for the steam of his meat with the tinkling of a coin. The subtitle *Libro di parlar gientile* is a perfect description of the style and the atmosphere that envelop events and characters as well as of the temperament of the author.

Quite different in content, but sharing the same quality of simplicity and naïveté are the fifty-two chapters of the *Fioretti*, an imaginative rehandling in the vernacular of the life of St. Francis of Assisi, executed around 1300[3] by a warm admirer of the Saint. His simple prose runs smoothly on, not unlike the chaste and limpid waters dear to the Saint. The author's name is unknown, but there is no doubt that he was a born artist, such is the power of expression he evidences in rendering the heroic figure of the Saint in his humility and goodness toward men and animals alike. Only an artist with high powers of observation can describe animals and their acts and motions in the manner offered by the author of the *Fioretti*.

The *Fioretti* is meant to keep the best, the flower, of the memories concerning St. Francis' holy life and deeds. To understand and to admire its legends one must abandon oneself to the flame of charity that St. Francis was capable of kindling in all those who knew him. The *Fioretti* is not a book of actualism. It abides in a sphere higher than actual life, although it never forsakes the human element in the events that it relates. We find in

The Saracen cook and the poor man.

the book a St. Francis who never forgot nature, although he chose to live on a plane above it. Memorable is the chapter on perfect bliss in which the most human Brother Leo, amidst the raging of a snowstorm, is told of the lofty goals that a Franciscan must reach in order to find happiness. Memorable, too, for the spirit that permeates them, are the legends of the conversion of the wolf of Gubbio and the sermon to the birds. The Saint, in his infinite compassion, understands the reason why the wolf destroys men and animals, and he makes a pact between it and the inhabitants of Gubbio, with the result that the fierce beast becomes a peaceful animal. The sermon to the birds is the counterpart of the episode of the wolf, for the tiny creatures are invited to express gratitude and praise to the Lord for all that He has given them. The beauty of the two episodes rests on the sense of observation and the power of description evidenced in etching the wolf which, when scolded by the Saint, lies reverent and repentant at his feet and accepts the pact of friendship with the inhabitants of Gubbio by raising his paw and placing it in the hand of the Saint. The sermon to the birds is enlivened by the description of the birds as they lower their heads to acknowledge agreement with the words of St. Francis, and flap their wings to express their joy. The familiarity of the wolf and the birds with the Saint envelops them in a halo of legend and love that lifts them to a higher plane than that of most animal stories, both ancient and modern. So convincingly are the two episodes conceived and executed

St. Francis, the wolf of Gubbio, and the birds.

that the modern reader does not find it difficult to rise to the level where the Franciscan spirit abides. The charm of the book lies in the atmosphere of peace and charity that emanate from every word and deed of the most understanding and lovable of all saints.

The *Milione* (Millions) recounts many stories of the strange lands, customs, and men observed by the famous merchant Marco Polo (1254-1324) when he went to the Orient. He belonged to one of those Venetian families that had accumulated great wealth by trading with the East. His father and his uncle, upon their return to the Orient in 1271, took Marco Polo with them when the lad was only seventeen years old. They visited Mongolia, China (Catai), Japan (Cipango), and other lands, and were received by Kublai Khan with such honor that Marco remained in the Khan's court for seventeen years. In 1298, after returning to his native city, Marco Polo manned his family galley and took part in the naval battle of Curzola in which Venice was defeated by Genoa. Many Venetians were taken prisoner, among them Marco Polo.

While he was in prison in Genoa, he dictated to Rusticiano or Rustichello of Pisa the story of his travels and adventures in the East. Rusticiano wrote them down in a rough French with which were mingled many words in the Venetian dialect. The title handed down to us by tradition is *Il libro di messer Marco Polo cittadino di Venezia, detto Milione, dove si raccontano le meraviglie del mondo* (The Book of Sir Marco Polo, a Citizen of Venice, Nicknamed Milione, Where the Marvels of the World Are Related). The title *Milione* was taken from the nickname that his fellow citizens ironically gave to the author upon hearing his extraordinary accounts of all that he had seen in the East, as if to say that he saw everything in terms of millions.

Marco Polo closed his book with the words *Deo gratias, Amen,* in the manner of the religious persons of that time. He attributes to Divine Providence the fact that he had been able to explore all the East and to return home safely. He appears conscious in his book of the uniqueness of his task in that he wishes to relate only what he and he only, Marco Polo, son of Niccolò Polo, a noble and outstanding citizen of the city of Venice, saw and observed. Aware of the wide audience his narration would attract, Marco Polo addresses himself to the whole world because he deemed his adventures worthy of being known to all.

If the essence of literary art lies in presenting to the reader a new reality, most certainly the *Milione* is a landmark in fictional literature in the new tongue. It is the product of a fancy kindled by the deep sense of wonder in an author who stands before a world that is constantly new to him, and that he makes new to the reader. Every page speaks of a new discovery, a discovery seen through the very human and penetrating eyes of an artist.

Marco Polo possessed a sort of elemental fancy to which he gave expression by the use of very general terms in his descriptions. The rooms in the palace of Kublai Khan, for example, were "all covered with gold and silver." The gardens of the same palace are described in the same indefinite manner: "There are beautiful meadows and trees, and many kinds of wild beasts." This procedure in its diffused character achieves extraordinary results in rendering the wondrous beauty and opulence of the palace.

An unforgettable page is that in which the Venetian traveler notices that when the Tartars venture into the obscure northern valleys in search of booty, pelts, and game, they ride mares and they take along the young colts. Before entering the mysterious North, they tie their colts to a tree and go on their expedition. Having found their loot, they load it on the mares and sleep while they ride back, sure that the mother instinct will guide their mounts back to the place of departure. This simple and direct account contains a moving and deep admiration for the power of instinct.

The *Milione* is a significant book for information concerning the economic and social conditions of the East at the end of the thirteenth century and for its description of the customs of various peoples: Tartars, Mongols, Russians, and many other different tribes. However, it is its imaginative quality and the power of observation that give to the book its enduring literary character.

HISTORICAL WORKS

By the end of the twelfth century, there already existed in Italy an outstanding Latin historical tradition.[4] During the thirteenth century significant historical works written in the vernacular appeared, although, as was to be expected, the Latin tradition continued.

The study of history in Latin is represented by a very impressive array of works written during the period studied here. There are significant books written on religious history, such as the *Historia ecclesiastica* (Ecclesiastical History) by Tolomeo of Lucca, which studies church history to the year 1312.

Many Latin works were dedicated to the study of contemporary history, a clear proof of the closeness of this generation to the events of their time. Bartolomeo of Neocastro wrote of the political vicissitudes of Sicily between 1250 and 1294 from a Ghibelline point of view. Niccolò Jamsilla dealt with the activity of Frederick II and his children between 1210 and 1258 in his *Historia de Rebus Federici II Eiusque Filiorum* (History of Events under Frederick II and His Sons). The same events (1250-1276) were discussed by Saba Malaspina in his *Rerum Sicularum Libri* (Books about Events in Sicily). Parisio of Cereta wrote the *Annales Veronenses* (Annals of Verona) up to the year 1297. Galvano Fiamma wrote about Milanese history in his *Manipulus Florum* (A Handful of Flowers), relating events up to 1334. Giovanni of Cermenate in his history of Milan discussed events that occurred in that city up to 1313. Venetian citizens continued to be interested in the history of their city and the Doge Andrea Dandolo wrote about the vicissitudes of the republic up to the year 1339.

Among the outstanding historians of Milan who wrote in Latin was Bonvesìn of Riva (*ca.* 1240-*ca.* 1314). He was a teacher of rhetoric and, among other works, left a history of Milan that Francesco Novati discovered in the National Library of Madrid in 1895.[5] The book is written from a scientific point of view and offers a good description of that city at the end of the thirteenth century through statistics and the personal observations of the author. The reader is introduced to Milan at the time that the despotism of the Signoria loomed amidst the weakening of Communal institutions.

Albertino Mussato (Padua, 1261-1329), a jurist and a classical scholar, wrote his *Historia Augusta* in which he very objectively presented the internal strife of Italian cities and especially of his native Padua during the expedition to Italy of Heinrich VII that ended with his death in 1313. The author continued to study the conditions of Italy after the death of the German emperor until 1329 in his book on the history of his own time. Mussato was one of the first scholars who tried to write in a style definitely molded on the pure classical form. However, he is remembered here not because he was a stylist, but because he possessed a penetrating mind and stood out as a keen observer of the historical events in which he played a very important role. He was a contemporary of Dino Compagni and Dante, and like them he fought to preserve the freedom of his city. He went as a legate to both Boniface VIII and Heinrich VII of Germany. When his native Padua fell under the lordship of Marsilio of Carrara, he went into exile to Chioggia, where he died in extreme poverty.

The masterpiece of historical writing from the point of view of insight and even humor is the *Chronica* (Chronicle) of the Franciscan Brother Salimbene of Parma (1221-1287). It deals with European as well as Italian events from the end of the twelfth century until the death of the author. He often quotes vernacular poems of the time and relates anecdotes that greatly enliven his writing. The significant part of the Chronicle is the visual power of Salimbene's style. He incisively etches men and landscapes observed during his travels in both Italy and France. Although written in faulty Latin, the book is one of the keenest and most vivid accounts of thirteen-century life.

Equally alive and interesting is the *Chronica* (Chronicle) by Rolandino of Padua that covers events from 1180 until 1260 and pivots around the awesome figure of Ezzelino of Romano.

Historical works in the vernacular, mostly Florentine, are of particular interest because they reflect the direct reactions of the authors to the tumultuous events in which they had been actors or of which they had been at least witnesses. It is most amazing to find in many of the works written in the epoch of Dante the basic traits of history as we conceive it in our time: an objective and keen record of events accompanied by the study of the causes that accounted for them.

The oldest and most revered example of this type of history was the *Cronaca fiorentina* (Florentine Chronicle), written by two members of the Malispini family, Ricordano and Giacotto. Ricordano, linking the birth of Florence to ancient Rome, studied Florentine history until 1282, the year of daring democratic reforms. Giacotto continued it until 1286. The first part of the book is legendary, but the section dealing with the division of the city into Whites and Blacks and the later vicissitudes of Florence offers a dramatic presentation of what happened in Florence under the very eyes of the aristocratic Malispini. Giovanni Villani, a few decades later, preserved this work for posterity by incorporating it in his own history of Florence, a sign of the high regard in which he held the Malispinis' record of Florentine history.

Infinitely superior was the work of Dino Compagni (*ca.* 1266-1324), a friend and contemporary of Dante, and, like Dante, deeply offended by the excesses and the maneuvers of the Black Party in their city. He, too, took an active part in the political life of Florence and, as a consul of the silk guild which he represented in the government, fostered democratic reforms. In 1289, Dino Compagni was elected to the office of the *priori* and, in 1293, became *gonfaloniere di giustizia*, the highest magistrate in Florence. In 1300, viewing with dismay the danger that menaced Florence because of the political strategy of Pope Boniface VIII, he followed the example of Dante and joined the White Party, opposing the Papal policies. He became a *priore* also of the White Party and had held that office only three months when the Whites were driven out of Florence. Compagni's moderation and proved honesty saved him from exile when he invoked the regulation that those who had been in office for less than a year could not be banished. During the years of the tenure of the Blacks in office, he lived quietly in Florence and dedicated himself to writing his famous book entitled *Cronica delle cose occorrenti ne' tempi suoi* (Chronicle of Things Taking Place in His Own Time). Dino Compagni is a most vivid writer. He is strictly factual in relating the clashes between the Whites and the Blacks, yet the dramatization of characters such as the demagogue Giano della Bella, the butcher Pecora, and the solitary and disdainful Guido Cavalcanti makes the reading as absorbing as that of a work of fiction. The historian's objective and fair temperament stood him in good stead in the events that he narrated with a faith in honesty and in God that never abandoned him. Unlike many of the historians of his time, he did not begin the history of Florence from the creation of the world. He offered the passionate recollection of the history of his own time only as seen by a noble and upright citizen. At his death in 1324, Compagni was buried in his family chapel in the old church of Santa Trinita.

Dino Compagni's work is a beautiful and outstanding exemplification of the same simplicity and nobility that one admires in the *Fioretti* and the *Novellino*. His style possesses the quality of purity that one finds in the art of Giotto and Arnolfo. All express the spirit of the democratic commune that animated one of the greatest periods of human history.

The Florentine Giovanni Villani (*ca.* 1276-1348), author of *La Nuova Cronica* (The New Chronicle), lived a few years later than Compagni. He was primarily a businessman and traveled on business in France and Flanders. Upon his return home, he took an interest in the politics of Florence from 1316 on. Villani was held in high esteem by his fellow citizens who bestowed important political offices upon him. He felt the effects of the economic crisis of the Bardi in 1346 and died in the famous plague of 1348.

Villani conceived the plan of writing the *Chronicle* of his times in 1300 upon his return from Rome where he went on the occasion of the Jubilee. His mind was filled with the memories of the greatness of classical Rome, and he viewed Florence as a child of ancient Rome. His *Chronicle* opens with the episode of the tower of Babel and continues to the year 1348, the year of his death. The first six books deal with the first two thousand years of human history and serve as an introduction to the history of a Florence that he really knew, that of his own time. This part, the best documented and most carefully studied, extends from 1260, the date of the battle of Montaperti, to his death. It deals with the division of the citizens of Florence into Whites and Blacks, a division that he, a Black, deprecates very sincerely, and the politics of Pope Boniface, which he condemned in spite of the fact that he was a member of the Black Party. Villani, unlike Compagni, shows interest in European affairs and in Eastern history, but he does not possess the dramatic quality of the latter. Although his style is rather flat, he offers a very accurate account of the conditions of Europe at the beginning of the fourteenth century. At his death, Giovanni's brother, Matteo, continued the chronicle until 1363. At Matteo's death in that year, the latter's son Filippo continued the work down to the year 1364.

The present sketch of the historical works of these years allows us to see their growth from primitive and legendary versions to dignified and rigorous historical accounts in which modern historiography can mirror itself and recognize its dawn.

DRAMATIC ACTIVITY

The history of drama in the early days of Italian literature was not very significant, for no outstanding personality used playwrighting as a means of self-expression. Nevertheless, the drama of this period has been very painstakingly studied by Italian as well as foreign critics who have seen in it the origin of modern drama and its forms. In our attitude of denying a connection between the early dramatic attempts and playwrighting of the present day, we simply say that the artistic instinct of the early age expressed itself in forms that differed radically in spirit, content, and aims from those of the drama of our time. Similarity of form, if any is found, was purely casual. Dialogue is a human attribute rather than a cultural influence exercised on the drama of our time.

CLASSICAL DRAMA

Before treating the main dramatic expressions of thirteenth-century drama, it is dutiful to mention the writings of Albertino Mussato whom we have just mentioned as a historian of distinction. He was a great admirer of Classicism and defended classical literature against the pious persons who wanted it abolished as contrary to Christianity. He evidenced his interest in classical drama by imitating the tragedies of Seneca. In this he was the forerunner of the learned and classical drama of the sixteenth century. Albertino Mussato belonged to a small group of scholars, active in both Padua and the neighboring Vicenza, who were interested in Latin literature. An inhabitant of Vicenza, Ferreto de' Ferreti (1294-1337), wrote Latin verse. In the city of Padua, a fellow citizen of Albertino Mussato, Lovato de' Lovati (1241-1309), produced a metrical commentary on Seneca's tragedies.

Albertino Mussato modeled a tragedy, to which he gave the Latin title *Ecerinis*, on the tragedies of the Roman playwright. It was finished in 1315 and its completion was celebrated in a public ceremony at the City Hall of Padua where the author was crowned poet laureate, the first recorded revival of the Roman custom. The theme developed in Mussato's tragedy was the awesome figure of Ezzelino of Romano, a tyrant (Ecerino) who terrorized Italy at the middle of the previous century. The Latin play can hardly be called drama in the modern sense of the word. It has no action nor development. It relies mainly on declamation, expressing noble feelings in favor of freedom and independence. In his work Mussato aimed also at serving the practical purpose of warning his city against the greed of conquest on the part of Can Grande della Scala. He exhorted his fellow citizens to be united that the freedom of Padua might be preserved. Although the play is outstanding for this noble aim, its artistic value is very small. It has historical value rather than aesthetic significance.

RELIGIOUS PLAY

According to the extant record, dramatic art in the thirteenth century assumed the twofold form of the religious play and the profane comedy.

The religious play represented a facet of a general European movement that is referred to as *auto-sacramental* in Spain, the *miracle* play in England, *le mystère* in France, and *Geistliches Schauspiel* in Germany. In Italy, the religious drama expressed itself in the simple *lauda* and the more complex *sacra rappresentazione*.

At a time in which the theaters did not exist, religious dramatic works, written largely by members of the church, were enacted in churches and monasteries as well as in public squares. The actors were members of the secular clergy or members of religious organizations called *confraternite*. The material was taken from the Gospel, legends of saints, and from the Bible.

The *lauda* was especially linked to the revival of religious fervor aroused by Raniero Fasani in the middle of the century at Perugia and later in the whole of Italy. His followers, the *Disciplinati*, *Flagellanti*, and *Battuti*, were responsible for enacting rudimentary religious sketches on such religious themes as the passion of Christ, the sorrow of the Virgin, the three Marias, St. John, and themes taken from the lives of the saints. There are about two hundred collections of *laude*, called *laudari*. Their great number testifies to the fact that religious organizations of the various cities were wont to exchange them. We can fully grasp the dramatic significance of the *lauda* if we picture large throngs of people imploring divine compassion as they crowded the public squares in front of the cathedrals or as they went on pilgrimages, singing the *laude* to express their joy or to break the monotony and weariness of the long journey.

The *laude* were mostly anonymous. Only two names have survived among those who composed them during this period: that of an obscure Garzo, who was linked with the town of Cortona, and that of Jacopone of Todi.

The *lauda* was usually written in the metrical form of the *ballata*. That it was sung as well as recited is proved by the fact that its lines are accompanied by music in the oldest manuscripts. Favorite tunes were often borrowed from popular music and adapted to this religious genre.

Although the outstanding quality of these compositions is that of being beautifully lyrical, they nevertheless represent a definite, though elementary, aspect of dramatic activity. That they are possessed of dramatic form, although strictly religious, is proved by the fact that the words of the main character are addressed to a chorus that responds much in the manner of the chorus at the dawn of Greek drama.

The *sacra rappresentazione,* containing a more complete action than did the *lauda,* had its heyday in the fifteenth century, although we have records of performances of works dealing with the passion of Christ at earlier dates.[6] Bartoli, quoting Zeno and Tiraboschi, states that in Padua there was a representation of the passion and resurrection of Christ in 1244. Treviso, Rome, Siena, as well as Cividale in northern Italy, enjoyed similar performances. Although the *sacra rappresentazione* was directly connected with the Church, its performance was, as with the *lauda,* entrusted to members of the religious societies or *confraternite,* a fact that explains how, with the passing of time, profane elements drifted into these religious plays.

From the titles of such works, variously called *devozione* (act of devotion), *lamento* (lament), *pianto* (plaintive song), we can deduce that they were especially performed during the Christmas season and Easter Week. In fact, two compositions bear the title of *Devozione del giovedì santo* and *Devozione del venerdì santo* (Act of Devotion for Holy Thursday and Act of Devotion for Good Friday).[7] Judging from the directions for the staging, it can be concluded that these performances were closely integrated with the religious services and were enacted before the altar.

PROFANE COMEDY

Historians have insisted on the uninterrupted presence of profane dramatic forms throughout the centuries of the Christian Era.[8] Mimes and pantomimes continued to delight and cheer the populace as in the days of the Romans, even though the age of the great creations of the Classical Era was over. Actors scoffed and jeered in the public squares at a time when the lords of the Renaissance had not opened their magnificent halls and democracy had not developed enough to permit the building of public theaters. However, no full-fledged work in the field of popular drama appeared in Italy in the thirteenth century. More than through significant works, its existence can be surmised and proved through the influence that it exercised on religious drama, changing its very nature by introducing into it scurrilous elements.

⟁ ⟁ ⟁ ⟁ ⟁

Conclusion

The Age of Dante marked one of the best-balanced periods of Italian history. It was characterized by a harmonious blending of religion and patriotism, healthy economic life and outstanding achievements in the field of the arts. Its sense of unity has rarely been repeated in Italian history. The gift of artistic instinct was lavished on such artists as Cimabue, Cavallini, Nicola Pisano, Giotto, Arnolfo, Compagni, Cavalcanti, Marco Polo, and the greatest of them all, Dante Alighieri. These artists determined new directions in the history of art and culture, unifying the temporal and the eternal in a manner not different from that in which Dante fused the two planes in the *Divina Commedia*. The terms "Primitive" and "Pre-Raphaelite" that in the English tradition have been bestowed on the painters of Giotto's generation apply as well to the poets and to the prose writers whom we have analyzed in our study.

The achievements of those glorious centuries, and especially of the last decades of the thirteenth century, were marked by a sincerity and simplicity that bound together the various arts and the social life of the time. Politically, the generation of Dante fought for the preservation of the spirit of the democratic Commune, then threatened by the ambition of the many local despots who were trying to establish the Signoria in many parts of Italy. Dante's contemporaries and the poet himself aimed at preserving the old democratic institutions even if they often turned their hope toward the Empire, seeing in it the only force that could save the independence of their free cities.

The history of this epoch offers numerous instances that are suggestive of a glorious sunset in whose rich hues one detects the anticipation of twilight and darkness. The most significant of these historical episodes was the attempt of Boniface VIII to establish theocratic rule over all of Europe. The Jubilee of 1300 was a tremendous success for Boniface, whose prestige seemed to rival that of his predecessor, Gregory VII, the great Hildebrand. Boniface's bull *Unam sanctam* issued in November of 1302 resounded like a clarion over all Christianity, but in spite of its impressive statements concerning the temporal and spiritual powers that Boniface claimed, it failed to gain him much. The temporal dream of Papacy vanished in the midst of the gloomy foreboding of sincerely religious thinkers like Dante. In 1305, a Frenchman, Bertrand of Goth, was elected to the throne of St. Peter under the name of Clement V, and he moved the seat of the Papacy to Avignon in southern France. The lines of Dante's *Divina Commedia* referring to the political plight of Florence and Italy were a dirge that accompanied the setting of the civilization of the Communes whose greatest citizen ended his life in exile.

With Dante's death in 1321, an age ended and a new one,
represented by two younger poets and learned men,
Petrarch and Boccaccio, arose.

⌂　⌂　⌂　⌂　⌂

Notes to Chapters

Introduction to the Literature of the Renaissance

1. R. A. Hall, *A Short History of Italian Literature* (Ithaca, 1951), Part I, 7-22.

2. *Medieval Cities* (Princeton, 1925), pp. 78-108, 109-134.

3. *Le satire* (Florence, 1911), pp. 181-190.

4. H. Baron, *The Crisis of the Early Renaissance* (Princeton, 1955), I, 285. Baron refers to the negative Humanists of the late Trecento by the term *literati*, the same term applied by Dante in the *Convivio* to the pseudo-Humanists of a century before.

CHAPTER ONE: *Italian Culture in the Eleventh and Twelfth Centuries*

1. E. Monaci, *Crestomazia* (Rome, 1888), A Florentine bankers' book dating back to 1211 is transcribed on pp. 19-28.

2. *Ibid.*, p. 1.

3. *Ibid.*, p. 5.

4. *Ibid.*, p. 8.

5. There is a translation executed in 1931 on the Latin text published by L. A. Muratori in 1721 (Cuneo, 1931).

CHAPTER TWO: *The Transmission of Culture in the Twelfth Century*

1. So Vico states in his book *De Sui Temporis Studiorum Ratione*, written in 1709. He writes contemptuously of such a fact.

2. G. Sarton, *Introduction to the History of Science* (Baltimore, 1931), II, part I, 338.

3. A. Bartoli, *I primi due secoli della letteratura italiana* (Milan, 1878), pp. 92-110. For translations into the vernacular, *see Volgarezzamenti del Due e Trecento*, edited by Cesare Segre, Turin, 1953.

CHAPTER THREE: *Contributions to Culture During the Thirteenth Century*

1. G. Pepe, *Lo stato Ghibellino di Federico II* (Bari, 1938), App., pp. 124-161.

2. *Opuscoli e testi filosofici*, edited by B. Nardi (Bari, 1920).

3. The complete works of Thomas Aquinas were published in Rome in 1882-1926 by order of Pope Leo XIII. The first edition of *De Regimine Principum* bears no date. Later editions:

Paris, 1509; Cologne, 1643. A good selection of the *Political Writings* of Aquinas is that edited by A. P. D'Entrèves, with translation by J. G. Dawson, Oxford, 1948.

4. Published again in 1858 by Francesco Corazzini in Florence, under the title of *Del regimento de' prìncipi*.

5. G. Sarton, *op. cit.*, II, Part II, 914-921.

6. P. Duhem, *Le système du monde* (Paris), III, 407-410. There is a good Italian translation by Auguste Hermet (Lanciano, 1928).

7. E. Monaci, *op. cit.*, pp. 32-35. It was published in 1863 at Munich by F. Rockinger.

8. The *Gemma Purpurea* was published in Rome by E. Monaci in 1901. The *Summa* appeared in the *Propugnatore*, edited by A. Gaudenzi, III, Bologna, 1870.

9. Published in 1821 at Venice by B. Gamba under the title of *Il fiore di Rettorica di Fra Guidotto da Bologna*.

10. *Il fiore* can be found in *Tutte le opere di Dante Alighieri* in the Barbera edition, E. Moore (Florence, 1921), pp. 185-223.

11. E. Monaci, *op. cit.*, pp. 387-393.

12. E. Gardner, *The Arthurian Legends in Italian Literature* (London, 1930), pp. 44-63.

13. *Ibid.*, pp. 152-190. Published in two volumes at Bologna in 1864-5 by F. L. Polidori.

14. Edited by Lucy Allen Paton in New York, 1926-27, from manuscript 593 of the Library of Rennes.

15. These Arthurian compilators in the Italian vernacular have been recently re-edited by F. Arese in *Prose di romanzi* (Utet, Turin, 1950).

16. The translation into the vernacular, based on the Latin text published by T. Graesse in 1846, was republished in three volumes by A. Levasti in 1924 in Milan.

17. Vincent de Beauvais used it by giving a summary of it in his *Speculum Historiale*. The first edition appeared in Paris in 1838 by d'Avezac. The first Italian translation appeared in Milan in 1929 under the title of *Viaggio ai tartari di frate Giovanni di Pian Carpine*.

18. G. Sarton, *op. cit.*, II, Part II, 611-613.

CHAPTER FOUR: *Poetry During the Thirteenth Century*

1. *De Vulgari Eloquentia*, Part II, i, 1.
2. *Ibid.*, Part II, iv, 6.

3. *Vita Nuova*, Ch. XXV.
4. *De Vulgari Eloquentia*, Part I, xii, 2.

CHAPTER FIVE: *Popular Poetry*

1. E. Monaci, *op. cit.*, 1912, p. 289. A. D'Ancona, *La poesia popolare in Italia* (Livorno, 1892; second edition, 1906), p. 10.

2. G. Carducci, *Intorno ad alcune rime dei secoli XIII e XIV ritrovate nei Memoriali dell' Archivio notarile di Bologna* (Imola, 1876).

3. *Id.*, *Cantilene e ballate, strambotti e madrigali nei secoli XIII e XIV* (Pisa, 1871), p. 56.

4. *Ibid.*, p. 59.

5. Camiola of Messina was a woman famous for her beauty and nobility and as such she was sung by the poets of the time.

6. *Ibid.*, pp. 59-69.

7. E. Monaci, *op. cit.*, p. 95.

8. *Ibid.*, p. 97.

9. *Ibid.*, p. 75.

10. *Ibid.*, p. 82.

11. A. D'Ancona., *op. cit.* (Livorno, 1900), p. 19.

12. E. Monaci, *op. cit.*, p. 288.

13. *Ibid.*, p. 273.

14. *Ibid.*, p. 280.

15. *Ibid.*, p. 281.

16. *Sonetti burleschi e realistici dei primi due secoli*, edited by A. F. Massera (Bari, 1920), Vols. I and II. For critical information: Vol. II, 121-149.

17. *Ibid.* I, 157-173. Also in F. Neri, *Folgore da San Gimignano, Sonetti*, pp. 25-38; 55-62.

18. *Sonetti burleschi e realistici dei primi*

due secoli, I, 175-181. F. Neri, *op. cit.*, pp. 39-51.

19. *Sonetti burleschi e realistici dei primi due secoli*, I, 1-30.

20. *Ibid.*, p. 136. Also in F. Neri, *op. cit.*, pp. 97-98. N. Sapegno, *Il Trecento* (Milan, 1939), pp. 401-404.

21. E. Monaci, *op. cit.*, pp. 512-518. *Sonetti burleschi e realistici*. l, 63-138; II, 82-92.

22. S. Santangelo, *Le tenzoni poetiche nella letteratura poetica delle origini* (Geneva, 1928).

23. A. D'Ancona, *op. cit.*, p. 10.

24. Uguccione wrote *Il libro* (The Book), a series of meditations on the fleeting character of human pleasures; Pierto da Bersagapè treated the same subject in his *Sermoni* (Sermons); Patecchio reflected on what caused petty annoyances in life in his *Noie* (Annoyances) and left a *Splanamento* (Explanation), a book of moral advice taken from the proverbs of Solomon and other sections of the Old Testament; Giacomino of Verona penned his idea of the suffering in Hell and the joys of Paradise; Bonvesìn of Riva, although more cultured than those mentioned above, wrote in the same cold, moralizing tone about the life of the Beyond. He also wrote a book on good table manners.

25. E. Monaci, *op. cit.*, p. 29.

26. F. Ageno, *Jacopone da Todi* (Florence, 1953).

CHAPTER SIX: *Courtly Poetry*

1. F. De Sanctis, *Storia della letteratura italiana* (Milan, 1924), I, 9-13.

2. E. Monaci, *op. cit.*, pp. 202-203.

3. *Ibid.*, p. 202.

4. *Ibid.*, p. 42.

5. *Ibid.*, pp. 88-89.

6. *Ibid.*, p. 83.

7. *Ibid.*, p. 84.

8. The *canzone* of Mazzeo di Ricco of Messina *Lo grande valore e lo spregio amoroso* (The great worth and high quality of your love), found in Monaci's *Crestomazia* (p. 216), bears witness to the fact that courtly lyrics in Sicily continued even after the court at Palermo lost its prestige. The poems of Guittone d'Arezzo, of Bonagiunta Urbiciani of Lucca as well as those of Guinizelli of Bologna show us that in every city courtly love was cultivated in poetic circles.

9. The poetry of this period is found in *Rimatori Siculi-Toscani del Dugento*, edited by G. Zaccagnini and A. Parducci (Bari, 1915).

10. E. Monaci, *op. cit.*, pp. 180-182.

11. These and other poets are translated into English by Dante Gabriel Rossetti and can be read in *No.* 627 of Everyman's Library.

12. E. Monaci, *op. cit.*, p. 253.

13. *Ibid.*, p. 252.

14. Dante's sonnet is in the *Vita Nuova*, Ch. III. The answers of the three poets can be read in the edition of the *Rime di Dante*, edited by Michele Barbi (Florence, 1921); also in the Barbera edition (Florence, 1921), pp. 174, 175, 179, where the sonnets by Cavalcanti, Cino and Dante of Maiano are published.

15. Dante glorified Guinizelli in the twenty-sixth canto of the *Purgatorio*, 91-148. He wrote words full of admiration of him also in *De Vulgari Eloquentia*, I, ix, 15; II, v, 6; and in *Convivio*, IV, 20. In the *Divina Commedia* he calls him "father," when he sees him in the flames of Purgatory.

16. *Rimatori del Dolce Stil Nuovo*, edited by Luigi di Benedetto (Bari, 1939), pp. 7-9.

17. *Ibid.*, p. 16.

18. *Ibid.*, pp. 20-21.

19. Dante was the author of *Donne ch'avete intelletto d'amore* which he placed in the center of the *Vita Nuova* (Ch. XIX); Cavalcanti wrote *Donna mi prega per ch'io voglio dire* (*Rimatori*, pp. 25-27). In these poems as well as in *Al cor gentil ripara sempre amore* by Guinizelli, the authors attempted to give a philosophical justification of love.

20. Those written by Dante to his friends include verses addressed to Forese, those to Cino of Pistoia, and those to Dante of Maiano (in *Tutte le opere*, Barbera edition, pp. 173-182).

21. *Tutte le opere*, Barbera edition, Sonetto XV, p. 153.

22. *Rimatori del Dolce Stil Nuovo*, pp. 193-195.

23. *Ibid.*, pp. 24-60.

24. *Ibid.*, pp. 25-27.

25. *Ibid.*, pp. 29-30.

26. *Ibid.*, pp. 46-47.

27. *Ibid.*, pp. 50-51.

28. *Ibid.*, pp. 61-82.

29. *Ibid.*, pp. 84-85.

30. *Ibid.*, p. 87.

31. *Ibid.*, p. 88.

32. *Ibid.*, pp. 111-235.

33. *Ibid.*, pp. 89-109.

34. *Ibid.*, p. 107.

35. Published by B. Wiese in Numbers 94 and 95 of the Biblioteca Romanica (Strasbourg, 1909). There is an Italian popular edition edited by R. Piccoli (Lanciano, 1910).

36. Published for the first time by Alzanaus in 1850, it is now to be found in a popular edition in the series *Scrittori Nostri*, edited by R. Piccoli (Lanciano, 1910).

CHAPTER SEVEN: *Dante Alighieri: His Minor Works*

1. *Vita Nuova*, edited by K. McKenzie (Boston, 1922), p. 2.

2. *Fabula* was the literature of lowly style or popular literature in contrast with the courtly.

3. In the Provençal tradition, the identity of the lady who was loved by the poet was hidden behind that of another woman to whom the lover dedicated himself in the court. This woman was referred to as the "woman of the foil."

4. D. Vittorini, "Luci ed ombre nella *Vita Nuova*," *Letterature moderne*, IV (1953), 518-523.

5. *Purgatorio*, XXIV, 34-63.

6. *Ibid.*, XXIV, 49-54.

7. *Tutte le opere*, Barbera edition, pp. 173-174.

8. *Purgatorio*, XXIII, 116-118.

9. *Tutte le opere*, p. 180.

10. *Ibid.*, pp. 161-163.

11. *Ibid.*, Canzone LXVI: *Amor, tu vedi ben che questa donna* (Love, you can clearly see that this woman).

12. *Purgatorio*, XXXII, 1-90.

13. *Tutte le opere*, pp. 165-172.

14. *Ibid.*, p. 165.

15. *Ibid.*, p. 152.

16. *Ibid.*, p. 152.

17. *Ibid.*, pp. 227-232.

18. *Ibid.*, pp. 423-442. Seventeen epistles are listed.

19. *Ibid.*, pp. 445-453.

CHAPTER EIGHT: *Dante as a Thinker*

1. *Purgatorio*, II, 76-133.

2. It was put on press for the first time in Paris in 1577 by Jacopo Corbinelli. Gian Giorgio Trissino translated it into Italian and published it in Venice in 1529. The critical edition was published by Pio Rajna in Florence in 1896. The best modern edition is that of A. Marigo in Vol. IV of the Florentine edition of 1921.

3. The oldest code bears the date 1334 and it is in the Berlin Library. It was printed at Basel in 1559. Marsilio Ficino (1433-1499) was the first to translate it into Italian. The best modern edition is found in the complete works of Dante, published in Florence in 1921.

CHAPTER NINE: *The Divine Comedy*

1. "Here Begins the Comedy of Dante Alighieri, a Florentine by Citizenship, Not By Morals."

2. A. Graf, *Miti, leggende e superstizioni del medio evo* (Torino, 1892; second edition, 1925).

3. There are no grounds in the *Commedia* for transforming this compassionate maiden into St. Lucia. Dante places her (*Inferno*, II) in the "court of Heaven" and courtly is the language of all persons concerned in that canto. *See* D. Vittorini, "La corte del cielo," *Italica*, XX (1943), 57-64.

4. *Convivio*, II, I, 5; *Epistle to Can Grande*, 7.

5. D. Vittorini, "Dante e il concetto d'amore," *Symposium*, V (1951), 22-37.

6. *Inferno*, II, 37-48; *Purgatorio*, V, 16-18.

7. D. Vittorini, *op. cit.*, pp. 22-27.

8. D. Vittorini, "Francesca da Rimini in the Dolce Stil Nuovo," *Romanic Review* (Apr.-June, 1930), pp. 116-127; "Dante e Francesca da Rimini," *Italica* (Sept., 1933), pp. 67-76.

9. Pope Celestine, a very saintly man and a lover of solitude, renounced Papacy in 1294 to return to his hermitage. As a consequence, Boniface VIII became Pope, the man whom Dante blamed for his exile.

10. D. Vittorini, "Dante e il concetto d'amore," *Symposium*, V (1951), 22-37.

11. *Convivio*, III, 5; *Paradiso*, IV, 49.

CHAPTER TEN: *Prose Writing in the Thirteenth Century*

1. E. Monaci, *op. cit.*, pp. 432-438.

2. *Le cento novelle* (Milan, Tosi, 1825), p. 5.

3. The Latin text was attributed to Brother Ugolino of Montegiorgio and bore the title of *Actus Beati Francisci et Sociorum Ejus* (Deeds of St. Francis and His Companions).

4. These books were made known by Ludovico Antonio Muratori in his work *Rerum Italicarum Scriptores* (1723-1751).

5. The work was translated into Italian by E. Verga in 1921.

6. A. Bartoli, *op. cit.*, p. 177.

7. *Ibid.*, pp. 173-183.

8. In Italy, Lorenzo Stoppato has carefully documented the presence of popular drama in *La commedia popolare italiana*, Padua, 1887. He claims that the *Commedia dell'arte* in the sixteenth century was the development of popular drama that had existed uninterruptedly in Italy.

⟁ ⟁ ⟁ ⟁ ⟁

Selected Bibliography

This selected bibliography attempts to present the best works on Dante and on Italian cultural and literary history of the period outlined in this study, with emphasis on the most important historical and critical problems. Place and date of publication are given only in the first citation of a work. Pages are given when referring to a specific problem.

Introduction to the Period

General Aids

ANTONI, C., AND MATTIOLI, R. (eds.). *Cinquant'anni di vita intellettuale italiana* (1896-1946). Naples, 1950.

BARTOLI, A. *I primi due secoli della letteratura italiana.* Milan, 1878.

———. *Storia della letteratura italiana.* Florence, 1878-1889.

CARETTI, L. *Avviamento allo studio della letteratura italiana.* Florence, 1953.

CASATI, G. *Dizionario degli scrittori d'Italia.* Milan, 1926-1929.

CESAREO, G. A. *Storia della letteratura italiana.* Catania, 1933.

CRESCIMBENI, G. M. *Storia della volgar poesia.* Venice, 1730-1731.

D'ANCONA, A., AND BACCI, O. *Manuale della letteratura italiana.* Florence, 1892. 2nd ed., Florence, 1925. Vol. I, 1-405.

DEL SECOLO, F., AND CASTELLANO, G. *Da Dante a Cuoco.* Bari, 1927. Vol. I.

DE SANCTIS, F. *Storia della letteratura italiana.* Naples, 1870-1871. New ed., Bari, 1930

DIONISOTTI, C. *Indici sistematici dei primi cento volumi del Giornale storico della letteratura italiana.* Turin, 1948.

Dizionario delle opere e dei personaggi Bompiani. Milan, 1949-1950.

Enciclopedia Italiana Treccani. Milan, 1929-1939.

EVOLA, N. D. *Bibliografia degli studi sulla letteratura italiana* (1920-1934). Milan, 1938.

FEDELE, P. *Grande dizionario enciclopedico.* Turin, 1933-1939.

FINZI, G., AND VALMAGGI, L. *Tavole storico-bibliografiche della letteratura italiana.* Turin, 1889.

FLORA, F. *Storia delle letteratura italiana.* Milan, 1940-1941. Latest ed., 1953.

FORNACIARI, R. *Disegno storico della letteratura italiana.* Florence, 1914.

FUBINI, M., AND BONORA, E. *Antologia della critica letteraria.* Turin, 1952. Vol. I.

FUCILLA, J. G. *A Bibliographical Guide to the Romance Languages and Literatures.* Evanston, 1939. Part III, 44-56.

GASPARY, A. *Storia della letteratura italiana.* Translated by U. ZINGARELLI and V. ROSSI. Turin, Vol. I, 1914; Vol. II, 1900-1901. First published in German under the title of *Geschichte der italienischen Literatur,* Berlin, 1884-1888.

GETTO, G. Storia delle storie letterarie. Milan, 1942.

GIUDICI, P. E. Compendio della Storia della letteratura italiana. Milan, 1864.

HALL, R. H. A Short History of Italian Literature. Ithaca, 1951.

MAZZAMUTO, P. Rassegna bibliografica critica della letteratura italiana. Florence, 1953. 2nd ed., 1954.

MAZZONI, G. Avviamento allo studio critico delle lettere italiane. Florence, 1923.

MOMIGLIANO, A. Storia della letteratura italiana. Messina, 1937. Pp. 3-5.

NOVATI, F., AND MONTEVERDI, A. Le origini in Storia letteraria d'Italia. Milan, 1906-1926. New ed. by A. VISCARDI, 1939.

PAPINI, G. Storia della letteratura italiana. Florence, 1937.

PEPE, G. "Gli studi di storia medievale" in Cinquant'anni. Vol. I, 109-124.

PREZZOLINI, G. Repertorio bibliografico (1902-1932). Rome, 1936. Supplemento (1932-1942). New York, 1946-1948.

Problemi e orientamenti critici di lingua e di letteratura italiana. Under the direction of A. MOMIGLIANO. Milan, 1948. Vol. II.

PUPPO, M. Manuale bibliografico-critico per lo studio della letteratura italiana. Genoa, 1954. Pp. 9-26.

———. Orientamenti critici generali di lingua e di letteratura generali. Genoa, 1952.

ROSSI, V. Storia della letteratura italiana. Latest ed. revised by U. Bosco, Milan, 1943. Vol. I.

RUSSO, L. Disegno storico della letteratura italiana: Dalle origini all'Umanesimo. Florence, 1946. Vol. I.

———. Problemi di metodo critico. Bari, 1929. 2nd ed., Bari, 1950.

———. Ritratti e disegni storici. Bari, 1951. Series III.

SAPEGNO, N. Il Trecento. Milan, 1934.

SARTON, G. Introduction to a History of Science. Baltimore, 1931. Vol. II, Parts I and II.

SCHERILLO, M. Le origini e lo svolgimento della letteratura italiana. Milan, 1919-1936. Vol. I.

Studi e testi. Edited by the Vatican Library. Rome, 1900-1955.

THORNDIKE, L. History of Medieval Europe. Boston, 1917.

TIRABOSCHI, G. Storia della letteratura italiana. Venice, 1823. Vols. V-X.

TRABALZA, C., ALLODOLI, E. AND TROMPEI, P. Esempi di analisi letteraria. Turin, 1926.

TURRI, V., AND RENDA, U. Dizionario storico critico della letteratura italiana. Turin, 1952.

VISCARDI, A. Le origini. Milan, 1939.

VOLPE, G. Il medioevo. Florence, 1932.

———. Il medioevo italiano. Florence, 1923.

WALSH, J. J. A Golden Treasury of Medieval Literature. Boston, 1930.

WILKENS, E. H. A History of Italian Literature. Cambridge, Mass., 1954.

ZONTA, G. Storia della letteratura italiana. Turin, 1928-1932.

The Christian Age

ADAMS, G. B. Medieval Civilization. New York, 1883. Pp. 92-142.

A Monument to St. Augustine. London, 1934.

BALZANI, U. Le cronache italiane del Medio Evo. Milan, 1884. Latest ed., Milan, 1909.

BERTONI, G. Poesie, leggende e costumanze del Medio Evo. Modena, 1917.

CESSI, R. Fonti per la storia medievale. Bologna, 1955.

———. Le vicende politiche dell'Italia medievale. Padua, 1956.

COPLESTON, F. C. Medieval Philosophy. Westminster, Md., 1952. Vol. II.

CURTIS, S. V. A Short History of Western Philosophy in the Middle Ages. Westminster, Md., 1950.

CURTIUS, E. European Literature and the Latin Middle Ages. Bern, 1948.

DE LABRIOLLE, F. Histoire de la littérature latine chrétienne. Paris, 1924. Translated into English by H. WILSON, London, 1924.

DEL LUNGO, I. La figurazione storica del Medio Evo italiano. Florence, 1891.

DE WULF, M. Histoire de la Philosophie Médiévale. Louvain, 1924-1925. Vols. I, II. Translated into English by E. C. MESSINGER, London, 1926; into Italian by V. MIANO, Florence, 1944.

EBERT, A. *Histoire Générale de la Littérature du Moyen Age en Occident.* Paris, 1833. Translated by J. AYMERIC and J. CONDAMIN, Paris, 1883-1889.

EGIDI, P. "Fonti, edizioni, studi" in *Storia Medioevale* in *Guide Bibliografiche Fondazione Leonardo.* Rome, 1922. Pp. 36-42.

———. *La Storia medioevale* in *Guide Bibliografiche Fondazione Leonardo.* Rome, 1922.

FIORENTINO, F. *Compendio di storia della filosofia.* 3rd ed., Florence, 1924. P. 230; 255-310.

GARIN, E. "La dignitas hominis e la letteratura patristica" in *Rinascita* (1938), pp. 102 and ff.

GETTO, G. *Op. cit.*

GIESEBRECHT, G. VON. *De Literarum Studiis Apud Italos Primi Medii Aevi Seculis.* Berlin, 1845.

GILSON, E. *La philosophie au Moyen Age.* Paris, 1944.

GRAF, A. *Miti, leggende e superstizioni del Medio Evo.* Turin, 1883.

HALL, R. H. *Op. cit.*, Part I, 7-45.

HARNACK, A. *Outline of the History of Dogma.* Translated by N. BUCHANAN. New York, 1905.

———. *The Mission and Expansion of Christianity.* Translated by J. MOFFATT. London, 1908.

MANITIUS, M. *Geschichte der Lateinischen Literatur des Mittelalters.* Munich, 1911.

———. *Monumenta Germaniae Historica.* Hanover, 1826.

MURATORI, L. A. *Rerum italicarum scriptores.* Milan, 1723-1751.

OZANAM, A. F. *La civilization au cinquième siècle.* Paris, 1885.

PAGANO, A. *Manuale di storia della letteratura latina nel Medio Evo.* Milan, 1943.

PIRENNE, H. *Maometto e Carlomagno.* Translated by M. VINCIGUERRA. Bari, 1939.

POTTHAST, A. *Bibliotheca Historica Medii Aevi.* Berlin, 1896.

SANDYS, J. E. *History of Classical Scholarship.* Cambridge, 1903-1908.

SAVIGNY, F. K. VON. *Geschichte des Romanischen Rechts in Mittelalter.* Heidelberg, 1815-1831.

TAYLOR, H. O. *The Medieval Mind.* London, 1911.

USSANI, V. "Lingua e lettere latine" in *Guide Bibliografiche Fondazione Leonardo.* Rome, 1921.

VIEUSSEUX, G. P. *Archivio storico italiano.* Florence, 1842.

WRIGHT, F. A. AND SINCLAIR, T. A. *A History of Later Latin Literature.* London, 1931. Pp. 201-269; 273-331.

Texts of the Christian Age

ANON. *The Imitation of Christ.* Italian translation by A. CESARE. Verona, 1785. New ed., Milan, 1945.

AUGUSTINE, ST. *The City of God* in *Writings of St. Augustine.* New York, 1947-1955. Vols. VI, VII, VIII. Translated into Italian, Milan, 1929.

———. *The Confessions* in *Writings of St. Augustine.* New York, 1947-1955. Vol. V. Translated into Italian, Florence, 1929.

BOETHIUS, A. M. S. *Of the Consolation of Philosophy.* Leipzig, 1871. Translated into English, London, 1902. Reprint, 1940.

Carmina Burana (Collection of the Poetry of the Wandering Students). Breslau, 1883.

COLOMBO, S. *La poesia cristiana antica.* Rome, 1910.

CORRADINO, C. *I canti dei Goliardi.* Turin, 1892.

DU MÉRIL, E. P. *Poésies inédites au Moyen Age.* Paris, 1845.

———. *Poésies populaires antérieures au XII* siècle.* Paris, 1843.

———. *Poésies populaires latines du Moyen Age.* Paris, 1847.

HILKA, A. AND SCHUMANN, O. *Carmina Burana.* Heidelburg, 1930-1941.

MONE, F. G. *Hymni Latini Medii Aevi.* Freiburg, 1852-1855.

PICCIONI, L. *Da Prudenzio a Dante.* Turin, 1916.

SYMONDS, J. A. *Wine, Women and Song. Medieval Songs.* New ed., London, 1925.

VECCHI, G. *Poesia latina medievale.* Modena, 1952.

VERTOVA, L. *Canti goliardici medievali.* Florence, 1929-1952.

New Approach to Linguistics

BERTOLDI, V. *La glottologia come storia della cultura*. Naples, 1947.

BERTONI, G. *Il Duecento*. Milan, 1910. 2nd ed., 1930.

———. *Lingua e pensiero*. Florence, 1932.

———. *Lingua e poesia*. Florence, 1937.

HATZFELD, H. A. "A Critical Bibliography of the New Stylistics Applied to Romance Literatures (1900-1952)" in *Studies in Comparative Literature of the University of North Carolina*, No. 5, Chapel Hill, 1953.

NENCIONI, G. *Idealismo e realismo nella scienza del linguaggio*. Florence, 1946.

———. "Orientamenti nel pensiero linguistico italiano" in *Belfagor* (May, 1952).

PUPPO, M. *Manuale*. Pp. 9-12.

SCHIAFFINI, A. "Gli studi di Filologia Romanza" in *Cinquant'anni*. Vol. II, 407-422.

New Approach to Criticism

ALLEN, G. W. AND CLARK, H. H. *Literary Criticism. From Pope to Croce*. New York, 1941.

ATTISANI, A. "Gli Studi di estetica" in *Cinquant'anni*. Vol. I, 289-331.

BARBI, M. *La nuova filologia e l'edizione dei nostri scrittori*. Florence, 1938.

BERTONI, G. *Il Duecento*.

CALOGERO, G. *Estetica, Semantica, Istorica*. Turin, 1947.

CROCE, B. *Estetica come scienza dell'espressione e linguistica generale*. Bari, 1902. 9th ed., 1950.

———. *La poesia*. 4th ed., Bari, 1946.

———. *Problemi di estetica e contributi alla storia dell'estetica italiana*. 4th ed., Bari, 1949.

FLORA, F. *Orfismo della parola*. Bologna, 1953.

FUBINI, M. "Critica e poesia" in *Belfagor* (Sept., 1950).

———. *Stile, linguaggio, poesia*. Milan, 1948.

GENTILE, G. *La filosofia dell'arte*. Milan, 1931.

MARZOT, G. "La critica e gli studi di letteratura italiana" in *Cinquant'anni*. Vol. I, 451-522.

MONTANARI, F. *Introduzione alla critica letteraria*. 2nd ed., Modena, 1942.

MONTANO, R. *Arte, realtà, storia*. Naples, 1951.

ROTA, E. (ed.). *Questioni di storia moderna*. Milan, 1951.

RUSSO, L. *La critica letteraria contemporanea*. 3rd ed., Bari, 1953-1954.

———. *Problemi di metodo critico*. Bari, 1929. 2nd ed., 1950.

SGROI, C. *Gli studi estetici in Italia nel primo trentennio del Novecento*. Florence, 1932.

Mysticism in the Christian Age

BIGG, C. *Christian Platonists of Alexandria*. Oxford, 1886.

DE WULF, M. *Histoire de la philosophie scolastique dans les Pays Bas et la principauté de Liège*. Louvain, 1895.

GRANDGEORGE, L. *Saint Augustin et les néoplatonisme*. Paris, 1896.

NARDI, B. "Studi di storia della filosofia medievale" in *Cinquant'anni*. Vol. I, 15-42.

UNDERHILL, E. *The Mystic Way*. New York, 1913.

Concept of the Renaissance

ANAGNINE, E. "Il concetto del Rinascimento attraverso la storia" in *Nuova Rivista Storica*, XVIII (1940).

———. "Il problema del Rinascimento" in *Nuova Rivista Storica*, XVIII (1934).

ANGELERI, C. *Il problema religioso del Rinascimento*. Florence, 1952.

BARTOLI, A. *I precursori del Rinascimento*. Milan, 1877.

BERTONI, G. "Le origini della civiltà italiana" in *Il Duecento*. 2nd ed., Milan, 1930. Pp. 1-12.

BURDACH, K. *Reformation, Renaissance, Humanismus*. Berlin, 1918. Translated into Italian by D. CANTAMORI, Florence, 1935.

CANTAMORI, D. "Sulla storia del concetto di Rinascimento" in *Annali della Regia Scuola Normale Superiore di Pisa*, Series II, 1, 1932.

CHABOD, F. "Gli studi di storia del Rinascimento" in *Cinquant'anni*. Vol. I, 127-207.

———. "Il Rinascimento" in *Questioni di storia moderna*. Milan, 1951. Article, pp. 53-91; bibliography, pp. 92-99.

CHAMARD, H. *Les origines de la poésie fran-çaise de la Renaissance.* Paris, 1932.

FALCO, G. *La polemica sul Medioevo.* Turin, 1933.

FERGUSON, W. K. *The Renaissance in Historical Thought.* Boston, 1948.

FIORENTINO, F. *Compendio di storia della filosofia.* 3rd ed., Florence, 1924. Pp. 255-310.

FUNCK-BRENTANO, F. *La Renaissance.* Paris, 1935.

GARIN, E. *Medioevo e Rinascimento.* Bari, 1947.

GENTILE, G. *Giordano Bruno e il pensiero del Rinascimento.* Florence, 1920.

GILSON, E. *Heloïse et Abelarde.* Translated into Italian, Turin, 1950.

———. "Humanisme mediéval et Renaissance" in *Les idées et les lettres.* Paris, 1932.

———. "Il Medioevo e il naturalismo antico" and "Filosofia medievale e umanesimo" in *Appendix of Eloisa e Abelardo.* Turin, 1950.

———. "Medieval Universalism and Its Present Value" in *Harvard Tercenary Conference of Arts and Sciences.* Cambridge, Mass., 1936.

HUNZINGA, J. *Autunno del Medio Evo.* Translation of 3rd Dutch ed. of 1928, Florence, 1944.

MONTEVERDI, A. "Medievo" in *Cultura* (July, 1927).

NERI, F. "La Rinascita medievale" in *Storia e Poesia.* Turin, 1936.

NORDSTRÖM, J. *Moyen Age et Renaissance.* Paris, 1933. P. 47.

PUPPO, M. *Manuale: Medioevo, Umanesimo, Rinascimento.* Genoa, 1954. Pp. 125-135.

———. "Prospettive sull'umanesimo e il Rinascimento" in *Studium* (Feb., 1954).

Rinascimento (Basic journal for Renaissance Studies in Italy). Formerly *La Rinascita.* 1938-1944.

ROSSI, V. *Il Quattrocento.* Milan, 1933. Ch. I.

———. "Il Rinascimento" in *Nuova Antologia,* (Nov., 1929).

SABBADINI, R. *Le scoperte dei codici latini e greci nei secoli XIV e XV.* Florence, 1905. 2nd ed., 1914, Vols. I, II.

SICILIANO, I. *Medioevo e Rinascimento.* Milan, 1936.

SIMONE, F. "Cultura medievale francese e umanesimo italiano" in *Rassegna della letteratura italiana* (Apr.-June, 1954).

SORRENTO, L. "Medioevo: il termine e il concetto" in *Annuario dell'Università cattolica di Milano,* Milan, 1930-1931.

SPAVENTA, B. *Rinascimento, Riforma, Contro-riforma ed altri saggi critici.* 2nd ed., Venice, 1928. First published under the title of *Saggi di critica filosofica, politica e religiosa* in 1867.

THODE, H. *Franz von Assisi und die Anfänge der Renaissance in Italien.* Berlin, 1885. 2nd ed., 1904.

CONTINUITY OF CULTURAL LIFE THROUGHOUT THE CHRISTIAN AGE

CHABOD, F. *Op. cit.*

GILSON, E. "Humanisme médieval et renaissance" in *Les idées et les lettres.* Paris, 1932. Pp. 171-196.

———. "La scholastique et l'esprit classique" in *Les idées et les lettres.* Pp. 243-316.

MONTEVERDI, A. "Medioevo" in *Cultura* (July, 1927).

OLSCHKI, L. *Struttura spirituale e linguistica del mondo neo-latino.* Bari, 1935.

RONCA, U. *Cultura medievale e poesia latina d'Italia nei secoli XI e XII.* Rome, 1891.

RUSSO, L. "Le origini" in *Ritratti e disegni storici.* P. 15.

VISCARDI, A. *Op. cit.,* pp. 14-42; 171-180; 200-237; 268-283; 524-555.

CONTINUITY OF POPULAR TRADITION

STOPPATO, L. *La commedia popolare in Italia.* Padua, 1887.

VISCARDI, A. *Op. cit.,* pp. 447-487.

Humanism

COMBÈS, G. *Saint Augustin et la culture classique.* Paris, 1927.

COMPARETTI, D. *Virgilio nel Medio Evo.* Florence, 1872. 2nd ed., 1896. New ed. by G. PASQUALE, 1937-1941.

CURTIUS, E. R. *Europäische Literatur und Lateinische Mittelalter*. Bern, 1948.

GRAF, A. *Roma nella memoria e nell'immaginazione del Medioevo*. Turin, 1882-1883. Reprinted, 1915.

MENGOZZI, G. *La scuola di Pavia nell'alto Medioevo*. Pavia, 1925.

NOVATI, F. *Attraverso il Medioevo*. Bari, 1905.

———. *L'influsso del pensiero latino sopra la civiltà italiana del Medio Evo*. Milan, 1899.

ROBERT, F. *L'umanisme. Essai de définition*. Paris, 1946.

ROLLA, A. *Storia delle idee estetiche in Italia*. Turin, 1905.

RONCAGLIA, A. "Problemi delle origini" in *Problemi e orientamenti critici*. Vol. III.

SABBADINI, R. *Classici e umanisti da codici ambrosiani*. Florence, 1933.

TOFFANIN, G. *Che cosa fu l'Umanesimo*. Florence, 1929.

———. *La fine dell'Umanesimo*. Turin, 1920.

———. *Storia dell'Umanesimo dal secolo XIII al secolo XVI*. Bologna, 1943.

VIGNAUX, P. *Il pensiero nel Medio Evo*. Translated by C. GIACON, Brescia, 1947. Pp. 13-23.

VISCARDI, A. *Op. cit.*, pp. 171-172.

ZABUGHIN, V. *Storia del Rinascimento cristiano in Italia*. Milan, 1924.

JOHN SCOTUS ERIGENA (FIRST HALF OF NINTH CENTURY)

VIGNAUX, P. *Op. cit.*, pp. 14-15.

CHAPTER ONE : *Italian Culture in the Eleventh and Twelfth Centuries*

Critical Appraisal of the Early Centuries of Italian Civilization and Literature

ANTONI, C. "Studi sulla teoria e la storia della storiografia" in *Cinquant'anni*. Vol. I, 63-81.

APOLLONIO, M. *Uomini e forme nella cultura italiana delle origini*. Florence, 1934.

BARTOLI, A. *I primi due secoli della letteratura italiana*. Pp. 184-219.

BERTONI, G. *Lingua e pensiero*. Florence, 1932.

———. *Il Duecento*. Pp. 4-7.

BETTINELLI, S. *Il Risorgimento d'Italia negli studi, nelle arti e nei costumi dopo il Mille*. Bassano, 1775.

CHABOD, F. "Il Rinascimento" in *Questioni di storia moderna*. Pp. 53-55; 57; 59; 61-62.

———. "Gli studi di storia del Rinascimento" in *Cinquant'anni*. Vol. I, 127-207.

DE RUGGIERO, G. *La filosofia del cristianesimo*. Bari, 1920.

———. *Storia della filosofia*. Bari, 1937. Vol. I.

DUHEM, P. *Système du monde*. Paris, 1913. Vol. III.

FLORA, F. *Storia della letteratura italiana*. Pp. 9-108.

FUNCK-BRENTANO, F. *Renaissance et Moyen Age*. Bari, 1935.

GARIN, E. *Dal Medioevo al Rinascimento*. Florence, 1950. Pp. 29-53.

———. *Il Rinascimento italiano*. Milan, 1941. Pp. 64-77.

HASKINS, C. H. *Studies in Medieval Science*. Cambridge, Mass., 1924.

———. *The Renaissance of the XIIth Century*. Cambridge, Mass., 1927.

MONDOLFO, R. "L'origine dell'ideale filosofico della vita" in *Rendiconti della Regia Accademia delle scienze di Bologna*. 1938. Series IV, Vol. I.

NARDI, B. "Studi di storia della filosofia medioevale" in *Cinquant'anni*. Vol. I, 15-42.

PUPPO, M. "Problemi delle origini" in *Manuale*. Pp. 113-123.

REDANÒ, U. "La storiografia dal Rinascimento all'Illuminismo" in *Questioni di storia moderna*. Pp. 855-856.

Russo, L. *Disegno storico della letteratura italiana.* Vol. I, Part I, 8, 11.

———. "Origini della civiltà e della lingua italiana" in *Studi sul Due é Trecento.* Rome, 1946. Republished in *Ritratti e disegni storici.* Bari, 1951, Series III, 7-35.

———. *Problemi di metodo critico.* Pp. 11-27.

Ruskin, J. *Mornings in Florence* in *Works.* London, 1903-1912. Vol. XXIII.

———. *Seven Lamps of Architecture* in *op. cit.,* Vol. VIII.

———. *Stones of Venice* in *op. cit.,* Vol. III.

Savj-Lopez, P. *Le origini neo-latine.* Milan, 1920.

Simone, F. "La coscienza della Rinascita negli umanisti" in *La Rinascita,* II (1939), 847-851.

Sismondi, S. *Histoire des républiques italiennes du Moyen Age.* Zurich, 1807-18.

Vignaux, P. *Il pensiero nel Medio Evo.* Part III, 19.

Viscardi, A. *Le origini.* Pp. 88-128; 176-177.

———. *Posizioni vecchie e nuove della storia letteraria romana.* Milan, 1944.

Political and Social History

Caggese, R. *Statuti della repubblica fiorentina.* Vol. I, Florence, 1910; Vol. II, Florence, 1921.

Egidi, P. "La storia medioevale" in *Storia medioevale* in *Guide Bibliografiche Fondazione Leonardo,* Rome, 1922. Pp. 49-57.

Falco, G. *Santa Romana Repubblica, Profilo storico del medioevo.* Naples, 1942.

Giesebrecht, G. von. *Geschichte des deutschen Kaiserzeit.* Leipzig, 1875-1895.

Haskins, C. H. *The Normans in European History.* Lowell Lectures. Cambridge, Mass., 1925. P. 265.

Luchaire, J. *Les sociétés italiennes du XIII au XV siècle.* Paris, 1933.

Mangozzi, G. *La città italiana nell'alto medioevo.* Florence, 1914. Latest ed., 1931.

Muratori, L. A. *Annali d'Italia.* Lucca, 1762. Vols. VI, VII.

Pepe, G. "Gli studi di storia medievale" in *Cinquant'anni.* Vol. I, 109-124.

———. *Il medioevo barbarico d'Italia.* in *Cinquant'anni.* Vol. I, 115.

Pirenne, H. *Medieval Cities.* Translated by F. H. Halsey, Princeton, 1925.

Salvatorelli, L. *A Concise History of Italy.* Translated by B. Miall. New York, 1939. Pp. 138-272.

———. *L'Italia comunale dal secolo XI alla metà del secolo XIV.* Milan, 1940.

———. *L'Italia medievale dalle invasioni barbariche al secolo XI.* Milan, 1938.

Salvemini, G. *Magnati e populari in Firenze dal 1280 al 1295.* Florence, 1899.

Staley, J. E. *The Guilds of Florence.* London, 1906.

Thorndike, L. *History of Medieval Europe.* Pp. 192-510.

Villari, P. "Il comune di Roma nel Medio Evo secondo le ultime ricierche" in *Saggi storici e critici.* Bologna, 1890. Pp. 97-263.

———. *I primi due secoli della storia di Firenze.* Florence, 1893. Translated into English, London, 1905.

———. *Le invasioni barbariche in Italia.* Milan, 1900. 2nd ed., 1905. Translated into English, London, 1914.

———. *L'Italia da Carlo Magno alla morte di Arrigo VII.* Milan, 1910.

Viscardi, A. *Le origini.* Pp. 128-151.

Volpe, G. *Medio evo italiano.* Florence, 1923.

———. "Storia politica, economica e giuridica" in *op. cit.,* pp. 131-200.

Religious Movements

Braun, S. M. "Movimenti politico-religiosi a Milano al tempo della pataria" in *Archivio Storico Italiano,* LVIII (1931).

Davison, G. S. *The Forerunners of St. Francis.* Boston, 1927. Pp. 96-167.

Di Stefano, A. *Riformatori e eretici nel Medio Evo.* Palermo, 1938.

Volpe, G. *Movimenti ereticali.* Florence, 1926.

The Italian Vernacular

TEXTS

Castellani, A. *Nuovi testi fiorentini del Dugento.* Florence, 1952.

Classici italiani Utet. Turin, 1911-1932.

De Bartholomaeis, V. *Rime antiche senesi*. Rome, 1902. Part I, 7-44.

Dionisotti, C., and Grayson, C. *Early Italian Texts*. Oxford, 1949.

Lazzeri, G. *Antologia dei primi secoli della nostra letteratura*. Milan, 1954.

Monaci, E. *Crestomazia italiana dei primi secoli*. Città di Castello, 1888. 2nd ed., 1912.

Monteverdi, A. *Testi volgari italiani anteriori al Duecento*. Rome, 1935.

———. *Testi volgari italiani dei primi tempi*. Modena, 1948.

Nannucci, V. *Manuale della letteratura del primo secolo della lingua italiana*. Florence, 1837-1839. 4th ed., Florence, 1883.

Schiaffini, A. *Momenti di storia della lingua italiana*. Bari, 1950.

———. *Testi fiorentini del Dugento e dei primi del Trecento*. Florence, 1926.

Trucchi, F. *Poesie inedite di duecento autori dall'origine della lingua infino al secolo decimosettimo*. Prato, 1846-1947.

Ugolini, F. A. *Testi antichi italiani*. Turin, 1942.

Vatican Codex 3793. Published by A. D'Ancona and D. Comparetti under the title of *Le antiche rime volgari*. Bologna, 1875-1888.

Wartburg, W. V. *Raccolta di testi antichi italiani*. Bern, 1946.

CRITICISM

Caretti, L. *Avviamento*. Pp. 9-12.

Devoto, G. *Profilo di storia linguistica italiana* in *Avviamento* by L. Caretti. Pp. 157-318.

Grandgent, C. H. *From Latin into Italian*. Cambridge, Mass., 1927. Pp. 157-313. Translated into Italian by N. Maccarone with the title of *Introduzione allo studio del latino volgare*.

Hall, R. O. *History of Italian Literature*. Pp. 15-26; 34-45.

Labande-Jeanroy, T. *La question de la langue en Italie*. New York, 1925.

Migliorini, B. "La questione della lingua" in *Problemi e orientamenti critici*. Vol. III.

———. "Storia della lingua italiana" in *Problemi e orientamenti critici*. Milan, 1948-1949. Vol. II.

Morandi, L. *Origini della lingua italiana*. 7th ed., Città di Castello, 1897.

Ozanam, A. F. *Documents inédits pour servir à l'histoire littéraire de l'Italie depuis le 8e siècle jusqu'au XIIIe siècle*. Paris, 1850.

Pernicone, V. "Storia e svolgimento della metrica" in *Problemi e orientamenti critici*. Vol. II.

Puppo, M. "Origine e carattere dell'italiano" in *Manuale*. Pp. 83-94.

Russo, L. *Disegno storico*. Vol. I, Part I, 15.

———. "La culla della lingua e della letteratura italiana" in *Problemi di metodo critico*. 2nd ed., Bari, 1950. Pp. 20-25.

Scherillo, M. *Le origini*. Milan, 1919. Ch. I.

Schiaffini, A. "Le origini dell'italiano letterario" in *L'Italia dialettale*, V (1929).

———. *Momenti di storia della lingua italiana*. Rome, 1953.

The Portolani and the Study of Geography

Sarton, G. *Introduction to a History of Science*. Vol. II, Part I, 33-41.

The Fine Arts

De Witt, A. (ed.). *Mosaici del Battistero di Firenze*. Florence, 1955.

Male, E. *L'art religieux du XIIe siècle en France*. Paris, 1922.

Mottini, G. E. *Storia dell'arte italiana*. Milan, 1937. Pp. 51-107.

Robb, D., and Garrison, J. J. *Art in the Western World*. New York, 1935. Pp. 75-104.

Salmi, M. *Dalle origini cristiane a tutto il periodo romanico* in *L'Arte Italiana*. Florence, 1943. Vol. I.

Venturi, A. *L'arte romanica* in *Storia dell'arte italiana*. Milan, 1909. Vol. III.

CHAPTER TWO: *The Transmission of Culture in the Twelfth Century*

Critical Appraisal

GILSON, E. *Les idées et les lettres.* Paris, 1932.

HASKINS, C. H. *Studies in Medieval Science.* Cambridge, Mass., 1924.

MANDONNET, P. F. *Etudes d'histoire littéraire et doctrinale du Moyen âge.* Paris, 1930.

SARTON, G. *Introduction to a History of Science.* Vol. II, Part I, 113-117.

TIRABOSCHI, G. *Storia della letteratura italiana.* Vol. VI, 500-506.

VIGNAUX, P. *Il Pensiero del Medio Evo.* P. 22.

RHETORIC AND POETICS

BALDWIN, S. *Medieval Rhetoric and Poetics.* New York, 1928.

FARAL, E. *Les arts poétiques du XII⁰ et du XIII⁰ siècle.* Paris, 1923.

SCHIAFFINI, A. *Tradizione e poesia.* Genoa, 1934.

VISCARDI, A. *Le origini.* Pp. 276-281.

TRANSLATORS

"Aristoteles Latinus" in *Corpus philosophorum medii aevi.* Rome, 1939. See B. NARDI in *Cinquant'anni,* Vol. I, 37.

BONCOMPAGNI, B. *Della vita e delle opere di Gherardo da Cremona, traduttore del secolo duodecimo e di Gherardo da Sabbionetta, astronomo del secolo decimoterzo.* Rome, 1951.

Dialogues of Plato, The. Translated by B. JOWETT. New York, 1937.

FRANCESCHINI, E. "Aristotile nel medioevo latino" in *Atti del Congresso nazionale di filosofia.* Padua, 1934.

———. "Il contributo dell'Italia alla trasmissione del pensiero greco in occidente nei secoli XI e XII e la questione di Giacomo Chierico di Venezia" in *Atti della Riunione della S.I.P.S.* Venice, 1937.

HASKINS, C. H. "The Sicilian Translators" in *op. cit.,* pp. 155-193.

MARCHESI, C. *L'etica nicomachea nella traduzione latina medievale.* Messina, 1905.

McKEON, R. (ed). *The Basic Works of Aristotle.* New York, 1941.

NARDI, B. "Studi di storia della filosofia medievale" in *Cinquant'anni.* Pp. 36-37.

SARTON, G. *Op. cit.,* Vol. II, Part I, 113-117; 167-181; 338-348.

VIGNAUX, P. *Op. cit.,* p. 4.

Schools and Universities

HASKINS, C. H. *The Rise of Universities.* New York, 1923.

MALAGOLA, C. *Statuti delle università e dei collegi dello Studio Bolognese.* Bologna, 1888.

MANACORDA, G. *Storia della scuola in Italia.* Palermo, 1914. Vol. I.

SARTON, G. *Op. cit.,* Vol. II, Part I, 350-351.

Study of Law

SARTON, G. *Op. cit.,* Vol. II, Part I, 316.

SOLMI, A. *Stato e Chiesa negli scritti politici da Carlo Magno al Concordato di Worm.* Modena, 1901.

VISCARDI. *Op. cit.,* pp. 200-237.

Study of Medicine

SARTON, G. *Op. cit.,* Vol. II, Part I, 67-70; 307-309.

Study of History

BALZANI, U. *Le cronache italiane nel Medio Evo.* Milan, 1884. New eds., 1900, 1909.

MURATORI, L. A. *Rerum Italicarum Scriptores.* Milan, 1723-1751. New ed. under the direction of G. CARDUCCI and V. FIORINI, 1917.

ORSI, P. *La storia d'Italia, narrata da scrittori contemporanei agli avvenimenti.* Turin, 1905.

VISCARDI, A. "Gregorio di Catino e gli esordi della storiografia documentale" in *op. cit.*, pp. 93-94.

Classical Influence

FLUTRE, L. A. *Li faits de romains dans la littérature francaise et italienne du XIII*e *siècle au XIV*e *siècle.* Paris, 1933.

GILSON, E. *La philosophie au Moyen Age.*

GORRA, A. *Testi inediti di storia troiana.* Turin, 1887.

MAGGINI, F. "Appunti sul *Sallustio Volgorizzato di Bartolomeo da San Concordio*" in *I primi volgarizzamenti.* Florence, 1952. Pp. 41-53.

———. "Il *Fiore di Rettorica*" in *I primi volgarizzamenti.* Pp. 16-40.

———. *I primi volgarizzamenti dei classici latini.* Florence, 1952.

MANDONNET, P. F. *Siger de Brabant et l'averroïsme latin au XIII*e *siècle.* Fribourg, Switzerland, 1899.

NARDI, B. *Cinquant'anni.* P. 37.

NOVATI, F. *L'influsso del pensiero latino.* Milan, 1899.

PARODI, E. G. "Le storie di Cesare nella letteratura italiana dei primi secoli" in *Studi di filologia romanza,* IV.

PELLEGRINI, C. "Relazioni fra la letteratura italiana e la letteratura francese" in *Problemi e orientamenti critici.* Vol. IV.

SAVJ-LOPEZ, P. *Storie tebane in Italia.* Bergamo, 1906.

SEGRE, C. *Volgarizzamenti del Due e Trecento.* Turin, 1953. Pp. 131-637.

SORBELLI, T. "Relazioni fra la letteratura italiana e la letteratura classica" in *Problemi e orientamenti critici.* Vol. IV.

UGOLINI, F. A. *I cantari d'argomento classico.* Florence, 1933.

Contacts with French and English Traditions

LABANDE-JEANROY, A. *La lirica francese in Italia nel periodo delle origini.* Translated by G. Rossi. Florence, 1897.

CAROLINGIAN LEGENDS

BERTONI, G. *Il Duecento.* Pp. 8-9; 13-37; 84-85; 320-326.

MEYER, P. "De l'expansion de la langue française en Italie pendant le Moyen âge" in *Atti del Congresso internazionale di Scienze storiche.* Rome, 1933.

NOVATI, F. "Il codice dell'amor profano" in *Freschi e mini del Dugento.* Pp. 207-240.

PELLEGRINI, C. "Il *Roman de la Rose* e la letteratura italiana" in *Beihefte z. Zeitschr. d. rom. Phil.,* XXI, Halle (1910).

———. "La littérature italienne d'expression française" in *Bulletin de l'Association Guillaume Budé* (June, 1949), pp. 95-99.

———. "Relazioni fra la letteratura italiana e la letteratura francese" in *Problemi e orientamenti critici.* Vol. IV.

RAJNA, P. *Le fonti dell'Orlando Furioso.* Florence, 1900.

RUSSO, L. *Disegno storico.* Pp. 11.

THOMAS, A. *Francesco da Barberino et la littérature au Moyen Age.* Paris, 1883.

PROVENCAL LORE

ANGLADE, J. *Les troubadours. Leur vie, leurs oeuvres, leur influence.* Paris, 1908.

BATTAGLIA, S. *Trattato d'amore. Testo latino del secolo XII con due traduzioni toscane inedite del secolo XIV.* Rome, 1947.

BERTONI, G. *I trovatori d'Italia.* Modena, 1915.

———. *La poesia provenzale nell'Italia superiore.* Pp. 13-37.

———. *Studi su vecchie e nuove poesie e prose d'amore e di romanzi.* Modena, 1922. P. 207.

———. "Trovatori italiani a Genova: Lanfranco Cigala" in *Il Duecento.* Pp. 28-33.

CANELLO, U. A. *Fiorita di liriche provenzali.* Bologna, 1881.

DE LOLLIS, C. *Vita e poesia di Sordello di Goito.* Halle, 1896.

NOVATI, F. "Sordello da Goito" in *Freschi e mini del Dugento.* Milan, 1908. New ed., 1925. Pp. 117-141.

PARRY, J. *The Art of Courtly Love by Andreas Capellanus.* New York, 1941.

TOJA, G. L. *Lanfranco Cigala.* Florence, 1952.

UGOLINI, F. A. *La poesia provenzale e l'Italia.* Modena, 1937.

VISCARDI, A. "La tradizione aulica e scolastica e la poesia trobadorica" in *Studi medievali*, Vol. VII.

ARTHURIAN LEGENDS

BERTONI, G. *Op. cit.*, pp. 85-87.
DE BARTHOLOMAEIS, V. *Tristano: Gli episodi principali della leggenda in versioni francesi, spagnole e italiane.* Rome, n.d.
GARDNER, G. E. *The Arthurian Legend in Italian Literature.* London, 1930.
MAZZONI, G., AND PAVOLINI, P. G. *Letterature Straniere.* Florence, 1915. Pp. 22-143.
NARDI, B. *Op. cit.*, pp. 35-36.

PARODI, E. G. *Il Tristano Riccardiano.* Bologna, 1896.
———. "Le storie di Cesare nella letteratura italiana nei primi secoli" in *Studi di Filologia Romanza*, IV.
POLIDORI, F. I. (ed.). *La Tavola Ritonda.* Bologna, 1864.
PRAZ, M. "Relazione fra la letteratura italiana e la letteratura inglese" in *Problemi e orientamenti critici.* Vol. IV.

NEOPLATONISM OF SCOTUS ERIUGENA, ST. AUGUSTINE, ECCARD OF HOCHHEIM

NARDI, B. *Op. cit.*, p. 37.

CHAPTER THREE: *Contributions to Culture During the Thirteenth Century*

Critical Appraisal of the Thirteenth Century

BERTONI, G. *Il Duecento.* P. 3.
GILSON, E. *La philosophie au Moyen Age.* Paris, 1914.
———. *La philosophie de St. Bonaventure.* Paris, 1924. Translated into English by D. I. TRETHOWAN and F. J. SHEED, New York, 1938.
———. *Le Thomisme.* Paris, 1947-1948.
———. *The Philosophy of St. Thomas Aquinas.* Translated by E. BULLOUGH, Cambridge, 1929.
NOVATI, F. *Freschi e mini del Duecento.* Milan, 1908. New ed., 1925.
SCHERILLO, M. *Le origini.* Pp. 14-192.
WALSH, J. J. *The Thirteenth, Greatest of Centuries.* New York, 1907. 2nd ed., 1909.

Historical Background

EGIDI, P. "Storia politica, economica, giuridica" in *La storia medievale.* Pp. 131-200.
SALVATORELLI, L. *A Concise History of Italy.* Pp. 138-265.
———. *L'Italia comunale del secolo XI alla metà del secolo XIV.* Milan, 1940.

———. *L'Italia medievale dalle invasioni barbariche al secolo XI.* Milan, 1938.
SALVEMINI, G. *Magnati e popolani in Firenze dal 1280 al 1295.* Florence, 1899.

FREDERICK II

DE STEFANO, A. *L'idea imperiale di Federico II.* Florence, 1927.
JUILLARD-BREHOLLES, J. L. A. *Historia diplomatica Friderici Secundi.* Paris, 1852-1861.
NOVATI, F. "Federico II e la cultura dell'età sua" in *Freschi e mini del Dugento.* Pp. 85-113.
PEPE, G. *Lo stato ghibellino di Federico II.* Bari, 1938.
SARTON, G. *Introduction to a History of Science.* Vol. II, Part II, 575-579.

Cultural Contributions

AMARI, M. *Storia dei Mussulmani di Sicilia.* Florence, 1854-1872.
BERTONI, G. *Op. cit.*, pp. 210-245.
OZANAM, A. F. *Dante et la philosophie catholique au XIII⁰ siècle.* Paris, 1840. Translated into Italian by P. MOLINELLI, Milan, 1841; into English by L. D. PYCHOWSKA, New York, 1913.

GLOSSATORS

SARTON, G. *Op. cit.*, Vol. II, Part I, 264-269; Part II, 688-690.

ARISTOTLE

FRANCESCHINI, E. "La poetica di Aristotile nel secolo XIII" in *Atti del Regio Istituto Veneto di Scienze, Lettere ed Arti* (1933-1934).

ST. THOMAS AQUINAS

BOURKE, V. J. *Thomistic Bibliography*. St. Louis, 1945.

CHESTERTON, G. K. *St. Thomas Aquinas*. London, 1933. 2nd ed., 1947.

D'ARCY, M. C. *Thomas Aquinas*. Dublin, 1953.

FRANCESCHINI, E. "S. Tommaso e l'etica nicomachea" in *Rivista di filosofia neoscolastica* (1936), pp. 4-5.

GENTILE, G. *I problemi della scolastica e il pensiero italiano*. Bari, 1913.

GILSON, E. *Le Thomisme*. Paris, 1944.

MALAGOLA, A. *Le teorie politiche di S. Tommaso d'Aquino*. Bologna, 1912.

NARDI, B. *Opuscoli e testi* in the *Collection of Laterza*, directed by G. GENTILE. Bari, 1915.

——. "Studi di storia della filosofia medievale" in *Cinquant'anni*. Vol. I, 15-42.

PEGIS, ANTON C. (ed.). *Basic Writings of St. Thomas*. (Two Volumes.) New York, 1945.

ROLLA, A. *Storia delle idee estetiche in Italia*. Turin, 1905. Pp. 39-44.

SARTON, G. *Op. cit.*, Vol. II, Part II, 914-922.

VIGNAUX, P. *Il Pensiero del Medio Evo*. Pp. 65-102.

TOCCO, F. *L'eresia nel medioevo*. Florence, 1884.

ST. BONAVENTURE OF BAGNOREA

Critical Edition of the Works of St. Bonaventure in the Franciscan Convent of Quaracchi. Quaracchi, 1882-1902.

SARTON, G. *Op. cit.*, Vol. II, Part II, 921-922.

SCHOOLS AND UNIVERSITIES

SARTON, G. *Op. cit.*, Vol. II, Part I, 350-353; Part II, 495-496; 570-572.

ARTES DICTANDI

BERTONI, G. *Op. cit.*, p. 338.

HASKINS, C. H. "The Early *Artes Dictandi* in Italy" in *Studies in Medieval Culture*. Oxford, 1929. Pp. 182 and ff.

NATHAN, S. *Amicitia di Maestro Boncompagno da Signa*. Rome, 1909. Part III, 3-88.

NOVATI, F., AND MONTEVERDI, A. "Artes Dictandi" in *Le origini*. Pp. 410-536.

SCHIAFFINI, A. "L'ars dictandi e la prosa di Guida Faba" in *Tradizione e poesia*. Pp. 41-55.

Use of French and the Translations into the Vernacular

BERTONI, G. *Op. cit.*, pp. 38-78.

——. "Nicola da Casola e la letteratura franco-italiana" in *Attila*. Fribourg, Switzerland, 1907.

Il Fiore e il Detto d'Amore. Introduction by G. MAZZONI. Florence, 1923.

"Il Fiore in Alighieri, D." in *Tutte le opere*. Barbera Edition. Florence, 1921.

MAZZONI, G. "Se possa il Fiore essere di Dante Alighieri" in *Raccolta di Studi critici in onore di Alessandro D'Ancona*. Florence, 1901.

PARODI, E. G. (ed.). *Il Fiore e il Detto d'Amore*. Florence, 1922.

SARTON, G. *Op. cit.*, Vol. II, Part II, 530-531; 803, 815.

SCHIAFFINI, A. "Traduttori di Cicerone, Ovidio, Virgilio" in *Tradizione e poesia*. Genoa, 1934. Pp. 200-217.

BRUNETTO LATINI

CHABAILLE, P. *Il Tesoro volgarizzato da B. Giamboni*. Bologna, 1878.

——. *Li livres dou trézor par Brunetto Latini*. Paris, 1863.

D'ANCONA, A. *Il Tesoro di Brunetto Latini versificato*. Rome, 1888.

GAITER, L. (ed.). *Il Tesoro*. Translated into the Italian vernacular by B. GIAMBONI. Bologna, 1878.

MAGGINI, F. (ed.). *La Rettorica*. Florence, 1915.

MARCHESINI, U. *Brunetto Latini notaio*. Verona, 1890.

SCHIAFFINI, A. *Tradizione e poesia*. Pp. 202-205.

SUNDBY, T. *Della vita e delle opere di Brunetto Latini*. Florence, 1884.

ZANNONI, G. B. (ed.). *Il Tesoretto e il favolello*. Florence, 1824.

FRA GUIDOTTO

SCHIAFFINI, A. *Op. cit.*, pp. 205-208.

Achievements in Practical Activities

SARTON, G. *Op. cit.*, Vol. II, Part I, 406.

Use of Arabic Numbers

LEONARDO FIBONACCI

SARTON, G. *Op. cit.*, Vol. II, Part II, 611-613.

Study of Medicine

MIELI, A. *Pagine di storia di chimica*. Rome, 1922.

SARTON, G. *Op. cit.*, Vol. II, Part I, 70; Part II, 1076-1088.

The Arts

HASKINS, C. H. *The Renaissance of the XIIth Century*. Cambridge, Mass., 1927. Ch. II.

MOTTINI, G. E. *Storia dell'arte italiana*. Pp. 111-175.

ROBB, D., AND GARRISON, J. J. *Art in the Western World*. Pp. 105-123; 467-490.

RUSKIN, J. *Giotto and His Work in Padua*. in *Works*. London, 1903-1912. Vol. 24.

SALMI, M. *L'arte gotica e l'arte del Primo Rinascimento* in *L'Arte Italiana*. Florence, 1942. Vol. II.

THODE, H. *Giotto*. Leipsig, 1899.

VENTURI, A. *La pittura del Trecento e le sue origini* in *Storia dell'arte italiana*. Milan, 1907. Vol. V.

———. *La scultura del Trecento e le sue origini* in *Storia dell'arte*. Milan, 1906. Vol. IV.

CHAPTER FOUR: *Poetry During the Thirteenth Century*

Texts

D'ANCONA, A., AND COMPARETTI, D. *Le antiche rime volgari secondo la lezione del codice vaticano 3793*. Bologna, 1875-1888.

LAZZARI, G. *Antologia dei primi secoli della nostra letteratura*. Milan, 1942. Latest ed., 1954.

MONACI, E. *Op. cit.*

NANNUCCI, V. *Manuale della letteratura del primo secolo*. Florence, 1878.

SALINARI, C. *La poesia lirica del Duecento*. Turin, 1951.

UGOLINI, F. A. *Testi antichi italiani*. Turin, 1942.

ZAMBRINI, F. *Le opere volgari a stampa dei secoli XIII e XIV*. Bologna, 1884.

General Aids

BERTONI, G. *Il Duecento*. Pp. 114-116; 206-209.

BRANCA, V. "Raccolta di scrittori e di rime" in *Problemi e orientamenti critici*. Vol. I.

CARDUCCI, G. "Dello svolgimento della letteratura nazionale" in *Prose*. Bologna, 1906. Pp. 265-410.

CROCE, B. *Poesia popolare e poesia d'arte*. Bari, 1939. New ed., 1946. Pp. 3-5.

D'ANCONA, A. *Saggi di letteratura popolare*. Livorno, 1913.

———. *Studi di critica e storia letteraria*. Bologna, 1880. 2nd ed., 1912.

———. *Studi sulla letteratura italiana dei primi secoli*. Ancona, 1887.

——. *Varietà storiche e letterarie*. Milan, 1883.

Fusco, E. *La lirica. Dalle origini all'Ottocento.* Milan, 1950. Vol. I, 1-93.

De Sanctis, F. *Storia della letteratura italiana.* Naples, 1870. New ed., Bari, 1930.

D'Ovidio, F. *Versificazione italiana e arte poetica medievale.* Milan, 1910.

Gimma, G. *Idea della storia dell'Italia letteraria.* Naples, 1723.

Monticelli, G. *Vita religiosa italiana nel secolo XIII.* Turin, 1932.

Morandi, L. *Antologia della nostra critica letteraria moderna.* Città di Castello, 1885.

Novati, F. "Lirica di popolo" in *Freschi e mini del Dugento.* Pp. 15-29.

Parodi, E. G. "L'eredità romana e l'alba della nostra poesia" in *Poesia e storia nella Divina Commedia.* Naples, 1921.

Puppo, M. *Manuale.* Pp. 113-123.

Quadrio, F. S. *Della storia e della ragione d'ogni poesia.* Bologna, 1739-1752.

Rossi, M. *Storia della letteratura italiana.* Vol. I.

Russo, L. "Genesi popolare o genesi dotta della letteratura italiana" in *Problemi di metodo critico.* 2nd ed., Bari, 1950. Pp. 11-20.

——. "I poeti del Duecento" in *Gli Scrittori d'Italia.* Vol. I, 3-32.

Santangelo, S. *Le tenzoni poetiche nella letteratura italiana delle origini.* Geneva, 1928.

Sapegno, N. "La corrente realistica nelle origini della nostra letteratura" in *Nuova Italia,* IV (1933).

Torraca, F. *Studi di storia letteraria.* Florence, 1923.

——. *Studi sulla lirica italiana del Duecento.* Bologna, 1902.

Viscardi, A. *Le origini.* Pp. 508-509.

Zingarelli, N. "Le tarde origini della poesia italiana" in *Nuova Antologia* (Jan. 16, 1923).

CHAPTER FIVE: *Popular Poetry*

Texts

Carducci, G. *Cantilene e ballate, strambotti e madrigali nel secoli XIII e XIV.* Pisa, 1871.

——. *Intorno ad alcune rime del secolo XIII ritrovate nei Memoriali dell'Archivio notarile di Bologna.* Imola, 1876.

D'Ancona, A. *La poesia popolare italiana.* Florence, 1887. 2nd ed., Livorno, 1906.

Massera, T. *Sonetti burleschi e realistici dei primi due secoli.* Bari, 1920. New ed. by L. Russo, 1933.

Monaci, E. *Crestomazia.*

Critical Appraisal

Bartoli, A. *I primi due secoli della letteratura italiana.* Pp. 127-172.

Bertoni, G. *Il Duecento.* Pp. 136-151.

Carducci, G. *Antica lirica italiana.* Florence, 1907.

Cian, V. *La satira.* Milan, 1923-1939.

——. *Studi sulla letteratura italiana dei primi secoli.* 2nd ed., Milan, 1891.

Guerri, D. *La corrente popolare nel Rinascimento.* Florence, 1931.

Grossi, T. *Cecco Angiolieri e i burleschi del 200 e del 300.* Turin, 1936.

Novati, F. *Freschi e mini del Duecento.*

Santoli, V. "Gli studi di letteratura popolare" in *Cinquant'anni.* Vol. II, 115-134.

Sapegno, N. *Il Trecento.* Pp. 65-111.

Schiaffini, A. "Le origini dell'italiano letterario" in *L'Italia dialettale,* V (1929).

Torraca, F. *Studi su la lirica italiana del Duecento.* Bologna, 1902.

Wilkins, E. H. *History of Italian Literature.* Cambridge, Mass., 1953.

Love Theme

Bertoni, G. *Op. cit.,* pp. 118-180.

CIELO D'ALCAMO

De Bartholomaeis, V. "Un mimo giullaresco del Duecento" in *Le origini della poesia drammatica italiana.* Bologna, 1924. Pp. 53-69.

LAZZARI, G. *Antologia dei primi secoli della nostra letteratura.*

MONACI, E. *Op. cit.,* pp. 106-109.

TUSCAN SONGSTERS OF THE MIDDLE CLASS

CROCE, B. *Poesia popolare e poesia d'arte.* Pp. 1-64.

RUSSO, L. *Disegno storico.* Pp. 77-108.

———. *Studi sul Due e Trecento.* Rome, 1946.

Folgore of San Gimignano

CAPPUCCIO, C. *Folgore da San Gimignano e Cenne de la Chitarra.* Siracusa, 1924.

ERRIGO, G. *Folgore da San Gimignano e "la Brigata Spendereccia."* Pisa, 1895.

FLAMINI, F. "Folgore da San Gimignano" in *Spigolature di erudizione e di critica.* Pisa, 1895.

MASTELLA, P. A. *Intorno a quel Niccolò cui Folgore da San Gimignano dedicò la corona dei sonetti de'mesi.* Venice, 1893.

NERI, F. (ed.). *Sonetti.* Città di Castello, 1914.

Rustico di Filippo

CASINI, T. "Un poeta umorista del secolo decimoterzo" in *Nuova Antologia* (Feb. 1, 1890).

DEL LUNGO, I. "Un realista fiorentino dei tempi di Dante" in *Rivista d'Italia* (Oct. 15, 1899).

RUSSO, L. "La letteratura comico-realistica del Due e Trecento: Rustico di Filippo" in *Belfagor* (March, 1946).

Cecco Angiolieri

D'ANCONA, A. "Cecco Angiolieri da Siena, poeta umorista del secolo XIII" in *Studi di critica e storia letteraria.* Bologna, 1880. New ed., 1912.

MARTI, Λ. *Cecco Angiolieri.* Galatina, 1946.

MOMIGLIANO, A. "L'anima e l'arte di Cecco Angiolieri" in *Italia moderna,* IV (1906).

NANETTI, E. *Cecco Angiolieri, la sua patria, i suoi tempi e la sua poesia.* Siena, 1923.

PIRANDELLO, L. *Umorismo.* Venice, 1908. Pp. 9-14.

———. "Un preteso poeta umorista del secolo XIII" in *Arte e scienze.* Rome, 1908.

RUSSO, L. "Cecco Angiolieri e la critica" in *Problemi di metodo critico.* Pp. 195-205.

STEINER, C. (ed.). *Il Canzoniere.* Turin, 1925. See L. RUSSO in *Problemi di metodo critico.* Pp. 271-281.

TODARO, A. *Sull'autenticità dei sonetti attribuiti a Cecco Angiolieri.* Palermo, 1934.

Religious Theme

BERTONI, G. *Op. cit.,* pp. 187-201.

DE LABRIOLLE, P. *Les sources de l'histoire du Montanisme.* Fribourg, 1913.

GETTO, G. "La letteratura religiosa" in *Problemi e orientamenti critici.* Vol. III.

LEVASTI, A. (ed.). *Mistici del Duecento e del Trecento* in *Classici Rizzoli.* Milan, n.d.

MONTEVERDI, A. "Lingue volgari e impulsi religiosi" in *Cultura neolatina,* VI-VII (1946-1947).

MONTICELLI, G. *Vita religiosa italiana nel secolo XIII.* Turin, 1932.

NOVATI, F. "Un poema francescano del Dugento" in *Attraverso il Medio Evo.* Pp. 7-115.

OZANAM, A. F. *Franciscan poets in Italy of the XIIIth Century.* Translated by A. E. NELLAN and N. C. CRAIG. London, 1914.

RUSSO, L. *Disegno storico.* Pp. 17-44.

———. "I flagellanti e altri movimenti religiosi" in *Ritratti e disegni storici.* Series III, 100-106.

———. "Letteratura religiosa del Duecento" in *Ritratti e disegni storici.* Series III, 69-158.

SAPEGNO, N. "La letteratura del Due e Trecento e la critica letteraria moderna" in *Studi cateriniani,* XII, 1937.

TOCCO, F. *L'eresia del medioevo.* Florence, 1884.

VISCARDI, A. *Le origini.* Pp. 511-516.

VOLPE, G. "Eretici e moti ereticali dell'XI secolo nei loro motivi e riferimenti sociali" in *Rinnovamento,* I (1907).

DIDACTIC POETS IN NORTHERN ITALY

BERTONI, G. "Uguccione da Lodi" in *Rendiconti della Regia Accademia dei Lincei,* Series V, 21.

CONTI, G. (ed.). *Le opere di Bonvesìn de la Riva*. (Società Filologica Romana.) Rome, 1941. Vol. I, Texts.

HABERTSTUMPFF, C. *La poesia morale e didatica di Bonvesìn de la Riva*. Naples, 1906.

LEVI, E. *Poeti antichi lombardi*. Milan, 1921.

———. *Uguccione da Lodi e i primordi della poesia italiana*. Florence, 1921.

RUSSO, L. "La letteratura religiosa lombarda" in *Disegno storico*. Pp. 31-43. Complete bibliography, pp. 43-44.

ST. FRANCIS OF ASSISI

CAPOZZI, F. C. *God's Fool*. New York, 1956.

COSMO, U. *Con Madonna Povertà*. Bari, 1940. Pp. 179-303.

CHESTERTON, G. K. *St. Francis of Assisi*. New York, 1924.

DAVISON, G. E. *Forerunners of St. Francis*. Boston, 1927.

MOMIGLIANO, A. *Storia della letteratura italiana*. Pp. 7-8.

NOVATI, F. "Dante e San Francesco d'Assisi" in *Freschi e mini del Dugento*. Pp. 169-183.

———. "L'amor mistico in S. Francesco d'Assisi ed in Jacopone da Todi" in *op. cit.*, pp. 187-204.

RAJNA, P. "San Francesco e gli spiriti cavallereschi" in *Nuova Antologia* (1926).

ROSSI, V. *Storia della letteratura italiana*. Vol. I, 69-71.

RUSSO, L. *Disegno storico*. Pp. 19-22.

SABATIER, P. *Vie de S. François d'Assise*. Paris, 1894. New ed., Paris, 1926.

SALVATORELLI, L. *Vita di San Francesco*. Bari, 1920. English translation, New York, 1928.

SAPEGNO, N. "Il sentimento francescano della natura" in *Leonardo*, V (1929).

SARTON, G. *Introduction to a History of Science*. Vol. II, Part II, 543-548.

THODE, H. *Franz von Assisi und die Anfänge der Renaissance in Italien*. Berlin, 1885. 2nd ed., 1904.

JACOPONE OF TODI

AGENO, F. *Jacopone da Todi*. Florence, 1923.

———. "Modi stilistici delle laude di Jacopone da Todi" in *Rassegna d'Italia* (May, 1946).

BAROLO, R. *Jacopone da Todi*. Turin, 1929.

BERTONI, G. *Il Duecento*. Pp. 201-206. Bibliography, pp. 208-209.

CASELLA, M. "Jacopone da Todi" in *Archivium romanicum*, IV (1920).

D'ASCOLI, P. E. *Il misticismo dei canti di Frate Jacopone da Todi*. Recanati, 1925.

FERRI, G. (ed.). *Le laude di Jacopone da Todi secondo la stampa fiorentina del 1490*. 2nd ed. by S. CARAMELLA. Bari, 1930.

GIULIOTTI, D. *Le più belle pagine di Jacopone da Todi*. Milan, 1922.

JACOPONE DA TODI. *Le laudi* in *Scrittori d'Italia*. Bari, 1915.

MASCIA, F. S. *La poesia di Jacopone da Todi*. Milan, 1932.

MOMIGLIANO, A. *Storia della letteratura italiana*. Pp. 8-11.

PAPINI, G. *Storia della letteratura italiana*. Florence, 1937. Pp. 39-67.

PARODI, E. G. *Poeti antichi e moderni*. Florence, 1923.

RUSSO, L. *Op. cit.*, pp. 28-31. Bibliography, p. 43.

———. *Ritratti e disegni storici*. Pp. 36-68.

———. "Jacopone da Todi, mistico poeta" in *Problemi di metodo critico*.

UNDERHILL, E. *Jacopone da Todi, Poet and Mystic*. London, 1919. Part II, 250-501.

CHAPTER SIX: *Courtly Poetry*

Critical Appraisal

BERTONI, G. *Il Dolce Stil Nuovo*. Bergamo, 1907.

DE BARTHOLOMAEIS, V. "Primordi della lirica d'arte" in *Italia*. Turin, 1943.

FIGURELLI, F. *Il Dolce Stil Nuovo*. Naples, 1933. Pp. 48-58.

NOVATI, F. "Vita e poesia di corte del Dugento" in *Freschi e mini del Dugento*. Pp. 33-54.

PARDUCCI, A. *Costumi ornati*. Bologna, 1928.

PELLEGRINI, C. "Relazioni fra la letteratura italiana e la letteratura francese" in *Problemi e orientamenti critici*. Vol. IV.

RUSSO, L. (ed.). *Gli scrittori d'Italia*. Florence, 1949-1951. Vol. I: *Dai Siciliani al Foscolo*, 3-214.

SAPEGNO, N. *Il Trecento*. Pp. 11-64.

SAVJ-LOPEZ, P. *Trovatori e poeti: Studi di lirica antica, Dolce Stil Nuovo*. Milan, 1906.

Sicilian School

TEXTS

GUERRERI CROCETTI, C. *La Magna Curia (La scuola poetica siciliana)*. Milan, 1947.

MONACI, E. *Op. cit.*

NANNUCCI, V. *Manuale della letteratura del primo secolo della lingua italiana*.

SALINARI, C. *La poesia lirica del Duecento*. Turin, 1951.

VITALE, M. *Poeti della prima scuola*. Milan, 1951.

CRITICISM

BERTONI, G. *Il Duecento*. Pp. 33-54; 88-117.

CESAREO, G. A. *Le origini della poesia lirica e la poesia sotto gli Svevi*. Palermo, 2nd ed., 1924.

GASPERY, A. *La scuola poetica siciliana del secolo XIII*. Florence, 1874.

JORIO, C. "L'imitazione provenzale in Pietro di Vigna" in *Studi in onore di Francesco Torraca*. 1922. P. 195.

PANVINI, B. *La scuola poetica siciliana.* Florence, 1955.

RUSSO, L. *Disegno storico*. Pp. 113-138.

——. (ed.). *Gli scrittori d'Italia*. Vol. I, 5-14.

Tuscan Poets

TEXTS

MONACI, E. *Op. cit.*

ROSSETTI, D. G. *Translations from the Italian Poets of the Thirteenth Century*. Everyman's Library, No. 627. New York, 1912.

ZACCAGNINI, G. AND PARDUCCI, A. (eds.). *Rimatori Siculi-Toscani del Dugento*. Bari, 1915.

CRITICISM

BARTOLI, A. *"La nuova lirica toscana"* in *Storia della letteratura italiana*. Vol. II.

FIGURELLI, F. *Op. cit.*, pp. 48-100.

——. *Gli scrittori d'Italia*. Vol. I, 14-19.

GUITTONE D'AREZZO

EGIDI, P. (ed.). *Le Rime di Guittone d'Arezzo*. Bari, 1940.

MERIANO, F. (ed.). *Le lettere di frate Guittone d'Arezzo*. Bologna, 1924.

PELLIZZARI, A. *La vita e le opere di Guittone d'Arezzo*. Pisa, 1906.

Terminology of the Dolce Stil Nuovo

BERTONI, G. *Op. cit.*, pp. 246-267.

FLORA, F. *Storia della letteratura italiana*. Vol. I, 32-34.

ROSSI, V. *Il Dolce Stil Nuovo*. Florence, 1921.

SHAW, J. E. "Cavalcanti's 'Canzone d'amore'" in *Italica*, XVI, No. 3 (Sept., 1939).

WILKINS, E. H. *History of Italian Literature*. Note on p. 74.

Florentine Poets

TEXTS

DI BENEDETTO, L. *Rimatori del Dolce Stil Nuovo*. Bari, 1939.

FIGURELLI, F. *Op. cit.*, pp. 233-399.

SAPEGNO, N. *Op. cit.*, pp. 11-64; 331.

CRITICISM

BERTONI, G. *Op. cit.*, pp. 246-267; 309-311; for extensive bibliography, p. 314.

FIGURELLI, F. *Op. cit.*, pp. 430-438.

Gli scrittori d'Italia. Vol. I, 28-32.

PHILOSOPHICAL ELEMENTS OF THE DOLCE STIL NUOVO

FIGURELLI, F. *Op. cit.*, pp. 131-147.

VOSSLER, K. *Die Philosophischen Gründlagen Zum Sussen Neuen Stil*. Heidelberg, 1904.

Allegorical Poets

EGIDI, P. Poemetti allegorici didattici del Duecento. Bari, 1940.

BRUNETTO LATINI

PICCOLI, R. "Il Tesoretto" in Scrittori Nostri.
Lanciano, 1920.

SUNDBY, T. Della vita e delle opere di Brunetto Latini. Translated by R. RENIER.
Florence, 1884.

WEISE, B. (ed.). Il Tesoretto. In Bibliotheca
Romanica, No. 94, 95. Strasbourg, 1909.

L'INTELLIGENZA

BIAGI, G. L'Intelligenza, che sia e di chi. Pisa,
1920.

CENZATTI, G. Sulle fonti dell'Intelligenza.
Vicenza, 1906.

GELLRICH, P. (ed.). Die Intelligenza. Breslau,
1883.

MISTRUZZI, V. (ed.). L'Intelligenza. Bologna,
1928.

TORRACA, F. "A proposito dell'Intelligenza" in
Studi di Storia letteraria. Florence, 1923.

FRANCESCO DA BARBERINO

BAUDI DI VESME, C. (ed.). Del Reggimento
e Costumi di donna. Bologna, 1875.

CRISTIANI, R. La questione cronologica nelle
opere di Francesco da Barberino. Pisa, 1918.

EGIDI, P. (ed.). I Documenti d'amore. Rome,
1905.

FESTA, G. Un galateo femminile italiano del
Trecento. Bari, 1910.

GORRA, E. "Il reggimento e costumi di donna
di Francesco da Barberino nei suoi rapporti
con la letteratura francese e provenzale" in
Studi di Critica Letteraria. Bologna, 1892.

ORTIZ, R. Francesco de Barberino e la letteratura didattica neolatina. Rome, 1948.

———. "Il Reggimento del Barberino nei suoi
rapporti colla letteratura didattico-morale
degli 'Ensenhamens'" in Zeitschr f. roman.
Philol., XXVIII.

———. "Le imitazioni dantesche e la questione
cronologica nelle opere di Francesco da Barberino" in Atti della Regia Accademia di
Architettura, Letteratura e Belle Arti di
Napoli, XXIII (1904).

THOMAS, A. Francesco da Barberino et la littérature provençale in Italie au Moyen âge.
Paris, 1883.

ZENATTI, A. Il trionfo d'amore di Francesco
da Barberino. Catania, 1901.

CHAPTER SEVEN: Dante Alighieri: His Minor Works

General Aids

BARBI, M. "Gli studi danteschi e il loro avvenire in Italia" in Problemi di critica dantesca. Florence, 1934. Pp. 1-27.

———. "La tenzone di Dante e Forese" in
Problemi di critica dantesca. Florence, 1941.

———. Un cinquantennio di studi danteschi.
Florence, 1937. Pp. 111-135.

———. Dante: Vita, opere e fortuna. Florence,
1946. 2nd ed., 1952.

CARDUCCI, G. "Dante e l'età che fu sua" in
Prose. Pp. 145-198.

———. "Dante, Petrarca e Boccaccio" in Prose.
Pp. 199-252.

———. "Opere di Dante" in Prose. Pp. 1131-
1160.

CARETTI, L. Avviamento. Pp. 35-43.

CASELLA, M. "Indice analitico dei nomi e delle
cose" in Opere di Dante. Florence, 1921.

COSMO, U. A Handbook to Dante's Studies.
Translated by D. C. MOORE. Oxford, 1950.
Pp. 50-51.

———. Guida a Dante. Turin, 1947. Translated
by D. MOORE, Oxford, 1950.

———. "Indicazioni bibliografiche" in Vita di
Dante. Bari, 1949. Pp. 297-324.

CROCE, B. La poesia di Dante. Bari, 6th ed.,
1948.

D'ANCONA, A. Scritti danteschi. Florence,
1912.

DE SANCTIS, F. *Pagine dantesche.* Edited by G. LAURINI. Naples, 1921.

——. *Saggi danteschi.* Edited by L. G. TENCONI. Milan, 1951.

DINSMORE, C. A. *Aids to the Study of Dante.* Boston, 1903.

——. *Life of Dante Alighieri.* Boston, 1917.

——. *The Teachings of Dante.* Boston, 1902.

EVOLA, N. D. *Bibliografia dantesca (1920-1930).* Florence, 1932.

——. "Bibliografia dantesca (1931-1934)" in *Bibliografia degli studi sulla letteratura italiana.* Milan, 1938.

——. "Bibliografia dantesca (1935-1939)" in *Aevum,* XV (1941).

FAY, E. A. *Concordance of the Divina Commedia.* Boston and London, 1888.

FIAMMAZZO, A. *Dizionario-concordanza delle opere latine e italiane.* Milan, 1905.

FISKE, W. *Catalogue of the Dante Collection.* Cornell University Library. Ithaca, 1898. P. 900. Additions by M. FOWLER, 1898-1921, Ithaca, 1921.

FOSCOLO, U. *La Commedia di Dante Alighieri.* Illustrata. Legano, 1827.

FRIEDRICH, W. P. *Dante's Fame Abroad.* Rome, 1950.

GENTILE, G. *Storia della filosofia in Italia.* Milan, 1905. Vol. I, Ch. IV.

GOZZI, G. *Opere.* Venice. 1812.

HILLEBRAND, K. *Etude historique et littéraire sur l'époque de Dante.* Paris, 1862.

HOLBROOK, R. T. *Portraits of Dante from Giotto to Raphael.* London, 1911.

LA PIANA, A. *Dante's American Pilgrimage.* New Haven, 1948.

MAGGINI, F. "La critica dantesca dal 300 ai giorni nostri" in *Problemi e orientamenti critici.* Vol. III.

MAMBELLI, G. *Gli annali delle edizioni dantesche.* Bologna, 1931.

MATHER, F. J., JR. *The Portraits of Dante.* Princeton, 1921.

MATTALIA, D. "Dante" in *I classici italiani nella storia della critica.* Florence, 1954. Vol. I.

——. *La critica dantesca.* Florence, 1950.

MOMIGLIANO, A. *Dante, Manzoni, Verga.* Messina, 1944.

MOORE, E. *Studies on Dante.* Oxford, 1889. Pp. 79-151.

NARDI, B. *Dante e la cultura medievale.* Bari, 1942.

OZANAM, A. F. *Dante et la philosophie catholique au XIIIᵉ siècle.* Paris. 1840. Translated into Italian by P. MOLINELLI, Milan, 1841; into English by L. D. PYCHOWSKA, New York, 1913.

PASSERINI, G. L. *Dante (1265-1321), note biografiche e storiche.* Milan, 1921.

POLETTO, G. *Dizionario dantesco.* Siena, 1885-1892.

PUPPO, M. "Dante" in *Manuale.* Pp. 183-201.

RAND, E. K., AND WILKINS, E. H. *Dantis Aligherii Operum latinorum concordantiae.* Oxford, 1912.

RENAUDET, A. *Dante humaniste.* Paris, 1952.

RUSSO, L. "La tenzone di Dante con Forese" in *Belfagor* (Sept. 15, 1946).

SANTANGELO, G. "Sole nuovo e sole usato, Dante e Guittone" in *Annuario del Regio Instituto Magistrale di Catania.* 1926-1927.

SCARTAZZINI, G. A. *Enciclopedia dantesca.* Milan, 1896-1899.

SCHERILLO, M. *Alcune fonti provenzali della Vita Nuova.* Naples, 1889.

SHELDON, E. S. *Concordanza delle opere italiane in prosa e del canzoniere di Dante Alighieri.* Oxford, 1905.

SOCIETÀ DANTESCA ITALIANA. *Opere.* Florence, 1921.

TOYNBEE, P. *A Dictionary of Proper Names and Notable Matters in the Works of Dante.* Oxford, 1898.

——. *Concise Dictionary* (smaller edition of the *op. cit.*). Oxford, 1914.

——. *Dante Alighieri: His Life and Work.* 4th ed., London, 1910.

——. *Dante in English Literature from Chaucer to Cary.* London, 1909.

VALLONE, A. *Gli studi danteschi dal 1940-1949.* Florence, 1950.

——. *La "cortesia" dai provenzali a Dante.* Palermo, 1950.

——. *La critica dantesca contemporanea.* Pisa, 1953.

——. *Studi sulla Divina Commedia.* Florence, 1955.

Vossler, K. *Medieval Culture.* Translated by W. C. Lawton. New York, 1929. Originally published under the title of *Die Göttliche Komödie.*

Zingarelli, N. *La vita, i tempi e le opere di Dante.* Milan, 1931. 2nd ed., 1947.

Dante's Life

Barbi, M. *Dante: vita, opere e fortuna.* Turin, 1952.
———. *Life of Dante.* Translated by P. G. Ruggiero. Berkeley, 1954.
———. "Le rime" in *Le opere di Dante,* edited by the *Società Dante Alighieri.* Florence, 1921.
Boccaccio, G. *Vita di Dante* in *Le vite di Dante, Petrarca e Boccaccio* by A. Solerti. Milan, 1904. Pp. 8-75.
Bosco, U. *Vita di Dante.* 2nd ed., Bari, 1949.
Del Lungo, I. *La donna fiorentina del buon tempo antico.* Florence, 1905. Pp. 112-115.
Livi, G. *Dante, suoi primi cultori, sua gente in Bologna.* Bologna, 1918.
Moore, E. *Dante and His Early Biographers.* London, 1890.
Renucci, P. *Dante, disciple et juge du monde gréco-latin.* Paris, 1954.
Scherillo, M. *Alcuni capitoli della biografia di Dante.* Turin, 1896.
Zingarelli, N. *La vita, i tempi e le opere di Dante.* Milan, 1931. 2nd ed., 1947.

Texts

Alighieri, D. *Le opere.* Edited by M. Barbi. Florence, 1921.
———. *Opere complete.* First ed. of complete works. Venice, 1757-1758.

Critical Appraisal

Benedetto, L. F. *Il "Roman de la Rose" e la letteratura italiana.* Halle, 1910.
Caretti, L. *Avviamento.* Pp. 37-43.
De Sanctis, B. *Pagine dantesche.* Edited by P. Arcari. Milan, 1921.
Farinelli, A. *Dante e la Francia dall'età media al secolo di Voltaire.* Milan, 1908.

Foscolo, U. *Saggi letterari.* Introduction and notes by M. Fubini. Turin, 1926.
Gozzi, G. *Difesa di Dante.* Venice, 1758. Verona, 1895.
Mambelli, G. *Gli annali delle edizioni dantesche.* Bologna, 1931.
Mattalia, D. "Dante Alighieri" in *I classici italiani nella storia della critica.* Florence, 1954. Vol. I.
———. *La critica dantesca.*
Montano, R. *Dante e il Rinascimento.* Naples, 1942.
Nardi, B. *Studi di storia della filosofia medievale* in *Cinquant'anni.* Vol. I, 15-42.
Ozanam, F. *Dante et la philosophie catholique.* Paris, 1839. P. 201.
Santangelo, S. *Dante e i trovatori provenzali.* Catania, 1921.
Sapegno, N. *Il Trecento.* P. 36-139.
Shaw, J. E. *Essays of the Vita Nuova.* Princeton, 1929.

Minor Works

LA VITA NUOVA

Texts

Alighieri, D. *Vita Nuova.* Edited by M. Barbi. Florence, 1907. 2nd ed., 1932.
———. *Vita Nuova.* Edited by T. Casini. Florence, 1885. New ed. by L. Pietrobono, 1922.
———. *Vita Nuova.* Edited by G. A. Cesareo. Messina, 1914.
———. *Vita Nuova.* Edited by A. D'Ancona. Pisa, 1872. 2nd ed., 1884.
———. *Vita Nuova.* Edited by L. Di Benedetto. Turin, 1928.
———. *Vita Nuova.* Edited by D. V. Guerri. Florence, 1922.
———. *Vita Nuova.* Edited by G. Manacorda. Florence, 1928.
———. *Vita Nuova.* Edited by D. Mattalia. Turin, 1936.
———. *Vita Nuova.* Translated by C. E. Norton. Boston, 1867.
———. *Vita Nuova.* Edited by N. Sapegno. Florence, 1931.

——. *Vita Nuova.* Edited by M. Scherillo. Milan, 1921.

Rossetti, D. G. *La Vita Nuova.* Everyman's Library, New York. Pp. 257-310.

Criticism

Cosmo, U. *A Handbook to Dante's Studies.* Pp. 32-49.

Marigo, A. *Mistica e scienza nella Vita Nuova di Dante.* Padua, 1914.

Pietrobono, L. "Il rifacimento della *Vita Nuova* e le due fasi del pensiero dantesco" in *Giornale Dantesco,* XXXV (1934). Pp. 1-82.

Santangelo, S. *Dante e i trovatori provenzali.* Catania, 1921.

Scherillo, M. *Alcune fonti provenzali della Vita Nuova.* Naples, 1889.

Schiaffini, A. *Il Gusto degli Stilnovisti. Tradizione e poesia.* Genoa, 1934. Pp. 123-153.

POEMS

Texts

Alighieri, D. *Il Canzoniere.* Edited by G. Zonta. Turin, 1923.

——. *Le opere minori.* Edited by G. L. Passerini. Florence, 1900.

——. *Le rime.* Edited by G. Contini. Turin, 1939.

——. *Rime.* Edited by D. Mattalia. Turin, 1943.

Cossio, A. *The Canzoniere of Dante.* New York, 1918.

Criticism

Barbi, M. *Studi sul Canzoniere di Dante.* Florence, 1915.

Grandgent, C. H. *The Ladies of Dante's Lyrics.* Cambridge, Mass., 1917.

EPISTLES

Monti, A. *Dantis Alighieri epistolae.* Milan, 1921.

Novati, F. "Le epistole" in *Lectura Dantis,* No. 108 (1905).

——. "Le epistole dantesche" in *Freschi e mini del Dugento.* Pp. 267-290.

Torri, A. *Epistole di Dante Alighieri.* Livorno, 1842.

Witte, C. *Epistolae quae extant.* Padua, 1827.

ECLOGUES

Albini, G. *Dantis Eclogae.* Florence, 1903.

——. *Italian version of the Eclogues in Exameters with comment.* Florence, 1903.

Alighieri, D. *Eclogues.* Edited by E. Pistelli in *Studi su Dante.* Florence, 1922.

Carrara, E. *La poesia pastorale.* Milan, 1908.

Macri, L. *La bucolica latina nella letteratura italiana del secolo XIV.* Turin, 1889.

Scolari, F. *I versi latini di Giovanni del Virgilio e di Dante Alighieri.* Florence, 1845.

Wicksteed, P. H., and Gardner, E. G. *Critical Text of the Poetic Remains of Giovanni del Virgilio and of Dante Alighieri's Eclogues.* Westminster, 1902.

Zingarelli, N. *La vita, i tempi e le opere di Dante.* Vol. II, 744-768.

CHAPTER EIGHT: *Dante as a Thinker*

Il Convivio

TEXTS

Alighieri, D. *Il Convivio.* Edited by G. Busnelli and G. Vandelli. Preface by M. Barbi. Florence, 1954. 1st ed., 1934.

CRITICISM

Pézard, A. *Le Convivio de Dante.* Paris, 1940.

Schiaffini, A. "Il *Convivio* dominato da filosofia" in *Tradizione e poesia.* Genoa, 1934. Pp. 157-181.

De Vulgari Eloquentia

TEXTS

ALIGHIERI, D. *De Vulgari Eloquentia*. Edited by F. CAPUA. Naples, 1944.

——. *De Vulgari Eloquentia*. Edited by A. MARIGO. Florence, 1921.

——. *De Vulgari Eloquentia*. Edited by P. RAINA. Florence, 1897.

CRITICISM

D'OVIDIO, F. "Sul trattato *De Vulgari Eloquentia*" in *Versificazione italiana e arte poetica*. Milan, 1910.

PAGLIARO, A. "La dottrina linguistica di Dante" in *Quaderni di Roma*, I (1947).

PARLANTI, E. *De Vulgari Eloquentia. Testo latino con versione a fronte*. Bologna, 1951.

TRISSINO, G. B. *De la volgari eloquentia*. Ferrara, 1583.

De Monarchia

TEXTS

ALIGHIERI, D. *De Monarchia*. Barbera Edition. Florence, 1921.

——. *Latin Works in English*. Temple Edition. London, 1904. Vol. V.

NICHOLL, D. *Monarchy and Three Political Letters*. London, 1954.

VIANELLO, N. *Il trattato della "Monarchia" di Dante*. Translated into Italian. Genoa, 1921.

CRITICISM

BATTAGLIA, F. *Impero, Chiesa e stati particolari nel pensiero di Dante*. Bologna, 1944.

CAPPA LEGORA, L. *Dante, S. Agostino ed Egidio Colonna*. Turin, 1906.

CAPOCASALI, D. *Il "De Monarchia" di Dante e i trattati politici del suo tempo*. Monteleone, 1920.

D'ANCONA, A. *Il "De Monarchia."* Florence, 1921.

D'ENTRÈVES, A. P. *Dante as a Political Thinker*. Oxford, 1952.

——. *La filosofia politica medievale*. Turin, 1934.

ERCOLE, F. *Il pensiero politico di Dante*. Milan, 1927.

MARIANI, U. "La posizione di Dante tra i teologi dell'imperialismo" in *Giornale Dantesco*, XXXIII, 2 (1927).

PARODI, E. G. "Del concetto dell'impero in Dante e del suo averroismo" in *Bulletino della Società Dantesca Italiana*, XXV (1918).

SOLMI, A. *Il pensiero politico di Dante*. Florence, 1922.

VINAY, G. *La Monarchia*. Florence, 1950.

CHAPTER NINE: *The Divine Comedy*

General Aids

APOLLONIO, M. *Storia della Commedia*. Milan, 1951.

BOCCACCIO, G. "Commento sopra la *Divina Commedia*" in *Opere volgari*. Florence, 1827-1834. Vols. X-XII.

CAMILLI, A. "La cronologia del viaggio dantesco" in *Studi Danteschi*, XXIX (1950).

D'OVIDIO, F. *L'ultimo volume dantesco*. Rome, 1926.

——. *Nuovo volume di studii danteschi*. Rome, 1926.

EGIDI, F. "L'argomento Barberiniano per la datazione della *Divina Commedia*" in *Studi romanzi*, XIX (1928).

FAY, E. A. *Concordance of the Divine Comedy*.

FOSCOLO, U. *Discorso sul testo e su le opinioni diverse prevalenti intorno alla storia e alla emendazione critica della Commedia di Dante*. London, 1825.

GARDNER, E. G. *Dante's Ten Heavens*. London, 1904.

GILBERT, A. H. *Dante's Conception of Justice*. Durham, N.C., 1925.

MOMIGLIANO, A. *La Divina Commedia*. Florence, 1945-1947.

PARRI, WALTER AND TERESA. *Anno del viaggio e giorno iniziale della Commedia*. Florence, 1956.

PIETROBONO, L. *Il poema sacro. Saggio d'una intepretazione generale della Divina Commedia. Inferno*. Bologna, 1925.

SANTAYANA, G. *Three philosophical poets: Lucretius, Dante and Goethe*. Cambridge, Mass., 1910. Reprint, 1944.

SINGLETON, C. S. *Dante Studies*. Cambridge, Mass., 1954. Vol. I.

Texts

ALIGHIERI, D. *Divina Commedia*. Edited by M. CASELLA. Bologna, 1923.

———. *La Divina Commedia*. Edited and annotated by C. H. GRANDGENT. Boston, 1909-1913.

———. *La Divina Commedia*. Translated and edited by C. E. NORTON with an Appendix by E. H. WILKINS. Boston, 1941.

———. *La Divina Commedia*. Translated and edited by J. D. SINCLAIR. London, 1939-1946.

Critical Appraisal

BORGOGNONI, A. *Matelda*. Città di Castello. 1887.

BUSNELLI, G. *Il concetto e l'ordine del Paradiso dantesco*. Città di Castello, 1911-1912.

———. *L'ordinamento morale del Purgatorio dantesco*. Rome, 1908.

FERRETTI, G. *I due tempi della composizione della Divina Commedia*. Bari, 1935.

GRANDGENT, C. H. *Dante*. New York, 1916.

———. *The Power of Dante*. Boston, 1913.

———. *The Ladies of Dante's Lyrics*. Cambridge, Mass., 1917.

MOMIGLIANO, A. "Il paesaggio della *Divina Commedia*" in *Dante, Manzoni, Verga*. Messina, 1944.

PARODI, E. G. *Poesia e storia nella Divina Commedia*. Naples, 1921.

RUSSO, L. "Genesi e unità della *Commedia*" in *Ritratti e disegni storici*. Pp. 224-263.

SCHIAFFINI, A. "A proposito dello stile comico di Dante" in *Momenti di storia della lingua italiana*. Bari, 1950.

Sources

ASIN, P. M. *La escatología musulmana en la Divina Comedia*. Madrid, 1919.

BUSNELLI, G. *Cosmogonia e antropogenesi secondo Dante Alighieri e le sue fonti*. Rome, 1922.

COSMO, U. *A Handbook to Dante's Studies*. Pp. 150-151.

D'ANCONA, A. *I precursori di Dante*. Florence, 1874.

GABRIELI, G. *Dante e l'Oriente*. Bologna, 1925.

———. *Intorno alle fonti orientali della Divina Commedia*. Rome, 1919.

ZINGARELLI, N. *Dante*. Milan, 1899-1904. New ed., 1947.

Dante and Classicism

ALBINI, G. "Stazio nella *Divina Commedia*" in *Atene e Roma* V (1902).

BUSNELLI, G. *L'etica nicomachea e l'ordinamento morale dell'Inferno*. Bologna, 1907.

D'OVIDIO, F. *Studi sulla Divina Commedia*. Naples, 1931-1932.

LANDI, G. "Sulla leggenda del Cristianesimo di Stazio" in *Atti e memorie Regia Università di Padova*. Padua, 1913.

MUSTARD, P. "Dante and Statius" in *Modern Languages Notes*, XXXIX, 2 (Feb., 1924).

RENUCCI, P. *Dante disciple et juge du monde gréco-latin*. Pp. 57-106; 125-128; 129-192.

SABBADINI, R. "Dante e l'Achilleide" in *Atene e Roma*, XII (1909).

SCHERILLO, M. "Stazio nella *Divina Commedia*" in *Studi di filologia, filosofia e storia*. Milan, 1913. Vol. I.

SZOMBATHELY, G. *Dante e Ovidio*. Trieste, 1888.

USSANI, V. *Dante e Lucano*. Florence, 1917.

Philosophy of Dante

CARLINI, A. *Del sistema filosofico dantesco nella Divina Commedia*. Bologna, 1902.

Cosmo, U. "La gran luce" in *Vita di Dante*. Bari, 1949. Pp. 169-188.

——. "Tra i sapienti della Sorbona" in *Vita di Dante*. 1st ed., Bari, 1930. 2nd ed., 1949.

——. *Vita di Dante*.

Gentile, G. *La filosofia di Dante*. Rome, 1921.

Gilson, E. *Dante, the Philosopher*. Translated into English by D. C. Moore. London, 1948., 2nd ed., New York, 1949.

Nardi, B. *Saggi di filosofia dantesca*. Milan, 1930.

Averroism in the Thirteenth Century

Aquinas, T. *Trattato dell'unità dell'intelletto contro gli Averroisti*. Introduction by B. Nardi. Florence, 1933.

Averreos (Ibn Rushd) in *Enciclopedia Italiana*. Milan, 1930. Vol. VIII, 624-628.

Mandonnet, P. F. *Etude d'histoire littéraire du Moyen âge*. Paris, 1930.

——. *Sigier de Brabant et l'averroïsme latin au XIIIᵉ siècle*. Fribourg, 1899.

Nardi, B. "Sigieri di Brabante nella *Divina Commedia* e le fonti della filosofia di Dante" in *Rivista di filosofia neoscolastica* (1911-1912).

——. *Saggi di filosofia dantesca*. Milan, 1930.

——. *Studi di studi della filosofia medievale*. in *Cinquant'anni*. Pp. 30-33.

Mysticism of Dante

Baldwin, G. E. *The New Beatrice and the Virtue That Counsels*. New York, 1928.

Barbi, M. "Razionalismo e misticismo in Dante" in *Problemi di critica dantesca*. Second series. Florence, 1941.

Burch, G. B. *Dante and St. Bernard*. Cambridge, Mass., 1940.

Carlini, A. *Del sistema filosofico dantesco nella Divina Commedia*. Bologna, 1902.

D'Ancona, A. *Beatrice di Dante*. Pisa, 1865.

Gardner, E. *Dante and the Mystics*. New York, 1933. Pp. 247-256.

Gilson, E. "La mystique cistercienne et le Jesu dulcis memoria" in *Les idées et les lettres*. Paris, 1932. Pp. 39-57.

——. *The Mystical Theology of Saint Bernard*. Translated by H. C. Downes. New York, 1940.

Hermet, A. *Itinerario della mente in Dio* and *La riduzione delle arti alla teologia*. Lanciano, 1928.

Nardi, B. *Dante e la cultura medievale*. Bari, 1942.

Pietrobono, L. "Filosofia e teologia nel *Convivio* e nella *Commedia*" in *Giornale Dantesco*, XLI (1940). Pp. 13-71.

Underhill, E. *The Mystic Way*.

Vignaux, P. *Il pensiero nel Medio Evo*.

Concept of Love

Figurelli, F. *Il Dolce Stil Nuovo*. Pp. 401-428.

Vittorini, D. "Dante ed il concetto d'amore" in *Symposium*, V (May, 1951). Pp. 22-37.

Dante's Influence

Apollonio, M. *Immagini dantesche nella poesia dell'età romantica*. Milan, 1947.

Barbi, M. "Gli studi danteschi e il loro avvenire in Italia" in *Problemi di critica dantesca*. Florence, 1934. I, 1-27.

Farinelli, A. *Dante in Spagna—Francia—Inghilterra—Germania*. Turin, 1922.

Renzulli, M. *Dante nella letteratura inglese*. Florence, 1925.

Sells, A. *The Italian Influence in English Poetry: From Chaucer to Southwell*. London, 1954.

Toynbee, P. *Dante in English Literature*. London, 1909.

CHAPTER TEN: *Prose Writing in the Thirteenth Century*

Critical Appraisal

BERTONI, G. *Il Duecento.* Pp. 86; 316-359.
CRANE, T. F. *Italian Popular Tales.* Boston, 1885.
CRESCINI, V. *Il cantare di Fiorio e Biancifiore.* Bologna, 1889-1899.
CROCIONI, G. *Il cantare di Fiorio e Biancofiore.* Rome, 1903. Part II, 3-34.
MARIGO, A. *Il "Cursus" nella prosa latina dalle origini cristiane ai tempi di Dante.* Padua, 1934.
ROSSI, V. "I primordi della prosa italiana" in *Storia della letteratura italiana.* Pp. 108-121.
RUSSO, L. "I prosatori del Duecento" in *Gli scrittori d'Italia.* Vol. I, 35-43.
SCHIAFFINI, A. "La tecnica della'prosa rimata' nel medioevo latino" in *Guido Faba, Guittone e Dante.* Rome, 1931.
———. *Tradizione e poesia nella prosa d'arte italiana dalla latinità medievale a Giovanni Boccaccio.* Genoa, 1934. 2nd ed., Rome, 1943.
———. "Gli stili prosastici" in *Tradizione e poesia.* Pp. 19-38.

Early Attempts at Fiction

SCHIAFFINI, A. *Testi fiorentini del Dugento e dei primordi del Trecento.*

LIBRO DEI SETTE SAVI

Texts

D'ANCONA, A. (ed.). *Il Libro dei setti savi.* Pisa, 1864.

CONTI DI ANTICHI CAVALIERI

Texts

MONACI, E. *Crestomazia.* Pp. 432-438.

NOVELLINO

Texts

FRANCIA, L. (ed.). *Cento Novelle Antiche.* Turin, 1930.

Le Cento Novelle Antiche. Secondo l'edizione del MDXXV. Corrette ed illustrate con note da C. GUALTERUZZI. Milan, 1825.
SECARDI, E. (ed.). *Il Novellino e altre novelle antiche.* Livorno, 1919.

Criticism

D'ANCONA, A. "Del *Novellino* e delle sue fonti" in *Studi di critica.*

FIORETTI

Texts

DELLA TORRE, A. (ed.). *Fioretti.* Turin, 1909.
Fioretti di S. Francesco. Preface by G. PAPINI. Florence, 1922.

Criticism

BONAVENTURA, ST. *Legendae duae de vita S. Francisci Seraphici.* Chiaravalle, 1923.
PENNACCHI, F. *Actus Sancti Francisci.* Foligno, 1911.

MARCO POLO

Texts

BENEDETTO, L. F. *Il libro di Marco Polo.* Critically reconstructed with complete Italian translation. Milan, 1932.
Il libro di Marco Polo detto Milione. Nella versione trecentesca dell'ottimo. With a preface by S. SOLMI. Turin, 1954.
POLO, MARCO. *Il Milione.* Edited by L. F. BENEDETTO. Florence, 1928.

Criticism

CASELLA, M. "Il ritorno di Marco Polo" in *Pegaso,* IV (1923).
RUSSO, L. *Disegno storico.* Pp. 45-46.

History

PALMAROCCHI, R. (ed.). *Cronisti del Trecento.* Milan, 1935.

ALBERTINO MUSSATO

Texts

MUSSATO, A. Sette libri inediti del "De Gestis Italicorum post Henrichum VII." Edited by L. PADRIN in Regia Deputazione. Venice, 1903.

Criticism

NOVATI, F. "Nuovi studii su Albertino Mussato" in Giornale Storico della letteratura italiana, IV-VIII (1885-1886).
WILKINS, E. H. A History of Italian Literature. Pp. 33-35.

SALIMBENE OF PARMA

Texts

SALIMBENE DA PARMA. La Chronica. Parma, 1857.
———. Chronica. Edited by A. BERTANI. 1856.
———. Cronica. Edited by F. BERNINI. Bari, 1942.
———. Cronica. Edited by V. FOLLINI. Florence, 1816.

Criticism

MOMIGLIANO, A. "Motivi e forme della Cronica di Salimbene" in Cinque Saggi. Florence, 1945.
SCIVOLETTO, N. Fra Salimbene da Parma e la storia politica e religiosa del secolo decimoterzo. Bari, 1950.

RICORDANO AND GIACOTTO MALISPINI

Texts

MALISPINI, RICORDANO. Cronica. Edited by V. FOLLINI. Florence, 1816.

Criticism

MAZZONI, G. "La questione malispiniana" in Nuova Antologia (June 1, 1922).

DINO COMPAGNI

Texts

CARBONA, D. La cronica fiorentina di Dino Compagni e l'Intelligenza. Florence, 1868.
COMPAGNI, D. La Cronica, le Rime e l'Intelligenza. Edited by R. PICCOLI. Lanciano, 1910.
———. The Chronicle. Translated by E. C. M. BENECKE and A. G. GERRERA. Everyman's Library, n.d.
DEL LUNGO, I. (ed.). Dino Compagni e la sua Cronica. Florence, 1889.

Criticism

DEL LUNGO, I. Dino Compagni e la sua Cronica. Florence, 1879-1887. Republished under the title of Storia esterna, vicende, avventure d'un piccolo libro de' tempi di Dante, Rome, 1917-1918.

GIOVANNI, MATTEO AND FILIPPO VILLANI

Texts

VILLANI, G. La Cronica. Florence, 1823.
———. Villani's Chronicle: Being Selections from the First Nine Books of the Croniche fiorentine. Translated by R. E. SELFE; Edited by P. H. WICKSTEED. London, 1896.

Criticism

MORGHEN, R. "Dante, Villani and Ricordano Malispini" in Bulletino dell'Istituto Storico Italiano, XL, XLI (1920).

Dramatic Activity

APOLLONIO, M. Storia del teatro italiano. 2nd ed., Florence, 1943. Vol. I.
BARTOLI, A. I primi due secoli. Pp. 173-183.
BERTONI, G. Op. cit., pp. 185-186.
D'AMICO, S. Storia del teatro drammatico. 2nd ed., Milan, 1950.

D'ANCONA, U. *Origini del teatro italiano.* Florence, 1877. 2nd ed., Turin, 1891, Vol. I, Ch. I-XII.

DE BARTHOLOMAEIS, V. *Le origini della poesia drammatica italiana.* Bologna, 1924.

DU MÉRIL, E. P. *Les origines latines du théâtre moderne.* Leipzig, 1897.

GIUDICI, E. P. *Storia del teatro in Italia.* Florence, 1869.

LEVI, C. "Il teatro" in *Guide Bibliografiche.* Rome, 1919.

ROSSI, V. *Storia della letteratura italiana.* Vol. I, 71-76.

STOPPATO, L. *La commedia popolare in Italia.* Padua, 1887.

TONELLI, L. *Il teatro italiano.* Milan, 1924.

TOSCHI, P. *L'antico dramma italiano.* Florence, 1926.

WILKINS, E. H. *Op. cit.,* pp. 35, 51, 78-79.

CLASSICAL DRAMA

MUSSATO, A. *Eccerinide.* Edited by L. PADRIN with Introduction by G. CARDUCCI. Bologna, 1900. Translated into Italian verse by M. T. DAZZI, Città di Castello, 1914.

RELIGIOUS PLAY

BERTONI, G. *Il laudario dei Battuti di Modena.* Halle, 1909.

D'ANCONA, A. *Sacre rappresentazioni dei secoli XIV, XV e XVI.* Florence, 1872.

GALLI, G. "I disciplinati dell'Umbria del 1260 e le loro laudi" in *Giornale storico della letteratura italiana,* Supplemento IX.

————. *Laudi inedite dei disciplinati umbri.* Bergamo, 1910.

MOMIGLIANO, A. *Storia della letteratura italiana.* P. 13.

MONACI, E. "Uffizi drammatici dei disciplinati" in *Appunti per la storia del teatro italiano.* Imola, 1874.

MONTI, G. M. *Bibliografia delle laude.* Florence, 1925.

ROSSI, V. *Op. cit.* Vol. I, 71-76.

RUSSO, L., "I laudesi umbri e il teatro religoso" in *Ritratti e disegni.* Series III. Pp. 89-100. First published in *Disegno storico.* Pp. 22-28.

UNDERHILL, E. *Jacopone da Todi, Poet and Mystic.* Part II, 339, 450.

WILKINS, E. H. *Op. cit.,* pp. 33-35.

YOUNG, K. *The Drama of the Medieval Church.* Oxford, 1933.

Index

U

V

W

Z